PREACHING
John's Gospel
The World It Imagines

David Fleer & Dave Bland, EDITORS

CHALICE
PRESS
ST. LOUIS, MISSOURI

Cover art: "Pieta", ca. 1550 by Michelangelo Buronarroti
    Photograph by Erich Lessing/Art Resource, NY
Cover and interior design: Elizabeth Wright

Visit Chalice Press on the World Wide Web at
www.chalicepress.com

10 9 8 7 6 5 4 3 2 1   08 09 10 11 12 13

Library of Congress Cataloging–in–Publication Data

(pending)

Printed in the United States of America

Contents

Contributors

DAVE BLAND is professor of preaching at Harding University Graduate School of Religion in Memphis, Tennessee, where he has taught for fifteen years and where he directs the Doctor of Ministry program. He also teaches classes in Europe for the Ministry of Theological Education. Dave complements his teaching activity with preaching responsibilities at the Church of Christ at White Station in Memphis, where he has served as one of the preaching ministers for the past eleven years.

DAVID FLEER's devotion to preaching first found expression through a long-tenured pulpit ministry with the Vancouver Church of Christ in Washington state. His Ph.D. in Speech Communication from the University of Washington moved him into teaching at Rochester College, where he served for twelve years as professor of religion and communication, vice president of church relations, and directed the sermon seminar. Currently he fills a dual role at Lipscomb University in Nashville as assistant to the president and professor of religion and communication.

THOMAS E. BOOMERSHINE is an internationally known speaker and author, interpreting biblical narratives as oral story. He served as the G. Ernest Thomas Distinguished Professor of Christianity and Communication at United Theological Seminary in Dayton, Ohio, from 2004–2006 and professor of New Testament from 1979–2000. He now writes and produces multimedia resources for the interpretation of the Bible in digital culture. Tom founded the Network of Biblical Storytellers in 1977 and in the last decade has lectured and led biblical storytelling workshops for over a dozen different denominational conferences. In 2004 he organized the NOBS Seminar, which explores the implications of storytelling for biblical scholarship. Tom founded and chaired (1982–89) the Society of Biblical Literature's Bible in Ancient and Modern Media group and authored *Story Journey: An Invitation to the Gospel as Storytelling* (Abingdon Press, 1988).

For all his professional life, **FRED B. CRADDOCK** has been a preacher, a teacher of preaching, and a writer on the subject of preaching. With his Ph.D. in New Testament (Vanderbilt), Fred has understood the sermon as the future of the biblical text. As word of God, the biblical text is to be interpreted appropriately to every time and place and listener. To do this in ways that honor both the form and the content of the text is the work of his life. Long identified with the "New Homiletic," Fred's more notable publications include *Preaching, Overhearing the Gospel,* and *As One Without Authority.* Fourteen years "deep into retirement," Fred continues an active work schedule and designed the sermon contained in this volume "in conversation with" the enclosed chapters by his former colleague, Gail O'Day.

For more than thirty years a dynamic United Methodist pastor and teacher in a variety of regional and national settings, **RICHARD ESLINGER** has sustained both pastoral and scholarly commitment toward the renewal of biblical preaching and liturgical celebration among God's people. He is author of seven books in the field of homiletics, including his latest, *The Web of Preaching,* which interprets current movements in preaching and approaches to homiletic method, especially as they intersect and complement a whole "web." Dick thrives in community life, and presently enjoys his work as professor of homiletics and worship at United Theological Seminary in Dayton, Ohio. He serves frequently as adjunct faculty for the Upper Room Academy for Spiritual Formation in its several expressions around the country. Soaring both as a glider pilot and as a preacher of the gospel are joyful life vocations.

STEPHEN FARRIS is dean of St. Andrew's Hall and professor of preaching at the Vancouver School of Theology in Vancouver, British Columbia. Prior to this, he served as professor of preaching and worship at Knox College, the University of Toronto. He was for five years minister of Trinity Presbyterian Church, Amherstview, Ontario. He is a graduate of the University of Toronto, Union Theological Seminary in Virginia, and Cambridge University, England, where he received his Ph.D. He is the author of three books. His most recent is *Grace: A Preaching Commentary.* Farris was President of the Academy of Homiletics for the year 2002.

Since 1978, **MARK FROST** has been the preaching minister for the Church of Christ in Trenton, Michigan, where he also serves as an elder. He holds a bachelor's degree from Harding University and a master's degree from Cincinnati Bible Seminary, with additional graduate studies at Harding University Graduate School of Religion and Ashland Theological Seminary. Mark's passion is gaining a renewed hearing for Scripture by presenting it in fresh and creative ways.

RICHARD B. HAYS is George Washington Ivey Professor of New Testament at Duke Divinity School and internationally recognized for his work on New Testament ethics. His scholarly work has bridged the disciplines of biblical criticism and literary studies, exploring the innovative ways in which early Christian writers interpreted Israel's Scripture. His book *The Moral Vision of the New Testament* was selected by *Christianity Today* as one of the 100 most important religious books of the twentieth century.

MORNA D. HOOKER is a New Testament scholar who, for twenty-two years, was Lady Margaret's Professor in the University of Cambridge. Before that, she taught at King's College, London, and the University of Oxford.

Now "retired," she continues to write, lecture, teach, and edit. Morna has written many books, including a *Commentary on St. Mark* (A. & C. Black, 1991), *Beginnings: Keys that Open the Gospels* (SCM, 1997), and *Endings: Invitations to Discipleship* (Hendricksen, 2003). For many years she was joint editor of The Journal of Theological Studies. She is a Methodist local preacher and one of a small group responsible for translating the New Testament for *The Revised English Bible*.

THOMAS G. LONG is the Bandy Professor of Preaching at Candler School of Theology in Atlanta. He has also taught at Columbia Theological Seminary and at Princeton Theological Seminary and has served as director of Geneva Press for the Presbyterian Publishing Corporation. His books include the widely used *Witness of Preaching, Preaching and the Literary Forms of the Bible,* and commentaries on Hebrews and Matthew.

D'ESTA LOVE is the university chaplain at Pepperdine University, where she also teaches New Testament and Christian ministry. She earned her M.A. in English Literature at Abilene Christian University and received her M.Div. from Pepperdine. She is the coeditor of Leaven, a quarterly journal for ministry among churches of the Stone-Campbell heritage, author of *John: Light in the Darkness* (ACU Press), and coauthor of a theology of marriage, *Good News For Marriage*. D'Esta is a popular speaker and author with a particular interest in writing about and proclaiming the message of John's gospel.

CLINTON MCCANN served as preacher and pastor for ten years in North Carolina, during which time he also received a Ph.D. in biblical studies from Duke University. Since 1987, he has taught biblical studies at Eden Theological Seminary in Webster Groves, Mo., where he is now the evangelical professor of biblical interpretation. Clint served from 1989 to 1998 as chair of the Psalms program unit for the Society of Biblical Literature. He is the author of several books and essays on the Psalms, including the Psalms commentary in *The New Interpreter's Bible* and *Preaching the Psalms* (coauthored with James Howell).

ALYCE M. MCKENZIE is associate professor of homiletics at Perkins Seminary, SMU. She received her Ph.D. from Princeton Theological Seminary in 1994 and her M.Div. from the Divinity School, Duke University, 1980. Her current research interests include the sayings and parables of the synoptic Jesus, the intersections between literature and preaching, and preaching on controversial public issues. She has authored Hear and Be Wise (Abingdon Press, 2004), *Preaching Biblical Wisdom in a Self-Help Society* (Abingdon Press, 2002), and *Preaching Proverbs: Wisdom for the Pulpit* (Westminster John Knox Press, 1996). She is an ordained elder in the United Methodist Church and coeditor of *Homiletic.*

GAIL R. O'DAY is associate dean of faculty and academic affairs and A.H. Shatford Professor of Preaching and New Testament at Candler Seminary,

Emory University. Her current research focuses on the gospel of John, the relationship between the Old and New Testaments, and the Bible and preaching. Of her several published volumes on the gospel of John, we consider her contribution in the *New Interpreter's Bible* (Volume 9, Abingdon Press, 1995) the most essential. O'Day's uncanny ability to move students and readers into the text and to allow them to be drawn into its world and its heuristic insights make her work invaluable.

THOMAS H. OLBRICHT has been intrigued by the writings of John in the New Testament for more than thirty years. His most recent publications on Johannine materials are: *Lifted Up and Life Together* (both by Covenant Press). Olbricht taught at Penn State, Abilene Christian University, and Pepperdine University, and taught some of the first classes at the newly founded Institute for Theology and Christian Ministry in St. Petersburg, Russia. Olbricht has lectured or taught courses for credit on all the continents except for Antarctica. He has written or helped edit twenty books, the most recent scholarly ones: *Rhetoric, Ethic and Moral Persuasion in Biblical Discourse* (T. & T. Clark, 2005) and *Early Christianity and Classical Culture: Comparative Studies in Honor of Abraham J. Malherbe* (SBL, 2005). More than two thousand of Olbricht's students serve as ministers and approximately two hundred as college professors.

CARSON E. REED is the senior minister for the Northlake Church of Christ in Tucker (Atlanta),. Prior to coming to Georgia in 2004, he served churches in Indiana, Tennessee, Kansas, and Oklahoma. Carson serves as an adjunct professor for Atlanta Christian College and provides consulting, training, and travel/study programs to individuals, churches, and businesses through Encounter Learning Services. He holds a M.Div. from Harding University Graduate School of Religion and a D.Min. from Abilene Christian University.

GREGORY STEVENSON is professor of religion and Greek at Rochester College. He holds a Ph.D. in New Testament from Emory University and a M.Div. from Harding University Graduate School of Religion. His primary research and writing interests lie in the areas of New Testament interpretation (particularly with respect to the use of archaeology and ancient culture in the act of interpretation) and the intersection of religion and popular culture. Among his publications are two books, *Power and Place: Temple and Identity in the Book of Revelation* (2001) and *Televised Morality* (2003); a forthcoming commentary on Matthew for the Restoration Bible Commentary; and articles on biblical interpretation for the *Journal of Biblical Literature* and *Restoration Quarterly*.

JERRY TAYLOR was honored with the Outstanding Leadership Award at the NAACP National Convention. Jerry preaches for the Highland Church of Christ in Abilene, Texas, and is assistant professor of Bible and ministry at Abilene Christian University. Taylor earned his D.Min. from SMU and has had a fruitful career in ministry. He speaks at college and church conferences around the country on the themes of preaching, leadership, and diversity. He is known for his engaging and challenging oratory crafted and delivered in the spirit of John's gospel.

PAUL SCOTT WILSON is professor of homiletics at Emmanuel College of Victoria University in the University of Toronto, where he has taught since 1981. He has published numerous books on preaching, including the widely used *Four Pages of a Sermon* (1999) and the most recent *Practice of Preaching* (Abingdon Press, 2007). Past president of the Academy of Homiletics, Paul is honorary minister at St. Stephen's-on-the-Hill United Church in Mississauga and has served churches in northern Ontario and Toronto. His M.Div. is from Emmanuel College and his Ph.D. is from King's College, University of London.

Moving into the World Envisioned in John's Gospel

DAVID FLEER AND DAVE BLAND

We recently visited a sophisticated congregation and sat in a Sunday morning adult Bible class led by a respected young professional man. We were covering the sixth chapter of John's gospel when the teacher asked us to define faith. After some discussion originating from all parts of Scripture and life, he turned to his notes and began working with *Webster's* and then proposed this apt analogy. He likened our Christian faith to his drive to church that morning. He said that if his car did not perform properly he had no "plan B." Having no "plan B" is the essence of faith, he claimed, and this analogy captured the class's attention and elicited affirmations. We thought, upon cursory check, that even Peter's comment in John 6 might fit this memorable definition. But before we could even consider the validity of such a connection, the teacher tantalized us with a dispute concerning whether Jesus walked *on* water as depicted in John 6, or if Jesus had merely hiked *around* the lake. Our teacher then took us on an alluring journey to various places in John's gospel where the particular Greek word seemed to allow the rendering he favored, *around.*

One student suggested that such a view might border on existentialism, as taught in the liberal universities. Others frowned and appeared concerned that if Jesus walked around the lake, traditional understandings might crumble. With the miracle in sufficient doubt, the teacher forged ahead and asked what might be faith's "lowest common denominator." He asked, "Must we believe the miracle to have faith in God?" It was an odd question, quite opposed to what one might expect from the vantage of John 6, in which several disciples

1

seem to realize the demanding implications of Jesus' teachings, cannot bear them, and walk away.

It was a lively and entertaining class. We could tell the teacher enjoyed the repartee and, evidently, so did the students. Every available seat in this room was filled, and each person successfully avoided entering the world imagined in John's gospel. We'd seen the text (even read portions of it), but spent the hour walking *around* the narrative, performing the precise movement our teacher claimed of Jesus.

Why the avoidance? Why not instead allow ourselves to be lured by the strangeness of reading so we can be captured by its life—not critique that life, but fully experience its reality and meaning? This is the imaginative work of the artist, as with the evangelist John and, twenty centuries later, the artists who preach the gospel on Sunday morning. How then do we move into the world envisioned in John's gospel?

This is a mutual effort, and if we work together, we might envisage possibilities to preach and inhabit the world John imagines. The work of preaching never gets easy. In fact, over time our better preaching often becomes harder and more demanding. As the difficulties increase, we are reminded how much is at stake and of our desperate need for friends along the journey who will hold us to high standards and tell us the truth, friends who love us enough to provide insight and critique, yet resist "enabling" us or doing the work for us. This volume introduces you, the reader, to essays and sermons that will prove to be true friends, guides who have in mind our destination and route, not *around* the text, but *into* its heart and life.

A Path to the World Envisioned in John

Richard Hays opens the volume by offering this basic strategy for preaching John: learn John's language and live within John's symbolic world. Hays explores what it might mean for preachers to learn John's "native tongue" and inhabit John's imaginative world so that—by the Spirit's guidance—we might use it to say new things to our time. Maintaining that John's aesthetic vision is rooted in the materiality of the Incarnation, he finds examples from particular pericopes, and outlines three "linguistic lessons": Jesus teaches us what to desire; teaches us how to read Scripture; and he gives himself, bodily, to the world. These lessons are rooted in Hays' memorable sermon "Standing by the Fire," which closes and illuminates his essay.

In the subsequent chapter, Gail O'Day convincingly demonstrates that friendship is the theological center of John's gospel. The theme of friendship serves as a lens through which to interpret Jesus' discourses. As she explores this theme, O'Day cautions against using a sentimental view of friendship to interpret John's theology of friendship. In John's gospel friendship is demanding. As friend, Jesus lays down his life for others and speaks frankly to his disciples. While Greek philosophers also identify these two qualities as characteristics of a true friend, Jesus' embodiment of the teaching sets him apart from the philosophers. Now, Jesus urges his followers to do the same.

In her sequel chapter, O'Day continues developing the friendship theme by focusing on the *Paraclete* as the spiritual power that continues Jesus' embodied friendship. In turn, the *Paraclete* enables the disciples to live out the fullness of what it means to be a friend. The *Paraclete* acts as friend by speaking honestly and openly to the disciples, reminding them of Jesus' teaching.

Tom Olbricht argues that proclamation dominates John's theology. For Jesus and his disciples, *words* lead to belief and life. With a riveting bevy of supporting evidence from John, Olbricht claims that Jesus consistently produces mighty works through his words and maintains that his disciples will do even greater works–through their proclamation. The implications for preaching are dynamic: more than our own or secondary narratives, what ultimately matters is that our proclamation center on *Jesus'* words and actions. Olbricht closes with stirring vignettes from Nathanael's story and the wedding at Cana.

In John's gospel belief is a slippery concept; and believers' encounters with Jesus often reveal a shallow, empty, or misguided faith. With this understanding, Gregory Stevenson proposes some clarifying imagery to label this common thread in John's gospel in which characters consistently operate on a different frequency than Jesus and struggle to appropriately understand Jesus. Stevenson traces this theme of opposing operating assumptions in individual characters and communities, which will resonate with twenty-first-century believers and provide theological grist for preaching.

In the final essay, Thomas Boomershine raises the intriguing question of how Jesus' voice sounded in the ancient performance of John's gospel and the significance for contemporary hearings. When Jesus' words are performed today, we often make his voice sound deep, solemn, monotone, and authoritative, effectively creating an arrogant Jesus. Challenging that performance's truthfulness, Boomershine believes that when we discover Jesus' audience we discover his voice. Through audience analysis, Boomershine concludes that Jesus' voice was sympathetic, inviting, and ultimately the honest voice of a friend.

Sermons follow each of these essays. These sermons develop by engaging the essays, the biblical text, and the audience to whom they speak. The sermons interact with more than one of the generative essays; however, each sermon follows the particular essay most influential to its development, theme, or theological perspective. We are thrilled that eight essayists from previous volumes in this series have returned as preachers to interact with the essayists of this volume. We believe the integration is unique and a witness to the generative nature of the essays and character and skill of the preachers.

In using this book, preachers might choose one of two approaches. Some may work through John's gospel in a linear sequence, relying on the essays and sermons as creative suggestions for preaching particular texts. Or, preachers might select a more thematic approach identified in the essays and work through the narrative of John thematically. For example, one could approach the theme of friendship, which O'Day compellingly argues is at the center of John's gospel. Or one might begin with the theology of word and works as suggested by Olbricht, or the concept of materiality as developed by Hays. Both approaches have merit. To stimulate creative and heuristic reflection, however, we organize around the latter paradigm.

You've undoubtedly selected this volume with a desire to live and preach in the world imagined in John's gospel. An enormous assortment of resources are available through the Web, over podcasts, and on the shelves of libraries and bookstores—which, together, provide an atlas of guides, promising to enhance and redefine what we know about John's gospel. We add this volume as entrée to the world created in John's gospel, challenging you to believe John on his terms, allowing John to provoke your imagination, so that when the words end, meaning will continue. May God use this work to change how we see, which will determine what we see and therefore impact how we live and how we preach.

1

The Materiality of John's Symbolic World

RICHARD B. HAYS

Inhabiting John's Narrative World

The gospel of John presents serious difficulties for the preacher, because the world it portrays seems strange to us. John's narrative world is disturbingly dualistic, positing sharp divisions between darkness and light, above and below, spirit and flesh. In this sharply dichotomous universe, Jesus appears to be an otherworldly figure who floats through the story about six inches off the ground. As Ernst Käsemann famously remarked, the christology of the Fourth Gospel seems to articulate a "naïve docetism": the glory of Jesus as portrayed in John threatens to overwhelm the fleshly reality of the Incarnation, with the result that Jesus appears in this gospel not as a human being but as "God going about on the earth."[1]

How then are we to preach on a gospel whose narrative world seems so remote from our experience of reality? When we confront a difficult text, we have three possible strategies for dealing with it.

1. *Don't* preach it. If you are a lectionary preacher, you will be familiar with this strategy. The lectionary itself has already scissored out most of the unpleasant or disturbing passages, including passages that speak of God's wrath or judgment. Even if the lectionary should give us a passage from John that we find confounding, we always retain the option of preaching instead on the Old Testament reading or the epistle. While this option has a certain sort of integrity, John is after all a part of the canon, and, historically, a critical component. So avoiding it altogether, while homiletically appealing, may be an act of theological bad faith.

2. *Translate* the text's language and imagery into some other conceptual vocabulary more accessible or appealing to our modern sensibilities. This was the strategy Rudolf Bultmann pursued in his program of demythologizing the New Testament. Bultmann's commentary on John's gospel expounds its meaning in terms of an understanding of "authentic existence" that is informed by twentieth-century existentialist philosophy.[2] While Bultmann's existentialist categories are no longer in fashion, the hermeneutical strategy of translation is widely influential; today we are likely to hear the New Testament "translated" into the categories of popular therapeutic psychology. Whatever the target language, every translational hermeneutic assumes that the text's own language is too strange or difficult for the hearers; consequently, it must be rendered in other terms.

3. The third option for dealing with difficult texts is to *learn the language* and live within the text's symbolic world.[3] Rather than translating John's language into some more familiar idiom, we instead undertake the hard work of learning to speak John's "native tongue." This is the approach to preaching that I want to commend to you. What would it mean for us as preachers to inhabit John's imaginative world? It would not mean that we simply repeat the text; rather, once we have learned the language, we can use it to say new things to our time—as we must—under the guidance of the Spirit.[4] Indeed, that is precisely what John himself has done: he has taken the traditions about Jesus and created a new "two-level drama" in which Jesus speaks not only to his own historical time but also to the author's own time and situation, perhaps fifty or sixty years after the death of Jesus.[5] Consequently, readers find themselves living *inside* the story. They become contemporary with Jesus, and he with them.

If we adopt this strategy of learning the language of the gospel, our preaching on John will come to share the texture of John's own language and vision: it will be symbolic, riddling, confrontational, and consoling. Our sermons will seek to create a new two-level drama, so that we find ourselves contemporaneous with Jesus. We will come to see our world in John's categories—or, perhaps better, we will come to see that the world we inhabit is most truly described and illuminated when we learn to see it as an extension of John's story.

In this chapter, I want to draw attention to one striking feature of John's symbolic world: its *materiality*. In light of the common perception of John as otherworldly and ethereal, this may be a surprising claim. But, I will argue that, in fact, this gospel's aesthetic vision is deeply grounded in the *particular,* the *palpable,* and the *embodied.* I suggest that this is necessarily so because of John's fundamental commitment to the *incarnation of the Word.* And I propose that this has significant implications for the way we preach on this text.

"Ars Poetica"[6]: Material Images in the Fourth Gospel

Our reflections will begin in what may seem an unlikely place: a poem by the twentieth-century American poet Archibald MacLeish, entitled "Ars Poetica." Perhaps you were required to read this poem in some long-forgotten high school English course. As its title indicates, it is a poem about the *art* of poetry. Specifically, it is about the way in which *images* constitute the vocabulary of the poem.

I want to propose to you that what MacLeish says of poetry is also true of preaching. So let us listen to MacLeish's poem as a starting point to think about how John communicates the gospel, and how our preaching might follow John's model.

> A poem should be palpable and mute
> As a globed fruit,
> Dumb
> As old medallions to the thumb,
> Silent as the sleeve-worn stone
> Of casement ledges where the moss has grown—
> A poem should be wordless
> As the flight of birds.
>
> A poem should be motionless in time
> As the moon climbs,
> Leaving, as the moon releases
> twig by twig the night-entangled trees,
> Leaving, as the moon behind the winter leaves,
> Memory by memory the mind—
> A poem should be motionless in time
> As the moon climbs.
>
> A poem should be equal to:
> Not true.
> For all the history of grief
> An empty doorway and a maple leaf.
> For love
> The leaning grasses and two lights above the sea—
> A poem should not mean
> But be.

There is a certain irony here: the poem asserts that poetry should not be didactic, but this poem is itself didactic. We will let that pass, for now, as an intentional paradox. But consider the contrast between the first stanza of MacLeish's poem above and the "translation" offered by John Ciardi: "A poem should be palpable, mute / Dumb, / Silent, / And wordless."[7] Ciardi is of course having some fun here, to show that the poem's images are integral to its meaning. He is not seriously suggesting that this paraphrase somehow clarifies or improves the poem as an act of communication. Quite the reverse: to strip away image and metaphor is to lose the force of the poem altogether. Unfortunately, however, many modern English translations do much the same thing to Scripture: they paraphrase the metaphors into direct, prosy statements. We preachers are often even worse. We seek to *extract* the message of the text from the story and images in which the gospel comes to us, supposing that it is somehow necessary to produce "translations" in dumbed-down *USA Today* prose, or in supposedly user-friendly language from which all the metaphors have been stripped away.

Laurence Perrine, writing about interpreting poetry, comments:

> [T]he message-hunter is likely to think that the whole object of reading the poem is to find the message–that the idea is really the only important thing in it. Like Little Jack Horner, he will reach in and pluck it out and say, "What a good boy am I!" as if the pie existed for the plum. The idea in a poem is only part of the total experience which it communicates.[8]

It is not clear to me why we preachers fall into the trap of Little Jack Horner hermeneutics. Madison Avenue understands and attempts to shape our consciousness in TV ads. The commercials are shot through with metaphors–both linguistic and visual. They think this is the *best* way to have an impact in few words. It is not clear why we, in contrast, fall into the trap of dumbed-down "explanation." But I know what the result is: the church's discourse is impoverished.

A few years ago, I was visiting the church built on the site of the garden of Gethsemane at the base of the Mount of Olives, just outside the walls of the Old City of Jerusalem. This is a place visited by many tourists. Apparently the caretakers of the building were concerned about the noise pollution caused by guides shouting out information for their tour groups, and so they had posted a large sign on the wall: "No explanations in the church." I have a photograph of that sign, and it is one of my favorite souvenirs of the Holy Land, because I think it reminds us, unintentionally, of what we ought to be doing as preachers: we should stop *explaining* and start *proclaiming*.

Why do we suppose that our secondary discursive translations are an improvement on the way that Jesus spoke? Why do we suppose that our translations are an improvement on the way that John wrote? Why do we suppose that our translations are an improvement on the way that God in God's providence has chosen to offer the gospel? Rudolf Bultmann thought John would have written a much better gospel if only he had known about modern science and had had the opportunity to read Heidegger! We laugh at this, but this is only one version of a fallacy we often commit in our preaching, in our well-intentioned efforts to put the cookies on a low enough shelf for what we suppose is the level of our congregations. We are making a serious mistake by doing this; all we succeed in doing is being boring–and impoverishing the church's ability to hear the complexity of the word of God.

Long before Archibald MacLeish, John understood the ars poetica very well. His gospel–perhaps more than any other text in the canon–narrates the gospel through the use of vivid, concrete images that *embody* the Word.

In the gospel of Luke, Jesus says, "I am among you as one who serves" (Lk. 22:27). But in the gospel of John, "[Jesus] got up from the table, took off his outer robe, and tied a towel around himself. Then he poured water into a basin and began to wash the disciples' feet and to wipe them with the towel that was tied around him." (Jn. 13:4–5). Do you see the point? I could almost stop right here!

At the most recent Duke University graduation, the speaker–G. Richard Wagoner Jr., the CEO of General Motors–recounted his experience of preparing to speak at a public event at which he was to be on the program along with Grant Hill, the great Duke basketball player who went on to become a star in the NBA. Before the proceedings started, Wagoner was clutching several pages of notes, but he noticed that Hill had nothing, not even an index card with notes for his talk. Hill looked over and said to him, "Hey, Rick you know the five B's of a good speech? Be brief, brother, be brief."

So, O.K., I'll be brief: Jesus stripping off his robe; wet dirty towel; the Lord on his knees. This is the gospel!

Or consider the man born blind in John 9: "[Jesus] put mud on my eyes. Then I washed, and now I see" (9:15b). When pressed for further elaboration, for some *theological* account of how to interpret this, here is what he says: "I do not know whether he is a sinner. One thing I do know, that though I was blind, now I see" (9:25). Amazing Grace! And the staying power of the hymn is rooted in the vivid *image*–which generations of Christians have readily understood as a *metaphor* for…well, if we must offer a translation: for the gift of new life that Jesus gives.

So here is my point: in the Fourth Gospel, the *materiality of incarnation* is the medium for the revelation of the Word. Contrary to Käsemann's opinion, John's theological vision is not docetic, not hostile to creation. Rather, it declares that creation is good because the Word was indeed made flesh. The life of the Logos, apart from whom there is no life, animates all creation. John masterfully embodies this truth by using earthy, material symbols to articulate the Word: water, wine, bread, light, door, sheep, seed, vine, blood, fish. These symbols are palpable and mute as a globed fruit. This kind of material imagining *transfigures* physical reality. Those who encounter the Jesus of the Fourth Gospel–the Jesus who washes filthy feet, rubs mud on the blind man's eyes, and weeps at the tomb of Lazarus–encounter a Lord who gives his own flesh for the life of the world (6:51).[9]

John 6: The Bread God Gives

And with that, we come to a passage in which the materiality of John finds particularly powerful expression. This is one of two passages in the Fourth Gospel in which Jesus *feeds* people. Interestingly, both occur at the shore of the Sea of Tiberias. And these are the only two scenes in the gospel set in this location. The stories are meant to *rhyme*. When we come to the ending in John 21, we are certainly meant to remember the earlier feeding story in John 6.

John built a strange tension into this story of the miraculous feeding. On the one hand, Jesus has compassion on the hungry crowd and miraculously multiplies five barley loaves and two fish to feed five thousand people at once;

he meets the concrete physical need of the people for food. On the other hand, Jesus scolds them: "Very truly, I tell you, you are looking for me, not because you saw signs, but because you ate your fill of the loaves" (6:26). He insists that the food itself is not the point; this strange feeding is a *sign* pointing beyond itself. But pointing to *what?* Let us look at the story more closely.

At the beginning of John 6, Jesus feeds the crowd. The people are so dazzled by this feat that they want to "take him by force to make him king" (6:15), but he ducks out of the crowd and withdraws alone to the mountain. Then, the night brings a mysterious interlude in which Jesus comes walking out on the Sea of Galilee to meet his terrified disciples out in a boat. He speaks to them: "*Egō eimi,* I am; do not be afraid" (6:20). Without saying it in so many words, the story portrays Jesus as the embodiment of the God of Israel, the same mysterious "I AM" who spoke to Moses from the burning bush. We are meant to hear the echo of Exodus 3. The next day, the puzzled crowd finds Jesus gone but tracks him down across the sea in Capernaum. And *this* is the point at which Jesus rebukes them for seeking the wrong thing; they are chasing him around the Sea of Galilee, he says, merely because they want him to keep producing free food. So Jesus says to the crowd, "Do not work for the food that perishes, but for the food that endures for eternal life, which the Son of Man will give you" (6:27).

Here we begin to learn the language of this gospel: *Jesus teaches us what to desire.* This may strike us as odd. Surely if we know anything, we know what we want and need. Isn't it just a question of asking God to provide what we want? Alas, no, because our desires are disordered. Our desires are far too easily manipulated—by advertising, by political propaganda, by the pressure of our circle of friends or colleagues. This is by no means a new problem created by the insidious power of modern media technology. Rather, the root of the problem lies in the human heart, and the problem itself goes all the way back to the garden of Eden. We have an astonishing capacity to take our God-given good desires for good things—for food, for beauty, for sex, for knowledge, for security—and to warp them into something distorted and destructive. Almost before we know it, we find ourselves eating to excess (to the detriment of our own bodies), becoming enslaved to our own passions, or committing acts of violence to protect what we think is rightly ours. The things that make for peace are hidden from our eyes.

Precisely because we have this propensity for messing up God's design, Jesus seeks to redirect the desires of his listeners. That is why he says, "Do not work for the food that perishes." He is echoing the prophet Isaiah, who cries out to Israel: "Why do you spend your money for that which is not bread, / and your labor for that which does not satisfy? (Isa. 55:2a).

Jesus is offering something better than perishable fish and barley loaves, but the crowd doesn't get it. They ask, "What sign are you going to give us then, so that we may see it and believe you?... Our ancestors ate the manna in the wilderness; as it is written, 'He gave them bread from heaven to eat'"

(6:30–31). *What sign are you going to give us?* Their question is strange, for just on the previous day Jesus provided them with food no less remarkable than the manna in the wilderness. What further sign could they possibly need? Perhaps they are simply good empiricists who want to see the results of the experiment replicated to make sure that the first time was not a fluke. More likely, though, their odd question is a symptom of deeper failure to understand what they have already witnessed. As T.S. Eliot writes, "We had the experience but missed the meaning."[10] They are expecting Jesus to fit the job description of the new prophet like Moses, and so their preconceived categories prevent them from seeing what is right before their eyes.

Our fixed categories can often create that sort of blockage. I'm reminded of a man who came up to me once after a public lecture and said, "I've read your book *Moral Vision of the New Testament,* and I thought it was wonderful, but I just have one question: Are you a conservative or a liberal?" He had waded through five hundred pages and thought he was enjoying it, but he missed the whole point because he kept expecting the book to fit into one or the other ideological pigeonholes in our contemporary culture wars. Something like that was happening with the crowd's response to Jesus.

So Jesus sets them straight. Here we come to the second lesson that helps us live within John's symbolic world: *Jesus teaches us how to read Scripture.* The crowd has the right text—they have linked Jesus' feeding of the multitude with Exodus 16, the story of the manna in the wilderness.[11] They have the right text, but the wrong reading. They seem to think the story is about Moses, about his skills as a charismatic wonder-worker. They want Jesus to do Moses' manna trick again. Jesus must explain: "Very truly, I tell you, it was not *Moses* who gave you the bread from heaven, but it is *my Father* who gives you the true bread from heaven" (6:32, emphasis added). Jesus is simply taking them back to exegesis class: when the text says, "He gave them bread from heaven to eat," the subject of the sentence is *God,* not Moses. So Jesus is saying what I always tell my first year students to remember when studying the Bible, "It's about God, stupid!"

But notice that Jesus' instruction in how to read goes beyond this simple corrective. Not only is it God the Father who is the true giver, but Jesus changes the tense of the verb from past to present and suggests that the manna must be interpreted as a prefiguration of another, truer bread still to come: "It is my Father who *gives* you the *true bread from heaven." Here* is the paradigm shift: the manna story is not just about a past event in salvation history; rather, it points forward *metaphorically* to a different kind of bread altogether. Even though the manna was divinely given, it was still "the food that perishes," Those who ate it still died (6:49). Jesus teaches us to read Israel's Scripture as pointing to *himself,* prefiguring himself. That is the hidden meaning of his cryptic statement: "For the bread of God is that which comes down from heaven and gives life to the world" (6:33).

In response to this, the crowd finally gets beyond the wrong questions and makes the right request: "Sir, give us this bread always" (6:34). They are like the Samaritan woman a little earlier in the gospel who asked Jesus, "Sir, give me this water, so that I may never be thirsty" (4:15). Jesus, no longer speaking cryptically, gives them a dramatic answer similar to the answer he gave her: *I am* [*Egō eimi*]—it's me. "I am the bread of life. Whoever comes to me will never be hungry, and whoever believes in me will never be thirsty" (6:35). I couldn't help thinking of these words when I saw on television last summer the image of a frail, parched old woman being carried out of a bombed building in Lebanon and given a life-sustaining drink of water; we are that woman, Jesus the water.

So this is the third impression as we learn to speak John's "native tongue": *by giving himself bodily, Jesus gives life to the world*. Jesus himself is the true bread from heaven. He is the bread toward which our desire should be directed; he is the true meaning of the manna story. Jesus, the one who came from heaven, is the giver of life. Only when we come to him will we be given the life that endures and overcomes death. When we come to him, we will find our desires directed to their true and proper end. That is the meaning of the Supper that the church celebrates: with open hands we receive Jesus, the enfleshed, material bread God gives.

From these insights about the *materiality* of the salvation God gives and the rich embodied imagery of John's gospel, we turn finally to a sermon that seeks to illustrate the sort of preaching that these observations might lead to in practice, a style of preaching that attends closely to the text's material images.[12]

SERMON _____

Standing by the Fire
John 21:1–19

RICHARD B. HAYS

The gospel of John has a trick ending. It looks as though the story has drawn to a close at the end of chapter 20 with a grand conclusion: "Now Jesus did many other signs in the presence of his disciples, which are not written in this book. But these are written so that you may come to believe that Jesus is the Messiah, the Son of God, and that through believing you may have life in his name" (20:30–31). The curtain falls, and the theme music starts to play. But then, suddenly, the curtain rises again. We find that there is more—another scene that wraps up some loose ends. This is a powerful dramatic device that calls special attention to the extra scene that comes at the end.

When the curtain rises again, the scene has shifted from Jerusalem back to Galilee. Jesus' disciples have returned home. They are seemingly seeking to return to the life they knew before the sudden violent end of their leader. Peter, not knowing what else to do, says, "I'm going fishing." It is a deep and understandable human impulse, after a tragic event, to return home and to seek the comfort of familiar activities. We saw this impulse at work recently at Virginia Tech, as a mourning campus, still numb from the shock of the horrible, senseless murders in their midst, slowly began returning to the reassuring routines of athletic practices and classes. We saw it after the grim tragedy of 9/11, as the city of New York and a stunned nation struggled to recover the rhythms of the life we had known before the unthinkable happened.

It seems that Jesus' disciples are doing something similar, returning to the waters where they had made their living as fishermen before, trying to get their balance back by doing the only thing they know how to do. It is as though they are trying to forget about the strange interlude in their lives that Jesus introduced. So Peter decides to go fishing, and the others join him.

But it's not so easy to go home again. After life with Jesus, nothing is quite the same any more. The disciples find that their effort to return to business as usual is marked by futility. They have spent the whole night in the boat and caught nothing.

Suddenly, just as light begins to dawn, a mysterious figure stands on the beach and calls out to them: "Children." Though he is a hundred yards away on the shore, he somehow knows they have caught nothing. He issues a word of command: "*Cast* the net to the right side of the boat, and you will find." (21:6, emphasis added). Our narrator, John, doesn't tell us what the weary disciples must have thought about this arbitrary instruction; he just tells us that for some reason they obeyed—and the consequence was a huge haul of fish, stuffing the net so full that they couldn't even get it back into their boat. This sign of miraculous superabundance in the changing dawn light causes the light to dawn also in the disciples' eyes. The "beloved disciple," always the quickest to understand, whispers to Peter, "It is the Lord!" And Peter, who just a few moments ago was throwing the net out of the boat, now, in a deft touch of storytelling, *throws himself* into the sea, thrashing toward shore in search of the Lord he longs to see again.

When the disciples arrive on the beach, they find the mysterious figure standing by a *charcoal fire*. Now I want you to think with me about this seemingly small narrative detail. I want to suggest to you that this strange, dreamlike story actually pivots on this image of fire.

The Greek word that John uses for "charcoal fire" is *anthrakia* (the root of our English word "anthracite"). Charcoal fire. This word occurs only one other time in John's gospel—indeed, only one other time in the whole New Testament. The one other appearance of the word is in John 18, John's account of the arrest and trial of Jesus. He tells us that Peter, who has followed the arresting party into the high priest's courtyard, has just denied being one of Jesus' disciples. Then John adds: "Now the slaves and the police had made a charcoal fire (*anthrakia*) because it was cold, and they were standing around it and warming themselves. Peter also was standing with them and warming himself" (18:18). So the one previous mention of the charcoal fire occurs precisely at the point where Peter denied Jesus. Peter cozied up to Jesus' captors to warm himself by the charcoal fire. Therefore, when, in this later post-Easter scene, Peter drags himself up shivering on the beach and finds there an *anthrakia,* we should imagine the camera zooming in and lingering on the shot. Charcoal fire.

The fire is a source of warmth in the chilly half-light, but it also illumines what is dark. The fire evokes again the scene of denial, the scene where Peter once stood by the fire and said, "I am not his disciple." The past comes rushing back. Perhaps in the distance we hear a cock crowing.

So this dramatic extra scene at the end of John's gospel turns out to be a story about memory and restoration. Many readers of the gospel recognize that Jesus' threefold question to Peter offers Peter a way of retracing the steps of his earlier threefold denial. "Simon, son of John, do you love me?" Three times, once for each knell of Peter's betrayal, Jesus offers a corresponding invitation for Peter to confess his renewed love and loyalty. But this healing confession does not come without pain. Confronting the risen Jesus is not easy, especially for those who have betrayed him. Standing in the flickering light of the charcoal fire, Peter must first remember his failure—and own it. The great Anglican theologian Rowan Williams, now Archbishop of Canterbury, describes the import of the scene:

> Simon has to recognize himself as betrayer: that is part of the past that
> makes him who he is. If he is to be called again, if he can again become
> a true apostle, the "Peter" that he is in the purpose of Jesus rather than
> the Simon who runs back into the cozy obscurity of "ordinary" life,

his failure must be assimilated, lived through again, and brought to good and not destructive issue.[1]

In this recognition of himself as betrayer, Simon Peter stands before the charcoal fire as a symbol for us all.

What is the truth about our pasts? What betrayals have we committed? Have we owned up to them? Our culture is notorious for its problem with truth-telling about the past. Celebrities such as Mel Gibson, Michael Richards, or Don Imus spew racist rants then later issue public "apologies," in which they say, "That wasn't me talking; I'm not like that." Notice that this is actually a non-apology; it disclaims responsibility, deflects guilt onto some other aberrant persona that isn't "the real me." But of course, forgiveness and restoration are possible only when we acknowledge that it *is* precisely the real me that has wronged others. It is the real me that has denied my Lord. During Holy Week, as we recall the passion and death of Jesus, we often sing the powerful hymn "Ah, Holy Jesus," in which we join together in singing this confession:

> Who was the guilty? Who brought this upon thee?
> Alas, my treason, Jesus, hath undone thee.
> 'Twas I, Lord Jesus, I it was denied thee;
> I crucified thee.[2]

We sing this way during Holy Week, but most of the time we find such radical self-assessment difficult. We choke on the words.

Consider the recent cautious lawyerly apology offered by Mike Nifong, the former District Attorney who blew the Duke lacrosse case into a national sensation by making inflammatory public accusations, issuing rape charges, and concealing evidence. He now offers the following public statement: "To the extent that I made judgments that ultimately proved incorrect, I apologize to the three students that were wrongly accused."[3] Let's try out how that would sound in Peter's mouth: "Simon, son of John, do you love me?" "To the extent that I made statements that seemed to deny you and that ultimately proved incorrect, I apologize to the Lord that was wrongly betrayed."

No, healing and restoration come only through looking in the mirror of memory and seeing our lies and evasions for what they really are. T. S. Eliot describes that wrenching moment of recognition:

> And last, the rending pain of re-enactment
> Of all that you have done and been; the shame
> Of motives late revealed, and the awareness
> Of things ill done and done to others' harm
> Which once you took for exercise of virtue…
> From wrong to wrong the exasperated spirit
> Proceeds, unless restored by that refining fire…[4]

We stand by the charcoal fire, and we can't help remembering, in the dawning light, things we had hoped to forget. We see, in the light of this fire, the self-deceptions that have masked our thousand little betrayals of the truth. This fire burns away our pretenses.

Precisely in this moment of memory, we also find restoration. It is Jesus standing on the beach. He has already prepared a meal of fish and bread. Another memory floods back: that other meal by the Sea of Tiberias when Jesus fed the multitude of five thousand with just five barley loaves and two fish. Where our situation seems hopeless, our resources insufficient, Jesus precedes us. He provides for us beyond all our imagining. This Jesus who provided vats full of wine, far more wine than the wedding guests could ever drink–this Jesus, who provided baskets full of bread, far more bread and fish than a hungry crowd could eat–*this* same Jesus now stands by the fire and says to us, "Come and have breakfast." Come and have breakfast. For us, perhaps that invitation evokes other memories: breakfast at the truck stop after the long night on the dark interstate, griddle cakes, butter, and syrup; or perhaps breakfast around the campfire, with fish sizzling in the morning chill. Jesus offers a breakfast to delight the senses: "Jesus came and took the bread and gave it to them, and did the same with the fish" (Jn. 21:13).

Let us see clearly what is at stake here. This offer of breakfast is also an offer of reconciliation. Standing by the fire we recognize ourselves not only as betrayers but also as prodigals welcomed home to a feast. Jesus, whom we have wronged and rejected, stands with us by the fire. He offers a restored relationship. "Weeping may linger for the night, / but joy comes with the morning" (Ps. 30:5). We take the bread and fish from his hands, and we remember something else, something Jesus said on the last evening before he was betrayed: "I do not call you servants any longer,...but I have called you friends" (Jn. 15:15). This offer of breakfast on the beach is an offer of renewed friendship beyond the betrayal. We stand by the fire and remember the truth about the past. We take the bread and fish from his hands, and we know that we are received back, made whole, given a new future in his love.

But Simon Peter discovers one more thing about this renewed relationship. The new relationship carries a new purpose. The risen Jesus has one repeated message for Peter: "Feed my sheep...Feed my sheep...Feed my sheep." Having been fed by Jesus, Peter and the disciples are not simply to bask on the beach in the rising Son. They are, in turn, to feed others. If our love for Jesus in this new resurrection relationship is real, it will spill out in a superabundance of gracious action for others. This charge evokes one final memory of something else Jesus had told them before: "As the Father has sent me, so I send you" (20:21).

So on the far side of resurrection we are given both a restored past and a new mission for the future. Jesus calls us by name as friends, summoned to the simple feast on the beach, by the charcoal fire. In that calling lies our new vocation. We are to tell the truth about our past, to eat the good breakfast that Jesus gives, and to share that life-giving food with others. So come, stand by the fire,...and have breakfast.

SERMON _____

God in the Flesh
John 1:1–18

CLINTON MCCANN

Compositional Comments

Richard Hays observes in his essay that the Logos animates all creation. John demonstrates this truth "by using earthy, material symbols to articulate the Word: water, wine, bread, light, door, sheep, seed, vine, blood, fish. These symbols are palpable and mute as a globed fruit. This kind of material imagining *transfigures* physical reality."

To understand the material nature of John's gospel, one must begin with the grand description of Logos in the prologue. For centuries Christian theologians have debated over the nature of the Incarnation. In this sermon McCann develops, not *how* the Incarnation happened, but *what* the Incarnation *means* for humans: that God has become one of us, with powerful implications for humans. McCann does not attempt to explain the Incarnation as much as he seeks to proclaim its good news.

Sermon

In the widely used, ecumenically oriented Revised Common Lectionary, John 1:1–18 is the gospel lesson for Christmas Day in each of the three yearly cycles, as well as the gospel lesson for the Second Sunday after Christmas in all three cycles. This exclusively Christmas orientation of John 1:1–18 is not inappropriate, of course; but it is somewhat unfortunate, especially since many Protestant congregations don't have Christmas Day services, unless the day falls on a Sunday, and since many Christmas seasons don't have a second Sunday. But even more to the point, John 1:1–18 should be a text for all seasons, because it communicates the very heart of the gospel. This is especially the case with 1:14–"the Word became flesh and lived among us,…full of grace and truth"–a verse that many would say is among the most important, if not the most important, in the entire Christian Scripture.

To begin to appreciate why this might be the case, consider author and preacher Frederick Buechner's suggestion that the Bible, despite the wide variety of traditions and voices and perspectives it contains, originating and compiled in various places and times spanning at least 1,000 years, contains a "single plot." He describes it this way: "God creates the world, the world gets lost; God seeks to restore the world to the glory for which he created it."[1]

If Buechner is right, and I think he is, then John 1:14 has to express the culmination of God's effort to reach a lost world, and to restore it, and us, to the glory that God intended "In the beginning," and still intends. Notice that phrase: "In the beginning"; it is the first phrase of John's gospel, reproducing Genesis 1:1, and thereby communicating very clearly that the God reaching out to the world in Word-made-flesh is the same God who created the world.

Now, notice, too, that the gospel of John does not say that Jesus of Nazareth was "In the beginning...with God." Rather, it is "the Word." The Greek is *Logos,* and the English cognate, of course, is "logic." In other words, "In the beginning," there was a logic or intent or purpose or will, apart from which God's own self cannot be understood. It is this "Divine Purpose" that "became flesh" in Jesus of Nazareth, who is, according to the gospel of John, just as the Word is, distinct from God yet inseparable from God, revealing God the Father's glory as only an only son can do...*in the flesh.* As Jesus would put it later in John's gospel, "Whoever has seen me has seen the Father" (14:9).

The Latin word for "in the flesh" is *incarnate.* Liturgically speaking, Christmas is the Festival of the Incarnation. The claim is striking! Jesus is God *with* or *in* the flesh! The gospel of John never explains *how* this is the case. As New Testament professor, Robin Scroggs, suggests, by portraying both the Word and the Son as distinct from yet inseparable from God, the gospel of John, chapter 1, provides the raw material or building blocks out of which the church eventually constructed a doctrine of the Trinity—Father, Son, Holy Spirit, three-in-one, and one-in-three—and its orthodox christology, or doctrine of Christ—Jesus is *both* "fully human" and "fully divine."[2] *However,* it took the church over 400 years to work out these formulations; and this meditation affords us only a few minutes. Plus, the church's formulations are couched in the language and conceptuality of Greek, Neo-Platonic philosophy, and they have often been a source of confusion over the past 1,500 years or so. I suspect, for instance, that for most contemporary Christians, the Trinity means, if it means anything at all, that the early church fathers were not very good at arithmetic! So, given the possible confusion, and given our limited time, we certainly will not penetrate all the mysteries of the Incarnation; but we may arrive at something constructive, helpful, and faithful if we focus less on how the Incarnation might have happened, and more on what it might *mean,* if we take it seriously.

What does it mean that "the Word," the "Divine Purpose" present "In the beginning," became flesh? What does it mean that, as one commentator paraphrases Word-made-flesh, "God moves in next door, just down the street"?[3] What does it mean that God has become "one of us," as a popular song put it several years ago? That song, "One of Us," sung by Joan Osborne and later used in part as the theme song for CBS's television show, *Joan of Arcadia,* is viewed as sacrilegious by some folk. But what the song asks as a question, "What if God was one of us?" the gospel of John clearly proclaims as a statement of the good news: God has become "one of us"—"the Word became flesh and lived among us"! That's why William Placher, one of the leading Reformed theologians and teachers in the United States today, chose to print a portion of the lyrics of "One of Us" on the flyleaf of his book, *Jesus the Savior.*[4]

In the video version of "One of Us," as Joan Osborne sings, the visuals portray what appears to be a cardboard or wooden cutout of God, patterned after Michelangelo's paintings on the ceiling of the Sistine Chapel. The face of God is a blank space; and in succession, a host of people, some of them pretty strange looking, take turns putting their faces in the space where the face of God belongs.

This seems to be the part of the song and video to which many people object; but the intent is not to say that we have become God. Rather, the intent is to say that God has honored us human beings by becoming *one of us*! Listen to how Placher in his book describes what the Incarnation *means*:

> The doctrine of the incarnation...implies that in Jesus we best learn what it means to be human. He is the one human being who got being human right...
>
> Jesus Christ united humanity with divinity, thereby transforming what it is to be human. We human beings turn away and separate ourselves from God, but in Christ divinity is reunited with humanity. In our culture, where many people are told, explicitly or implicitly, that they are worthless, Christian faith must declare all the more boldly that the humanity of every single human being has been united to God in Christ.[5]

Wow! Do you see what that means? The Word-made-flesh means that God values, God loves every single human being! Isn't that incredibly extraordinary?! Why, I can't even manage to love certain members of my extended family a good deal of the time, not to mention the folks next door and the people down the street—now I'm not talking about Aunt Vickie or Barb or any of the good Chautauqua folk on Jersey Avenue! Think back home, maybe your neighborhood, and perhaps you'll know what I'm talking about. But in contrast to me or us, who have trouble loving those near us, God loves everybody! "For God so loved the world"—the whole world!—"that he gave his only Son..." (Jn. 3:16).

> Remember that little song that you may have learned in Sunday school:
>
> Jesus loves the little children, *all* the children of the world.
> Red and yellow, black and white, they are precious in his sight.
> Jesus loves the little children of the world.

It's true!...*all* the children of the world—not just Annalise and Ian and all our precious little ones here at Chautauqua, but the abandoned children on the streets of Guatemala City, or any major world city, and the starving babies in

Darfur, and the shell-shocked little ones in Gaza and Beirut and Afghanistan and Iraq. And not just the children, but also their parents and grandparents and aunts and uncles and cousins! God loves every single human being!

One contemplative thinker and writer said that when he found himself on a crowded street corner in a busy city, he would be overwhelmed by the realization that God *loved* all those people surrounding him. Try it sometime, when you find yourself on a crowded street corner, or in a busy mall, or stranded in traffic at rush hour with thousands of other motorists. Instead of being aggravated by the crowd, or annoyed by the confusion, or frustrated by the chaos, like I usually am and probably you, too, contemplate the astounding reality that God *loves* all those people around you.

Love…that's what the Incarnation is ultimately all about. That's what it *means*. Love is "the Word," the Divine Purpose, that Jesus fleshed out for us! The First Letter of John, which most scholars believe derives from the same ancient church community as the gospel of John, puts it simply: "God is love, and those who abide in love abide in God, and God abides in them" (4:16b).

As this verse suggests, love is not only God's essence and purpose, but also our calling, our mission, our way to experience the full, authentic humanity that Jesus embodied, including the joy that God wills for God's children. As Jesus said to his disciples in John 15, and says to us as we read John's gospel: "I have said these things to you so that my joy may be in you, and that your joy may be complete. This is my commandment, that you love one another as I have loved you" (15:11–12).

The next verse goes on to define the greatest possible love as "lay[ing] down one's life for one's friends." Jesus, of course, literally laid down his life for others on the cross. More likely, for us, our calling will be not to die for others, but to live for others, as Jesus also did.

Dietrich Bonhoeffer, the German pastor and theologian who gave his life for others by way of his participation in the resistance to Hitler during World War II—he was executed by the Nazis—called Jesus "the man for others," an apt description of Jesus in all four gospels.

Living for others—love, in a word—was not the most popular thing to do in Jesus' time. Indeed, the opening verses of John's gospel already inform us that Jesus' "own people did not accept him" (1:11).

Living for others—love, in a word—is not the most popular thing to do in our time either. What our culture generally commends in the way of pursuing the so-called "good life" is the way of aggressive self-aggrandizement. If that pursuit has left you empty and dissatisfied, as it eventually will if it hasn't already, then rejoice and thank God that God has shown us in Jesus Christ a more excellent and joy-filled way—the way to a life that the gospel of John calls "abundant" and "eternal."

It's simple really; it's the way of the Word, the Word-become-flesh in Jesus, who loved the world unfailingly all the way to a cross, and who invites us simply to love one another as he has loved us. So be it! Amen.

SERMON _____

The Andrew Option
John 6:1–71

STEPHEN FARRIS

Compositional Comments

Stephen Farris proclaims the narrative of the feeding of the five thousand, pointing out the realities of the story. A realist might explain this miracle story, but "a miracle explained is a miracle explained away." Let John tell it in his own terms, let the preacher learn to speak John's language, and let the congregation live in John's world. The reality is Philip doesn't have access to enough money to buy food for the crowd. The reality is Andrew doesn't have much faith in the five loaves and two fish to feed the crowd. The reality is that both the resources and the faith are not much. But not much does not equal nothing. Farris explores this equation in his sermon. Using the material world as a starting point, John points to the true reality of Jesus, who opens for us new possibilities.

Sermon

Here's a piece of Bible trivia: the feeding of the five thousand is the one miracle story that makes it into all four gospels, even the gospel of John. It says something so important that none of the gospel writers could leave it out, and maybe it says something so important that we shouldn't leave it out either.

The way John tells it, the story takes place around Passover, the feast that celebrates that ancient time when God led the people out of Egypt, through the sea, into the wilderness. There they received the law of God on a mountain, and there they were miraculously fed with manna in the wilderness. Now the people have followed Jesus across the sea, the Sea of Galilee in this case, and there they will go hungry if they are not fed. Echoes! In John's story there is no long day of teaching and healing, no growing hunger as the sun sets over the hills to the west. Jesus is seated on a mountain—where else?—and as the crowd comes towards him, he turns to Philip and says, "Where are we to buy bread for these people to eat?" (6:5).

Now John's Jesus is great and glorious; he knows all things. Of course, he already knows what he will do. So this is a test. It's a test for Philip, and it's a test for the disciples. Perhaps it's a test for us. Philip gives his answer: "Six months' wages would not buy enough bread for each of them to get a little" (6:7). He quickly counts heads, does a little mental arithmetic, and comes up with a real world answer. Six months wages, say $25,000 (five thousand people, five bucks a head—can't fault the arithmetic). He doesn't have a spare 25 grand. This is a realistic answer. Philip's a realist. Don't be hard on Philip. He sees the gap between the need out there and the resources at hand and gives a real world answer. Call it the "Philip Option."

It's our real world, too… We also have to be realistic about what we can do. The need is so great and the resources so small. Take, for example, the problem facing Philip in this story, the problem of hunger. Hunger is still a problem in our world. One calculation is that 750 million people will go to bed hungry tonight, if they have beds. Many of them will be children. Of course, we would like to do something about it. We're decent folks, after all. In one way it's a simple problem. Hunger isn't like cancer or AIDS; we've known the cure for hunger for some time now. But the hunger problem is so complicated–environmental degradations, corrupt governments, inadequate transportation, agricultural practices of the developed world, a hundred and one factors. What is one person or even one little church to do? In real world terms, the need is so great, and our resources are so small.

A story floating around claims that the dictator Stalin was once warned that the pope would not like some action he was contemplating. "How many divisions does the pope have?" he sneered.

Why, none, just some Swiss Guards in ridiculous medieval outfits, and we Protestants don't even have that much. The problems are so great, and our resources are so small.

So, what *do* we have in the church?

A few voices, some eloquent and strong, but more of them stumbling.

A few minds, some sharp, but some getting a little tired with advancing years.

A few hands, a few feet, few dollars saved from providing for the necessities of life.

Not very much.

It's time to get realistic. "We can't do very much. Send them away. Let someone else deal with the problem."

"Send them away," says Philip to Jesus. "It's clear that there's not very much that people like us can do."

But "not very much" is not the same as "nothing at all." Here's the other problem. Saying, "*We* can do nothing," to Jesus is perilously close to saying, "*You* can do nothing."

Give the Philip Option an "A" for arithmetic, but an "F" for faith.

Then there's Andrew. Andrew is an interesting character in the gospels, particularly in John. There's not much special about Andrew. Like Philip, he's not a front row disciple. He doesn't get invited up the mountaintop or deep into the heart of the garden, as do Peter or James or John in the other gospels. He and Philip are a tag team. They just always seem to be doing the little things, such as bringing others to Jesus. Andrew brings his own brother, Peter, to Jesus. Philip brings Nathanael in the same manner. Some curious Greeks want to meet Jesus, and they approach Philip. Philip takes them to Andrew who, in turn, takes them to Jesus.

But this time Philip says, "Send them away," while Andrew says, "There is a boy here who has five barley loaves and two fish" (6:9). Five loaves, two fish—not very much for five thousand! That's the point of it being a boy's lunch. Five barley loaves, the food of the poor, and they're more like rolls than loaves, to be accurate. And two fish. They're not Moby Dick; they're more like sardines. Not very much to give! But "not very much" is not the same as "nothing at all."

Don't make Andrew a hero of the faith. He offers the fish and the loaves, but almost in the same breath he takes them back verbally, "But what are they among so many people?"

He doesn't have very much faith. But not very much faith is not the same as no faith at all.

He has faith the size of a mustard seed. He has five loaves and two fish worth of faith. He has faith the size of a small boy's lunch. That amount of faith, Jesus says, is able to move the mountain they're sitting on. It may even be enough to feed five thousand.

I'm a Canadian Presbyterian. Anybody who knows my denomination knows there's something odd about our church names. Every other Canadian Presbyterian church, at least, is called "St. Andrew's." All those homesick Scots named their churches after the patron saint of their homeland. It's such a consistent pattern that it's almost funny. In truth I wish they all could be St. Andrew's Churches, and the churches of all the other denominations too, if that could mean that these churches could be filled not with heroes of the faith but with people like Andrew! People like Andrew with five loaves and two fish worth of faith.

The smart guys in the back of the crowd, the realistic ones who know the price of everything and the value of nothing, must have been hooting and hollering in derision. Five loaves and two fish for five thousand! Weird! But Jesus doesn't think it is peculiar to try to feed five thousand with a small boy's lunch. In Philip's world, it's impossible, but in Jesus' world... So Jesus does the ordinary thing any pious Jew does at a meal. He takes the bread, says the prayer of blessing, and gives the loaves to those around him, and then the fish also.

And there's enough. There's more than enough.

I ought to tell you the rationalizing explanation for this miracle. According to this explanation, more than one person was prudent enough not to go out into the wilderness without a good lunch. Actually, of course, it would have been the boy's mother, not the boy himself. But maybe other mothers, or wives, or sisters planned ahead. When Jesus shared the five loaves and two fish, all these people with good lunches hidden in their robes were shamed by the generosity or strangely moved by Jesus' confidence. They fished out their fish or their bread or their cheese and shared with those around them.

And there was enough. More than enough. Did it happen that way? A miracle explained is a miracle explained away. I tell you this, not because I think this is what happened then. I tell you it because I think that's partly the way this miracle can happen now.

Call it the "Andrew Option," to bring the little bit we have to Jesus, even when our faith is as small as a boy's lunch, to see what Jesus can do. When that happens, there just may be a…well, let me tell you a story.

A number of years ago I attended a committee meeting hosted by a large church in central Sao Paulo, Brazil. Sao Paulo is an enormous city–29 million people by some estimates–with great shack cities called *favelas,* home to millions of the desperately poor. One day, I noticed a man lying in the open gallery covering the sidewalk outside the church door. His clothes were torn and stained; to all appearances he was sleeping it off. I saw nothing unusual in this. The like could be seen in any large city in North America. But this was different: near his head, laid against the hour in which he should awake, there was a cloth handkerchief, white as the linen on the Holy Table. On that cloth were five small loaves. I asked about what I had seen and was told that he had been an educated man from a wealthy family, fluent in three foreign languages, but had drunk away his life. From time to time, if sober, he would do a little outside work at the church, but he refused steadfastly ever to enter the church itself. It was as if he felt unworthy to come into the house of God.

I suppose it was foolish to lay out the loaves for the man. There were poor in the millions in that city. What were five small loaves compared to that mass of misery? And were not many of those millions more deserving than this man who had wasted his life in a bottle? So a realist might think. To lay a table for this man might seem truly foolish–as foolish, perhaps, as trying to feed 5,000 with a small boy's lunch. I was called on to give thanks to our hosts at the conclusion of the meetings. I spoke of what I had seen and of how touched I was, how touched we all were, by the faith and courage of the church to venture what they had even in the face of overwhelming poverty. I think our hosts were touched in their turn by what I said.

The next year, that same committee met in another country. The minister of the Sao Paulo church, who was also a member of the committee, approached me.

"Do you remember the man you spoke of last year?"

"Yes," I replied.

"He died," said the minister. "But before that he allowed us to carry him inside, and he died surrounded by friends, in the church."

In a realist's world, it was not much. Surely, it was not the feeding of five thousand, not much at all. But in Jesus' world, this is what it was…a miracle, a sign of the glory and the power of Jesus. And sometimes, sometimes when my small supply of faith is strong, Jesus' world seems more powerful and more real than any world the realist may know.

I ought to end the sermon here. But there is just one thing more. One of the greatest mysteries of the New Testament is that John doesn't have a Lord's supper story. This story, the feeding of the 5,000 and the sermon that follows it, take its place. Jesus took the loaves, and when he had given thanks, he distributed them. Do you hear the echo, not of the exodus, but of the eucharist? In the end, the story isn't about Philip. It isn't even about Andrew. It's about Jesus and what he gives. What he gives is not just bread or fish, here today and landfill tomorrow. The bread and the fish and the faith they represent matter only because they are entrusted to Jesus. Jesus knows all there is to know about giving. In the end, he gives himself. Call that the Jesus option. In a world in which the most real thing of all is that Jesus gave himself, anything is possible.

SERMON _____

The Empty Net Syndrome
John 21:1–14

JERRY TAYLOR

Compositional Comments

Richard B. Hays' chapter on "The Materiality of John's Symbolic World" shows the importance of John's usage of symbol in his gospel. Symbols and images in John serve as tangible fingers that point to the expansive context of Spirit that both encompasses and extends the world of concrete reality. Hays emphasizes that in John's gospel the Spirit makes its way incarnationally into the concrete world through the materiality of symbols, images, and metaphors. Though Hays' emphasis is correct, I think the materiality of symbols, images, and metaphors can become a distraction from the world of Spirit to which they are intended to point. My sermon seeks to make this point indirectly.

The physicality of Jesus' body serves as the supreme symbol in John's gospel. As most religionists do, the disciples had become attached to symbol. They became overly dependent upon the physical presence or "materiality" of Jesus' body. When Jesus is no longer physically present with the disciples, they experience insecurity and lack of vision. They unthinkingly enter into unproductive activity unrelated to the business of the kingdom of God. The disciples have to learn how to relate to Jesus beyond the parameter of materiality. He is spirit and must be experienced in spirit.

Contemporary disciples gather in community today heavily relying upon images, symbols, and metaphors as dependable means whereby they can encounter God's Presence. In some cases these things have become ends within themselves, leaving believers to believe that since Jesus is out of sight he is not a part of true reality. This sermon is developed under the scrutiny of this particular insight. It challenges the hearer to become weaned from ritualistic attachment to external religious symbols and to truly experience God in the context of Spirit.

Hays' third option for preaching a difficult text in John seems most reasonable. My intention from the earliest development of the sermon was to live comfortably within John's imaginative world. My intention, as Hays' suggests, according to Thomas Olbricht, was to go beyond simply repeating the text to actually using John's language to say something new to our present time under the guidance of the Spirit. My intention was that the sermon would share the texture of John's own language and vision and would therefore be "symbolic, riddling, confrontational, and consoling," as Hays puts it.

Sermon

The fat of consumerism surrounds the weak heart of the church, destroying its awareness of the presence of the resurrected Christ. Its worship is stiffly bound by boring routine that attempts to regulate the spontaneity of God. The consumer church forgets that the Holy Spirit is as free and is as formless as the wind. The Holy Spirit blows where it wills without regard to the religious boundaries fabricated by human beings. Jesus is one with the Holy Spirit.

Therefore, Jesus, like the Holy Spirit, is unpredictable and uncontrollable. The unpredictable Christ promises to meet the disciples in Galilee, but he does not forward his itinerary. The unpredictable Christ is spontaneous and sudden. He shows up in ways and at times least expected.

In our text the disciples are waiting in Galilee. John says that the disciples are gathered together in the absence of Jesus' physical presence. In their minds Jesus is not present because they cannot see him in his recognizable form of human flesh. The disciples face a serious challenge. They face the difficulty of not knowing what to do since Jesus is no longer physically present with them.

Similar to the disciples in John 21, Christians sometimes assemble together with no awareness of the Presence of Christ. Because Jesus is out of sight, he is out of mind. Sometimes Christians gather as a group of strangers in self-service worship. In our gatherings we hardly ever sit facing one another. The seating arrangement often allows us to see one another only from the back. This explains why in some cases we find it easy to talk behind one another's back.

How will the gathered disciples in our text spend their time while they are together without the physical presence of Jesus?

- While they are together, will they reflect upon the spiritual teachings of their master?
- While they are together, will they learn to live in the Spirit without an unhealthy dependence on the physical presence of Jesus' body?
- While they are together, will they become the community of the courageous that speaks truth to power in high places and that speaks power to the weak held captive in low places?

What will the disciples become in the physical absence of their Lord? Will they become Christians built upon the rock of Jesus Christ, or will they become religious consumers built upon militaristic mammon? Will they become the church of the risen Savior, or will they become the consumer church preoccupied with its wealth and stock portfolios? Will they as a church become more committed to Truth or to Trade? Will they promote the "free-market" or the "free-gospel"? Will they promote ministry or industry?

We see which direction the disciples take as a result of Peter's great influence. Without an awareness of the spiritual Presence of Christ, Christians become vulnerable to uninspired instructions and ideas. Peter says, "I am going fishing." Peter does not mention anything about the keys to the Kingdom that Christ promised him. Peter is more focused on his boat than he is on the kingdom of God. Like Peter, Christians today seem more concerned about their yachts than they are about the old ship of Zion.

Peter could use this free time in productive ways for the Kingdom. Instead he uses his time engaging in consumer activity. John tells us that Peter and the other disciples went fishing, and they fished all night long. Though they were experienced fishermen, still they caught nothing. The disciples experienced colossal failure in the area of their expertise. Sometimes it is necessary for us to experience humiliating failure in the area of our expertise. Sometimes failure is the best route to be taken that humbly puts us in harmony with God's will.

The good news is that the disciples in our story are not completely abandoned in the grips of failure. At the deepest point of their discouraging failure, Jesus shows up as an unidentified stranger on the shore of Lake Galilee. Thank God that after every fruitless night of self-effort, and after every moral oil spill of personal disaster upon the lake of life, Jesus stands ready to speak to us. He stands prepared to clean up our moral oil spills even when we fail to recognize his identity.

John tells us that Jesus calls out to the disciples even though they do not realize that it is Jesus. Jesus comes to his own disciples, and they do not recognize him. John here hints that the disciples must develop a spiritual method of establishing Jesus' identity. They will no longer have the luxury of identifying Jesus on the basis of physical form. They must learn to relate to Jesus beyond the physicality of a fleshly body. Christ is no longer confined to a physical body. Christ is omnipresent in the church and in the world. He shows up spontaneously in places and in ways least expected.

Although the disciples fail to recognize Jesus as the shadowy figure on the shore, he still calls out to them. Though today we can't see him physically, he still calls out to us.

His voice breaks through the eternal ages to gain the hearing of our hearts.

Can we hear his voice? His voice is not a passive voice. The voice of Christ is an active voice. It is a creative voice.

It is the Creative Voice that stepped out on the platform of nothingness in the beginning and spoke all of creation into existence.

It is the Creative Voice that speaks to the winds and the waves on a storm-tossed sea, bringing peace where there is turbulence.

It is the Creative Voice that calls Lazarus forth from the cold black stillness of the tomb, liberating him from the grip of death.

It is the Creative Voice in Egypt that says to an arrogant Pharaoh, "Let my people go."

It is the Creative Voice that cries out from the U.S. Congress to the Oval Office for truth to be spoken despite the present climate of tolerated lies and national deception.

It is the Creative Voice that demands the church of Jesus Christ assist blind justice in her walk throughout American institutions and international corporations.

It is the Creative Voice that demands the church desists from holding hands with only the rich and powerful.

It is the Creative Voice that demands the church get out of bed with regimes of injustice, covert operations of unchained greed, and global economic exploitation that's carried out in the name of global democracy.

According to John, Jesus says, "Friends, haven't you any fish?" (Jn. 21:25, NIV). Jesus speaks to them at the point of their exhausted depletion. Jesus is not ignorant of what the disciples are lacking in their lives. Unlike Jesus, the consumer church promotes a prosperity gospel that is impatient with people suffering from lack. We need more friends like Jesus.

Friends like Jesus care about people who have exhausted all their means of survival and still have nothing to show for it.

Friends like Jesus care about people who are struggling to find jobs, shelter, and decent living wages.

Friends like Jesus care about the Iraqi people that have to watch the never-ending horror movie being played out in the Iraqi theater of war.

Friends like Jesus care about how the poor in Third World nations are being crushed to death underneath the heavy weight of an imperialistic global economy.

Friends like Jesus care about how the astronomical gas prices are impacting the working poor while major oil companies are greedily pumping billion dollar profits into their coffers.

Friends like Jesus care about the children who are being left behind in the political rhetoric of politicians who care more for the rich and powerful than they do for the poor and weak.

Jesus says to his disciples, "Friends, haven't you any fish?" Have you caught anything?

They reply, "No!" They were not about to start making up fish stories.

Once the disciples admit their lack, Jesus instructs them to throw their net on the right side of the boat. As a result of obeying the master's command, the disciples caught such a large number of fish that they were unable to haul in the net.

In this story we see the clear demand of discipleship. Discipleship demands that we be motivated by the master's word and not by uninspired human ideas. When we abide in his word and his word abides in us, we will bear much fruit. He is the vine, and we are the branches. Without him we can do nothing.

In response to this miraculous catch of fish, the disciple whom Jesus loved proclaimed to Peter, "It is the Lord!" (21:7). What a magnificent word to proclaim. "It is the Lord."

When the stormy trials surround us in the darkness of night, we shall proclaim, "It is the Lord."

Who is the source of our unspeakable joy? "It is the Lord."

Who gives us the audacity to hope for life beyond the grips of the grave? "It is the Lord."

Who puts clothing on our backs and food on our tables and health in our bodies? "It is the Lord."

Who is the lifter of our heads in moments of depression and the securer of our souls in times of distress? "It is the Lord."

"It is the Lord" should be our everlasting refrain.

Upon hearing the phrase, "It is the Lord," Peter is the first to respond. He hears the word and immediately jumps into the water. Peter does not analyze or evaluate the proclaimed word. He does not commend the beloved disciple for being intellectually stimulating and entertaining. Proclamation of the word demands more than short-lived admiration. Proclamation of the word demands action.

We see a similar active response to the proclaimed word on the day of Pentecost in Acts 2, when Peter uses the keys to the Kingdom to unlock the understanding of those who witness the outpouring of the Holy Spirit. Peter's Pentecostal sermon is entitled, "It is the Lord." As a result of witnessing the outpouring of the Holy Spirit and hearing the preached word, three thousand souls actively respond by jumping into the waters of baptism.

Let me ask you some personal questions. How is your fishing expedition going? Have you found what you have been fishing for? Do you have any fish in your net? Have you, like the disciples, been fishing all night and still have come up with an empty net? Are you spiritually exhausted from all the self-effort of fishing for spiritual food to feed yourself? Maybe you feel you are the one on a hook being reeled in by a consumer society. Maybe spiritual forces are eating you. Are you called upon to give and to be all things to all people all the time? Do these demands leave your net empty? Are you filling your empty net with workshops, conferences, lectures, religious books, religious television and radio shows?

We may fish for all the things of this world, but they can never adequately fill our empty nets. Though our self-efforts leave us continuously empty, our hope is revived when we hear the voice of the master. He says "throw your net on the right side of the boat and you will find what you are fishing for." The good news is that Jesus knows exactly what we are fishing for even when we don't.

The story reveals that Jesus is already preparing what the disciples are fishing for. Not only does Jesus already possess what his disciples are fishing for, but he is preparing it and invites them to receive it. It is often true that, while we are fishing for results, Jesus is already cooking fish. Can you imagine what

Jesus' cooking tasted like? Some might say that Jesus was not only a master carpenter but he was also a master chef.

The disciples are now gathered together, sharing a meal with Jesus in their midst. As they eat fish and break bread together, the meal is suddenly transformed into communion. While eating the common elements of fish and bread with Jesus, his very own presence becomes the real meal. In our communion with Jesus the common elements of bread and wine are transcended to a feasting of the actual spiritual presence of the resurrected Christ.

The narrative says, "None of the disciples dared to ask him, 'Who are you?' because they knew it was the Lord" (21:12). In communion the mystery is resolved. In communion the shadowy figure on a distant lakeshore gives way to the unmistaken identity of the risen Savior. In communion we know with certainty that he who calls out in the darkness of dawn is the same as he who invites us to the meal. We know that, "It is the Lord."

In communion we share supper with Jesus as he sits at the head of the table. His table is not segregated. No system of apartheid governs the seating arrangement around the Lord's table. Only in communion with Christ do we come to genuinely know our real brothers and sisters who have responded to the same invitation we have accepted.

Let this narrative remind us that we shall encounter some disappointing failures as we fish upon the lake of life. But as we experience our fishing failures, remember that Jesus is already on that heavenly shore preparing an eternal feast for his followers.

On that shore we shall see him in full disclosure. On that shore we shall no longer see through a glass darkly. On that shore we shall be a part of the largest praise team that ever existed. On that shore we shall be in full communion with our brothers and sisters from every nation, including believers from Russia, China, North Korea, Iran, and Iraq. On that shore we shall sit in uninterrupted company with our Lord, eternally enjoying the feast of his glorious presence.

In the meantime we crave his presence. In the meantime we sing, "Bread of heaven feed me till I want no more."

Friendship as the Theological Center of the Gospel of John

Gail R. O'Day

Jesus as Friend: Courage for the Present

In the two essays I contribute to this volume, I want to explore what can happen to our reading of the gospel of John and our appropriation of it for the life of faith if we take friendship as the theological center of this gospel. To do this, we will need to re-imagine the very word *friend* and the way it is used—and perhaps overused—in contemporary American rhetoric. In Greek, language of friendship is automatically language of love, since one of the main Greek roots for love—*philos*—is the Greek word for friend. English vocabulary no longer maintains the essential connection of friendship and love. We may remember that the city of Philadelphia derives its name from the combination of two Greek words—those for "love" and "brother," hence "the city of brotherly love"—and that its original Quaker settlers were called "friends"; but in most usages of "friendship" in English, the intrinsic connection between love and friendship is obscured.

"Friendship" tends most often, in current U.S. parlance, to be the vocabulary of greeting cards and television sitcoms, rather than a term with the potential to inform many of the essential doctrines of the church—theology, christology, pneumatology, ecclesiology, and perhaps even eschatology. Friendship is essential to how Christians talk about God, Christ, their communities, and their future. The gospel of John is a pivotal resource in the reclaiming of friendship for the life of faith, as the vocabulary of friendship, especially the noun *philos* and the related verb *phileō*, occurs at key moments in the gospel story.[1]

Given the prominence of friendship language in the gospel of John, the Fourth Evangelist would have agreed with the central claim of the popular American hymn, "What a Friend We Have in Jesus,"[2] but the cultural conventions surrounding friendship as embodied in John and as praised in this hymn are quite distinct. The hymn reflects the sentiments of its time and culture. It was written by a son to comfort his mother whom he had left behind in Ireland when he came to the United States in the 1850s. Its image of friendship is thoroughly Victorian. According to this hymn, Jesus is our friend because he bears our burdens and cares, troubles, sins, and griefs. Jesus is the person to whom the hymn writer's mother could turn when her loneliness for her son became too much to bear. This hymn was written to let her know that Jesus is there for her even when no one else seems to be—and if Jesus is her friend, she needs no other.

The image of Jesus as friend in this hymn is powerful and remains comforting for Christians in all the ways that the son intended it to be comforting for his mother when he wrote it in 1855: "We should never be discouraged; take it to the Lord in prayer! / Can we find a friend so faithful, who will all our sorrows share?" This hymn's image of Jesus as friend is powerful and has brought strength and comfort to many generations of Christians. I want to propose, however, that the Johannine Jesus articulates a much more expansive way to enact friendship than presence in times of emotional distress. The Johannine Jesus articulates the heart of friendship this way: "No one has greater love than this, to lay down one's life for one's friends" (Jn. 15:13).

In my two essays, I want to probe what it means if we take the definition of love and friendship in John 15:13 as beginning and end, as our theological starting point and as the goal of the Christian life. To do that, I want to focus first on Jesus, "Jesus as Friend: Courage for the Present," and then in the next chapter to focus on the Paraclete, "The Paraclete as Friend: Hope for the Future." I have chosen to focus the essays in this way because friendship in John is not simply about Jesus. It is also about the community that forms itself around Jesus. As we will see, friendship is one of the ways in which the revelation of God in Jesus is extended beyond the work of Jesus to the work of the disciples.

Friendship in Greek and Roman Antiquity

In recent years, friendship has become an important category of theological reflection, especially among feminist theologians who are drawn to the patterns of reciprocity found in friendship.[3] God as friend and the Christian community as a community of friends are important themes that emerge. Friendship as a social and theological motif has been given considerable attention by New Testament scholars in recent years as well,[4] because it is a motif that the NT shares with the Greek and Roman cultures in which the early church took shape and in which the NT documents were written. Friendship was an especially popular topic in ancient Greece and Rome, as philosophers and storytellers attempted to define the social and moral virtues and the characteristics of a good society. When the New Testament talks about friends (Greek, *philoi*), it is using a vocabulary current in its cultural context. Modern readers cannot completely recapture those associations for their own reading, but can at least recognize that John is not creating the theme of friendship out of whole cloth.[5]

For classical Greek philosophers in Athens in the fifth and fourth centuries B.C.E., for example, most notably Aristotle, "friend" or *philos* played a pivotal social role in the maintenance of the *polis,* the city-state. For Aristotle and classical philosophers who followed him, friendship was a key social relationship; it exemplified the mutual social obligation on which the *polis* depended.[6] In the democratic ideal of the Athenian *polis,* the relationship between friends, *philoi,* was a relationship between equals contributing together to the public ethos of citizenship.[7]

The following quote from Aristotle about the ideal conduct of a friend illustrates the public and civic dimensions of friendship:

> But it is also true the virtuous man's conduct is often guided by the interests of his friends and of his country, and that he will if necessary *lay down his life in their behalf…* And this is doubtless the case with those who give their lives for others; thus they choose great nobility for themselves.[8]

This quotation from Aristotle highlights an important difference between ancient and modern understandings of friendship. Most contemporary language about friendship, perhaps best represented in the language of greeting cards adorned with roses, kittens, and butterflies, does not place as the ideal of friendship to "lay down one's life for a friend." Given the sentimental and emotional content of most contemporary language of friendship, the claim of Jesus' words in John 15:13 seems completely unprecedented for a modern friend. As this quote from Aristotle shows, however, Jesus' saying has precedent in the model for the ultimate friend in antiquity. In the *Symposium,* Plato writes, "Only those who love wish to die for others." Aristotle writes, "But it is also true that the virtuous man's conduct is often guided by the interests of his friends and of his country, and that he will if necessary lay down his life in their behalf." Lucian, a Hellenistic philosopher and storyteller, promises to tell his readers of "many deeds of blood and battles and deaths for the sake of friends."[9] This does not mean, of course, that any more people laid down their lives for their friends in the first century than are inclined to do so today—but it does show that the ideal of doing so belonged to the ancient rhetoric of friendship.

In the Hellenistic age under the Roman Empire, the period of the New Testament, the lens of democratic citizenship was no longer the center of the social dimension of friendship. Instead, a new set of social relationships, that of patron-client, informed philosophical reflection on friendship. Discussions of friendship in this period focused on the more pragmatic realities of patron-client relationships and on the political expediency captured in expressions such as "friends of the emperor." (Interestingly, this very phrase occurs in John 19:12.)

One of the main distinguishing marks of a friend in this context was the use of "frank speech" (*parrēsia*),[10] as philosophers counseled the patron to be on the lookout for whether "friends" were speaking honestly and openly, or whether they were engaging in flattery to further their own ends:

> *Frankness of speech,* by common report and belief, *is the language of friendship especially* (*as an animal has its peculiar cry*), and on the other hand, that lack of frankness is unfriendly and ignoble...[11]

Definitions of friendship concerned not only what it means to be a friend but how to distinguish between a true friend and its opposite, the flatterer.[12] According to the Hellenistic philosophers, to be someone's friend was to speak frankly and honestly to that person and to hold nothing back. As Plutarch wrote:

> [T]he friend is always found on the better side as counsel and advocate, trying, after the manner of a physician, to foster the growth of what is sound and to preserve it; but the flatterer takes his place on the side of the emotional and irrational.[13]

Two Friendship Motifs

These two dimensions of friendship in the ancient world—*the gift of one's life for one's friends* and *the use of frank and open speech*—provide the essential social and historical background for looking at friendship as a theological motif in John.[14] The first motif, the offer of one's life for one's friends, receives the most attention in studies of friendship in John, as it is widely recognized among Johannine scholars that the language of Jesus' laying down his life for his friends (Jn. 10:15; 15:13) is resonant with this classical motif of friendship.[15] The implications of the second motif, the use of frank and open speech, have been largely unexplored.[16] As we shall see, especially when we turn to study the Paraclete as friend, this is a costly oversight.

Jesus as Friend

Friendship, Love, and Death

For the first readers of John's gospel, the link with the friendship motifs mentioned above in all likelihood informed their understanding of John's teachings about Jesus' death. Since both classical and popular philosophy held up the noble death as the ultimate act of friendship,[17] Jesus' words in John 15:13 evoke the friendship maxims from any number of philosophical treatises on friendship: "No one has greater love than this, to lay down one's life for one's friends." The gospel's first readers would recognize in these words that Jesus is evoking a world in which the greatest moral good prevails. He is calling them into a world that is shaped by looking to the interests of others. The words of John 15:13 in and of themselves would sound familiar.

John 15:13 is distinguished from the philosophical teachings on friendship and death in that Jesus does not merely talk about laying down his life for his friends. Instead, his life is an incarnation of this teaching. Jesus did what the philosophers only talked about—he laid down his life for his friends. This makes all the difference in appropriating friendship as a theological category. Remember the words that introduce this teaching on friendship in chapter 15: "This is my commandment, that you love one another as I have loved you" (v. 12). Jesus' words about friendship in 15:13 are not ideal philosophical reflection or speculation. Rather, they are grounded in the lived reality of Jesus' love. The pattern of Jesus' own life and death moves the teaching of John 15:13 from philosophical ideal to an embodied promise and gift.

At the heart of friendship as a theological category, then, is the fact that Jesus' life transforms ideal models of friendship into realized and embodied grace. In John 10:11–18 (a central section of the Good Shepherd discourse), Jesus combines figurative and discursive language to evoke the type of friendship he offers the community. In 10:11a, Jesus says, "I am the good shepherd," but immediately moves away from first person language to describe more generalized activities of "the good shepherd." The good shepherd "lays down his life for the sheep" (v.11b), as opposed to the hireling who would put the sheep at risk rather than risk his own life (vv. 12–13). This mini-parable could be taken as an illustration of the classical distinction between the true and the false friend—the false friend will not be around in a time of crisis, but the true friend will be. Lucian, for example, writes, "Just so in calm weather a man cannot tell whether his sailing master is good; he will need a storm to determine that."[18]

What moves Jesus' teaching here from philosophical maxim to theological promise is his return to first person language ("I lay down my life for the sheep," v. 15) and his move away from figurative language to talk directly about his own life and death: "For this reason the Father loves me, because I lay down my life in order to take it up again. No one takes it from me, but I lay it down of my own accord" (vv. 17–18a). The first person language makes clear that Jesus is not speaking generally about the gift of one's life for others but that he is making a specific promise about his own life.

Jesus has already pointed figuratively toward his death earlier in the gospel narrative. At 3:14 and 8:28 he has spoken of the lifting up of the Son of Man. What is new in John 10 is the direct and explicit way that he speaks in the first person about his death and the element of volition and choice that he highlights. Jesus announces that he will choose to give his life for the sheep. John 10:17–18 resonates with the philosopher's teachings about the noble friend, choosing to lay down his life; but Jesus' words are not generalized friendship teachings. They are about the conduct and promise of his own life.

The foot washing in John 13 also takes on new dimensions when read through the lens of friendship. At the beginning of John 13, right before the foot washing, the Fourth Evangelist has told the reader that Jesus loved his own "to the end" (13:1). "To the end" (*eis to telos*) can mean simultaneously "to the end of time" and "to the full extent of love." John 13:1 invites the reader to understand the foot washing narrative as a symbolic enactment of the full extent of Jesus' love. To see the foot washing is to see the shape of Jesus' love. The verb used to describe Jesus' removal of his outer robe at 13:4 (*tithēmi*) is the same verb used in John 10 to describe Jesus' laying down his life (10:15, 17–18). This verb choice signals the connection between the foot washing and Jesus' gift of his life–and hence the connection between the foot washing and friendship.

This connection is also at the heart of Jesus' description of the foot washing in 13:8–10. Jesus first explains the foot washing to his disciples by saying, "Unless I wash you, you have no share in me." This description of the foot washing is often rushed past in interpretations of John 13 to get to Jesus' second description of the foot washing in 13:12–15–that in the foot washing Jesus sets an example of what it means to serve one another. While most interpretations of the foot washing, scholarly and popular, focus solely on this second description, the foot washing as Jesus' example of service makes no sense without the first description, that in the foot washing the disciples receive a share in Jesus. Service is defined by what Jesus has done, and what Jesus has done is share himself completely with the disciples through the symbolic act of foot washing.[19] Through the foot washing, the disciples share in Jesus' offer of his life. A paraphrase of 13:8 in the language of friendship would be, "Unless I wash you, you are not my friend."

The promises that Jesus makes in John 10 and the symbolic pre-enactment of his gift of his life in John 13 are shown to be trustworthy by stories of Jesus' arrest and death. The scene of the arrest in the garden in John 18:1–14 has interesting echoes of John 10. Jesus leads his disciples into an enclosed garden, recalling the shepherd and the sheepfold of John 10:1–5; a thief is in the garden (Judas, 18:2; described as *kleptēs* in 12:6), like the bandit in the sheepfold (*kleptēs*, 10:1). Jesus does not wait for Judas to identify him with a kiss in John, thereby robbing the "thief" of any access to the shepherd and his flock. When John 18 is read in light of John 10, Jesus' act of volition, in which he steps forward to meet those who come to arrest him (18:4–6), can only be read as showing the truth of his announcement and promise in 10:17–18: he lays down his life of his own accord. At 18:11, Jesus states explicitly that he chooses the death that is before him ("the cup that the Father has given me"; cf. 12:27). Jesus' life is not taken from him, but he willingly chooses the ultimate act of friendship. Jesus also directly links the offer of his life to his care for his "sheep" (cf. 10:11–13), because his offer of himself is accompanied by the protective instruction to "let these men go" (18:8).[20]

Jesus' free offer of his life for his friends is also illustrated in many details of the crucifixion story in John. Jesus carries his own cross to Golgotha (Jn. 19:17). His free offer of his life is reinforced in the quiet dignity of his death scene (19:28–30). From the cross, Jesus announces the end of his own life and work. ("It is finished" [19:30a].) The description of Jesus' moment of dying positions him as the actor in laying down his life, not as one acted upon: "Then he bowed his head and gave up his spirit" (19:30b).

The arrest and crucifixion narratives confirm that Jesus' words about laying down his life for others are much more than the articulation of the ideal situation. In the life and death of Jesus, the friendship convention of loving another enough to give one's life moves from philosophical or moral possibility to incarnated actuality. Jesus' words about laying down his life articulate the very real choices that he makes for his own life and that guide his relationships in the world. What once was recognizable to at least some of John's readers as a standard part of philosophical rhetoric loses its conventional quality and becomes a distinctive description of who Jesus is. Jesus does not merely talk the language of friendship; he lives out his life and death as a friend.

Equally important, the convergence of Jesus' words with his actions shows that his words and promises can be trusted. Jesus does what he says. There is complete consistency between what Jesus says about laying down his life and what Jesus does. Because Jesus is the Word-made-flesh, speaking and doing are inextricably linked in John (14:10). Jesus both says and does what he receives from God: he speaks God's words, and he does God's works (5:19–24; 10:38; 12:49–50; 17:7–8). Jesus' teaching about laying down one's life in John 10 is a reliable promise because his subsequent enactment of these words shows that Jesus' promises can be trusted.

Jesus' incarnation of limitless love in his life and death moves the teaching of John 15:13 from the realm of the general ("Only those who love wish to die for others") into the very specific. Jesus' disciples are urged to live the same way Jesus has lived, to be the kind of friend that Jesus has been. He is not simply asking them to be good citizens or moral exemplars. He is commanding them to embody the very promises that he has embodied for them (15:14, 17).

The connection between Jesus' offer of his life and the conventions of friendship, love, and death in antiquity is not often recognized when Christian theology and piety interpret the death of Jesus in John. Perhaps it is feared that the resonance with the friendship conventions of John's time somehow diminishes the significance of Jesus' teaching about his own death or routinizes the death itself. It is also the case that the distinctive soteriology of the gospel of John is often subsumed under the models of vicarious suffering or Jesus' death as a ransom for sins. John does not subscribe to either of those dominant understandings of the death of Jesus, but those perspectives so dominate most Christian theology and piety that the Johannine voice of friendship as the language of redemption is not heard.[21]

Christian faith—and its theological articulations of the meaning of Jesus' death—is diminished both in terms of christology and soteriology when the Johannine theology of friendship is overlooked. Instead of reflecting on Jesus' death as an act of gift and grace, of love embodied, the categories of law, sacrifice, and execution tend to set the contours of the theological conversation. When that happens, love and friendship disappear as means of redemption and salvation, and John's witness about the life and death of Jesus as friend is silenced. Jesus as friend in John invites us to reclaim those categories and so enrich the life of faith. Friendship is love in action, love in practice, and through John's witness we come to know that in acts of friendship, one sees God.

Friendship as Boldness of Speech and Action

Perhaps because this friendship motif of boldness of speech does not have the same emotional resonance that is associated with language about love and laying down one's life, most studies of friendship in John have not lingered on this topic. Given the importance of speech and speaking in the gospel of John, however, a friendship motif that focuses on the nature of speaking seems worthy of study. The word *parrēsia* (boldness) occurs nine times in the gospel of John (7:4, 13, 26; 10:24; 11:14, 54; 16:25, 29; 18:20), more times than in any other book of the NT.

Of the nine occurrences of *parrēsia* in John, three refer to his instruction of the disciples (11:14; 16:25, 29). The first, 11:14, seems relatively straightforward and as such its potential significance for understanding friendship is overlooked. At 11:11, Jesus tells his disciples, "Our friend (*ho philos hēmōn*) Lazarus has fallen asleep (*kekoimētai*)." "To fall asleep," in Greek, as in English, can function as a euphemism for death. Jesus' disciples do not recognize Jesus' words as a euphemism, and so do not understand why Jesus should put himself at risk by returning to Judea if Lazarus is only sleeping (v. 12). The narrator explains the euphemism to the gospel's readers, drawing attention to the disciples' lack of understanding (v. 13). In 11:14, Jesus explains to his disciples what he meant by the euphemism and explicitly names Lazarus' death. The narrator describes the speech act by which Jesus informs the disciples about the truth of Lazarus' situation as speaking *parrēsia* ("then Jesus told them plainly").

Perhaps this "plain speech" here is only the decoding of a figurative expression by a non-figurative one. Two aspects of the text argue against assigning this function to *parrēsia,* however. First, Jesus uses a standard euphemism ("fall asleep"), so it is not even clear that he was trying to mask his meaning. Then as now, the use of "sleep" as a euphemism for death would be readily recognized and understood. Second, unlike other sections of the Fourth Gospel in which misunderstanding, irony, and metaphor are intentional literary strategies to move characters to deepening levels of theological understanding (Jn. 4),[22] here the misunderstanding is corrected as soon as Jesus realizes it has occurred.

The role of *parrēsia* in Hellenistic friendship conventions suggests another way of looking at the exchange between Jesus and his disciples in 11:11–15. It seems fair to ask if Jesus' direct speech to his disciples might be an act of friendship, through which Jesus informs the disciples of the hard truth of the death of their friend Lazarus and prepares them for the consequences of this death. The disciples need to face squarely Lazarus' death in order to begin to contemplate the significance of what is to come. That is impossible unless they realize that Lazarus is dead, not merely ill and sleeping. Jesus himself links his "plain speaking" to the disciples' welfare. ("For your sake I am glad I was not there, so that you may believe" [v. 15].) Jesus must speak frankly to the disciples about Lazarus' death to equip them for the role of disciple that the situation may demand of them. (In this case, to see a revelation of God's glory in the raising of Lazarus and so come to believe, cf. 11:2 and 15.) Jesus treats the disciples as equals by speaking plainly to them.

The importance of *parrēsia* as a mode of speaking and instruction in John can also be seen in 16:25–33. This passage, set at the end of the Farewell Discourse and immediately preceding the Farewell Prayer of John 17, contains Jesus' last words of instruction to his disciples. In verse 25, Jesus contrasts his present speaking to his disciples, which has been "in figures of speech" (*en paroimais*), with his eschatological teaching ("the hour is coming"), in which he "will tell you plainly (*parrēsia*) of the Father." The contrast between figurative and direct speech tends to shape the interpretation of these verses,[23] but again one wonders if Hellenistic friendship conventions suggest another context in which to read Jesus' words here, especially since the vocabulary of friendship (*phileō*) occurs twice in verses 26–27. In those verses, Jesus links the effects of the eschatological teaching ("you will ask in my name") with the Father's love of the disciples (*autos gar ho patēr philei hymas*) and the disciples' love of Jesus (*hymeis eme pephilēkate*).

Love and friendship are the goal of Jesus' "plain speaking." Jesus' speech is not simply intended to lead to fresh comprehension on the disciples' part. Instead, Jesus intends to lead them to trust the relationship of love and friendship that they have with God and Jesus and thus to speak to God on their own, without the intermediary of Jesus' speech on their behalf (v. 26). Jesus speaks plainly, with *parrēsia*, to point the disciples to a different way of being with God and one another. This is why in verses 30–33 Jesus disputes the disciples' claim to comprehend his plain speaking and hence to believe (v. 29). Comprehension without enactment misses the point of speaking *parrēsia*. Plain speaking has its effect when the disciples act on God's love of them and their love of Jesus.

The combination of plain speaking and love is also found in Jesus' words about friendship in 15:15. Although the word *parrēsia* does not occur, the sense of plain speaking does. Jesus gives the following rationale for calling the disciples friends: "I do not call you servants any longer, because the servant does not know what the master is doing; but I have called you friends, because I *have made known to you everything* that I have heard from my Father" (emphasis added). The disciples are Jesus' friends because he has spoken to them openly; he has made known to them everything (*panta*) that he has heard from the Father. As Schnackenburg has noted about 15:15, "In our present text, Jesus enables his disciples to participate in the intimacy and trust of the Father, by means of which they acquire that 'openness' (*parrēsia*) which is the privilege of a free man and a friend."[24]

In this verse, the two friendship motifs, love and open speech, come together in Jesus' relationship with his disciples. They are his friends because he speaks plainly and openly to them and tells them everything about God (15:15; 16:25) and because he loves them and gives his life for them (13:1; 15:12–13). They will remain his friends if they keep his commandment and love one another as he has loved them (15:14, 17). They are empowered to keep his commandment because he has told them everything, and so they have their own new relationship with God who loves them (16:26–27).

Conclusion

In Jesus, the two friendship motifs we have looked at are inseparable. Jesus is willing to speak and act boldly throughout his life because he is willing to lay down his life. Jesus is the ultimate friend. Friendship in John is the enactment of the love of God that is incarnate in Jesus and that Jesus boldly and courageously makes available to the world.

SERMON _____

Blessed If You Do Them
John 13:1–30

RICHARD ESLINGER

Compositional Comments

In a powerful symbol of the radical friendship he demonstrates to his disciples, Jesus washes their feet. He even washes the feet of the denier and the betrayer. Jesus lays down his life for friend and foe. Here is no sentimental view of friendship but an expression of its fanatical nature.

A version of this pericope (John 13:1–17, 31b–35) is the gospel lesson for Maundy Thursday in each year of the Revised Common Lectionary. The sermon, "Blessed If You Do Them," assumes this context in Holy Week and projects two other pastoral and liturgical assumptions. First, I assume that the listeners do participate in the ritual of foot washing on Maundy Thursday along with their celebrating the Lord's supper. Second, I assume that the congregation also has been introduced to the Easter Vigil, and that the Great Vigil will, in fact, be the first service of Easter for this parish. Of course, if either or both of these assumptions do not apply to the listeners, then some reworking of the sermon will be necessary.

The strategy for preaching John 13:1–30 is somewhat of a challenge by virtue of the structure of the pericope. This passage does not progress with a step-by-step narrative logic, but rather spirals back through themes and images already developed. At its foundation, the text has a rather chiastic structure: A and A' deal with the meal and its imagery (including the foot washing); B and B' focus on clean, unclean, and betrayal; and the central fulcrum, C, is the self-disclosure of Jesus as "Teacher and Lord." The plot of the sermon, however, follows a sequence that adjusts but echoes the spirals of the chiasm. (So we begin with the text's Holy Meal and conclude with the assembly's Holy Meal.) Each of the moves of the sermon, though, is derived from the pericope. Another chiastic structure relates to those two distinctive terms employed by the Fourth Evangelist: Jesus "rises" (*egeiretai*) and "lays down" or "lays aside" (*tithēsi*) his garments. Each is initially developed within its Johannine larger meaning, while the inverted sequence will be applied to the church in the conclusion. *One final note:* The sermon lacks an immediacy to a particular congregation's life and work. Preached on Maundy Thursday at one church I have served, specific examples of servanthood would have been listed including a ministry to homeless persons. In another setting, that congregation's day care ministry to low-income parents and their children would have been mentioned. Such examples need to be included and need to be quite concrete.

Sermon

Like our Lord and his disciples on this night, we will soon begin our meal, our holy meal. We will take bread, give thanks. The bread will be broken and shared. And, once again, we will know a holy communion with our living Lord and a deepened bond in Christ with one another. Then, it will be time for the other "sacrament" of this night, one also commanded by our Lord Jesus. On this night, while at supper with his friends, Jesus washed their feet.

John takes great care in describing this rite we call the "foot washing." So much is occurring here and at so many levels. The meanings swirl among each other as John describes Jesus' actions. Knowing that his hour had finally come—the hour when he would "depart from this world and go to the Father" (13:1)—Jesus "rose" from the table, "laid aside" his robe, "girded" himself with a towel, and began to "wash" the feet of the disciples. Now, right away, this swirl of meanings goes on high speed. First, Jesus "rose" from the table. That's right, he "rose." This is the only place in the whole gospel where the word does not specifically refer to the resurrection. But does that Easter mystery also infuse the events of this night? We don't know, do we?

Then, Jesus "laid aside" his outer robe, or, as others translate, "laid down" that robe. Either way, the action reverberates with others in the gospel. To "lay aside" his robe certainly echoes with the scene in the empty tomb on Easter morning when Peter and the beloved disciple entered and saw a garment laid aside from the others. And how many times have we heard Jesus speak of laying down his life in order to pick it up again? Either way, we wonder, "Is this the risen Christ who presides at the meal and washes the feet of the disciples?" Remember, Jesus began by announcing that his "hour" had come, the hour when he would be lifted up—on a cross and in glory. Maybe it's not too hard to understand why, at the cathedral at Milan, they still begin the Easter Vigil the way their bishop, Saint Ambrose, taught them—with a service of foot washing! Baptized into Jesus' death and rising, the new babes in Christ of whatever age then receive the ritual of foot washing. Jesus "rose" from the table and "laid aside" his garments. The meanings swirl deeper and deeper. Life laid down follows rising to new and everlasting life. It is a mystery.

The next two movements in the drama seem to have more clarity about them. Here we come to the servant-Messiah scene: Jesus girding himself with a towel and washing the feet of the disciples. He poured water into a basin, began to wash their feet, and wiped them with the towel. The hymn, "*Jesu, Jesu*,"[1] sums it up: "master who acts as a slave to them." And, of course, Peter balks at this demeaning act by his Lord, and probably resists having his feet washed more because…well, he would have to submit to having his feet washed! And if it was true for Peter, it is maybe even more the case for us, isn't it? I mean, this business of submitting ourselves to having someone wash our feet. There is something too intimate and embarrassing about being subject to such a thing.

One writer told of a nurse friend who commented on this ritual: "Many people in the hospital," the nurse said, "will willingly undress for an examination or treatment but will hesitate to take their socks off!"[2] No wonder Peter speaks for so many church folk, too—"You will never wash my feet" (13:8). And you know who have the most trouble with allowing their own feet to be washed? I mean, after we hear from those who do not care for the intimacy or feel embarrassed in public? In my experience, it is the "Marthas" in the congregation who find this such an ordeal, the women and the men whose usual role is serving others. What a challenge it is for these "Marthas" to *receive* such servant ministry instead of *giving* it! This is true for clergy and laity, men and women. But Jesus insists, telling Peter he will have no share with him if he continues to refuse. With the tension building, Peter caves in, caves in completely and comically. "Lord, not my feet only but also my hands and my head!" Peter is now ready for a complete head to toe scrubbing by his Teacher. He would walk through a car wash for Jesus if needed. But that is not necessary, Jesus tells him. He has already bathed, is clean, and needs only his feet washed. Only those feet that are such a problem for Peter and for us.

Jesus disrupts whatever humor remains from Peter's turnabout on this washing business. Jesus adds that Peter is indeed clean, and adds, "[but] not all of you are clean." In fact, he adds a bit later, "One of you will betray me" (13:21). In addition to the other oppositions in John's gospel, we now have one more. We first heard of light and darkness, and later of earthly and heavenly. But now, the opposites have become clean and betrayer. It is a disturbing note for the disciples to hear; "Lord, who is it?" they ask.

It is always profoundly disturbing to learn that one of the flock has become a wolf. The discovery of such an unclean one in the midst of the community leaves everyone wounded, anxious, and suspicious. This upheaval within the family of Christ's followers can permanently damage or even destroy that sense of community. Some scholars have suggested that the community of the beloved disciple never did recover from this discovery of a betrayer. At the very minimum, this revelation of a betrayer in their midst jolted that New Testament church to its core. But Jesus' words come to us with their disturbing message every Holy Week, every Maundy Thursday, demanding that we at least consider the possibility. "One of you will betray me," Jesus tells us just as we are about to share in holy communion and in this most deeply touching rite of foot washing.

It seems that our Lord wants to gird us with the knowledge of such a possibility. To be sure, churches have discovered the truth of Jesus' words again and again. For some, it is the horrible discovery of past clergy sexual misconduct. "Not all of you are clean," our Lord announces. For other congregations, perhaps it is a dishonest financial officer. Not all are clean. Or let persecution rise up against a church and those Christians may find that some "Judas" or other has reported them to the authorities. "One of you will betray me," Jesus says. The wounds from such betrayals cut deep and are hard to heal. So it is interesting to remember that Jesus has already washed the feet of all of his disciples. He came to Judas, knowing all things, and knelt down and bathed and dried the feet of this one who remained unclean in his heart.

Has John provided us with yet another glimpse of this upside-down gospel? Does Jesus love and forgive this Judas, and does he do so even before the betrayer goes out into the night? We don't know. But this much is certain: a community in Christ can never heal from its wounds without forgiveness and without such loving care of each other. Jesus washes the feet of his friends…all of them…all of us.

So Jesus washes the feet of his disciples—he washes *all* their feet; he washes the clean and the unclean. Having completed this duty, he takes up his robe again and sits down. Jesus now takes the stance of their teacher, for it is time for the disciples to know what he has done to them. His teaching moment begins with his identity. The disciples have referred to him as "Teacher" and as "Lord," and Jesus tells them that they are right so to do. He is our Teacher and Lord. The lesson continues with some very direct application of these titles. If he, Teacher and Lord, has washed the feet of the disciples, they are to wash one another's feet. He has given them an example, adding, "servants are not greater than their master…" (13:16). Jesus adds, "If you know these things, you are blessed if you do them."

Here is a beatitude right at the heart of this lesson. We are blessed if we do these things. But I would guess that Peter might blurt out on behalf of us all, if he had not been so embarrassed by the washing business, "But what things are we to do?" Good question Peter, if you only muttered it or even just thought it. Blessed if we do what? Well, the obvious answer has to do with this Maundy Thursday evening. We are to wash each other's feet. That is about as direct a commandment from our Teacher and Lord as we can receive. And so we will kneel at the feet of our friends. After all, servants are not greater than their master.

Jesus, sitting there before us as Teacher and Lord, cannot have in mind only what we do this night. He says he is setting an example for us, and his example includes his faithfulness to his Father's will in the face of betrayal, suffering, and death. His example will include forgiveness, not only of those who betray, but those of us with wobbly faith like Peter. He gives us the fullest example of what it means to be light in a world of darkness, and truth in the midst of this world's lies. "Teacher," "Lord," and "example." "For I have set you an example, that you also should do as I have done to you" (13:15). Those are the words of our Teacher and Lord. On this night, then, we will be blessed if we do them.

Washing each other's feet—and, for some of us even more troubling, allowing another to wash our feet—follows our Lord's command. The ministry that radiates out from this service of foot washing will be an example to our neighbors that this is a church of Jesus' servants. But one is already scurrying out into the darkness. He will betray our Teacher and Lord. Tomorrow is the day in which Jesus' hour does come, and he is lifted up on a cross. He will set us an example to imitate: how to persist in love even when bearing witness to the light means scorn or suffering or death.

Now, if Peter's quiet question has been answered—about what things we are to do—the other question is whether we have the strength and courage to do them. By ourselves, honest to God, the answer is "probably not." But Jesus knows all things, including our wavering faith and uncertain courage. That is why he now invites us to this holy meal with him—to eat his flesh and drink his blood and be given life. See, Jesus, our Teacher and Lord, will raise us up before we have to lay down our lives. The good news of this night is the eternal life that is a gift right here in the darkness.

Amen.

SERMON _____

Being a Friend of Jesus
John 15:9–17

FRED B. CRADDOCK

Compositional Comments

Gail O'Day argues for friendship being the theological center of the gospel of John. She interprets the discourses of Jesus through the template or lens of friendship. In this first essay, O'Day references the well-known hymn, "What a Friend We Have in Jesus." The origin of the hymn indicates that it expresses a more sentimental and emotional view of friend. Jesus is there when we need him; he bears our burdens and cares for us. All we need to do is take these burdens to him in prayer. According to this hymn, it is relatively easy to be a friend of Jesus. O'Day points out that this stands in stark contrast to John's view of friendship. In John's view, friendship involves laying down one's life for a friend and bold honest speech. Both of these qualities come together in this text.

Fred Craddock accepted our invitation to write a sermon for this volume when the request paired him with this chapter from his former colleague, Gail O'Day. In the following sermon, Craddock fleshes out the Johannine theme in his usual creative and challenging way. Yes, he says, we can sing with strong emotion, "What a Friend We Have in Jesus," but then he reverses the relationship and wonders if we should consider, "What a friend Jesus has in me."

Initially, Craddock observes, Jesus' invitation to his disciples sounds like a promotion, you are no longer servants but friends. But the new relationship brings with it heavy responsibility. Servants are not privy to the information of their masters. Neither do they share the responsibilities. However, when we become a friend, we lose our naïveté, we are told the truth about God's will, and we come to share in God's burden. This provocative sermon challenges our view of friendship and will require readers to reexamine their relationship to Christ.

Sermon

It strikes me as strange that I have never heard a sermon on this text. Stranger still, I myself have not until now prepared a sermon on this text. Who knows why? Here is a passage with depth, with sufficient density to tease the mind of the preacher, with an extraordinary offer to the listener, hiding in plain sight. Maybe it is avoided because its promise is too magnificent and, therefore, too demanding. Some texts are like that. Even Martin Luther found the story of Abraham offering Isaac simply too much for a sermon. Or it could be that John 15:9–17 makes an offer to which the heart feels it must say, "No." Listen: "I do not call you servants any longer, because the servant does not know what the master is doing; but I have called you friends, because I have made known to you everything that I have heard from my Father" (Jn. 15:15). From servant to friend–do you welcome, will you accept, the promotion?

I must acknowledge that my trembling before John 15:15 has an antecedent in a sermon heard almost twenty years ago on a kindred theme: Abraham was called a friend of God (Jas. 2:23). A combination of misfortunes put me in the fortunate position to hear the sermon. A cancelled flight; a last minute reservation in a motel near the airport; a search for a church within walking distance, since the next morning was Sunday; a housekeeper at the motel pointing in the direction of one six blocks away; my arrival at a cinder block building in which a few tired souls had already begun singing gospel songs. The preacher, a large man, made painfully awkward by a number of maladies, including poor eyesight, moved to the pulpit and read in crippled speech his sermon text: James 2:23. His opening words were, "Abraham was a friend of God. I'm sure glad I am not a friend of God." His sermon was an explanation of why he was pleased not to be a friend of God.

I cannot recall being so engaged in a sermon. His delivery was without animation; his physical condition denied him that. His speech was a bit halting, but each word was clear and pronounced with respect. All of us in the small congregation were helping him preach by our total silence and attention to what he said. He recalled the story of Abraham, pilgrim and wanderer who after years of homelessness, died and was buried in a land not his own. "Abraham was a friend of God," he said; "I'm glad I'm not." He then spoke of others who had been called friends of God, faithful in spite of dungeon, fire, and sword. He concluded with a story of Teresa of Avila, remembered by the church as a friend of God. He recalled her begging in public to raise funds for an orphanage. After a series of setbacks–flood, storm, and fire repeatedly destroying the orphanage–Teresa in her evening prayers said to God, "So this is how you treat your friends; no wonder you have so few." The sermon closed with counsel: if you find yourself being drawn into the inner circle of the friends of God, blessed are you. But pray for the strength to bear the burden of it.

Because of that extraordinary sermon in that little church (I do not remember its name, nor that of the preacher), I am somewhat prepared to hear Jesus' words, "I do not call you servants any longer...but I have called you friends."

No longer servants but friends: it sounds like a promotion. One could make a case for such a reading. Had not Jesus, in that very room, on that very night, dramatically impressed upon the disciples the posture and action of a servant by washing their feet? Had he not said plainly that they were to wash one another's feet? Had he not reminded them of a fact not to be overlooked in the life of a disciple. "servants are not greater than their master"? (13:14–16).

"Servant" is the operative word to speak of our relation to Christ and to the community of faith. Nothing strikes us as so unbecoming a follower of Christ as arrogance, as the pursuit of position and power, as the desire to be served rather than to serve. Such living is a stark contradiction of the teaching and the example of Jesus. Of course, we sing with feeling "What a Friend We Have in Jesus," but who among us would say, "What a friend Jesus has in me"? None of us would or should claim that position.

Now, suddenly and shockingly, Jesus bestows the title that no one among us could claim: *friend.* It feels like a title; but, in fact, the word describes a relationship. It implies love and mutuality. Even if it is not a title, it still feels like a title. If you have been all your life a servant of Jesus; if you have chosen that role; if being a servant of Jesus faithful in word and deed has been the total definition of who you are, then to be called by Jesus his friend is an overwhelming gift. "Jesus has called me his friend"; who can pronounce the words? It is too much.

Of course, "friend" is heard as a promotion. No longer servant but friend—receive it for what it obviously is, a promotion from one station to another. Think of it: out of the cabin into the big house; off the back porch to the patio; off the bench up to the dining hall; out of the field onto the lawn; off the floor and into the big bed. No more, "Tote that barge, lift that bale"; instead, "Come, friend, let us walk together." Can there be in all God's kingdom a delight greater than this? No, absolutely not; it is impossible.

Jesus continues: "I do not call you servants any longer, because the servant does not know what the master is doing." That's the truth; the whole of my life was to do what I was told. Plough, plant, weed, harvest; that is what I did when told to do it. I did not know what went on in the big house; I did not know what went on in the master's head. Deals, trades, profit and loss: these were his responsibilities, not mine. His lamp burned late, not mine. When my day's work was done, it was done. After that, it was bread and bed for me. Don't ask me any questions about my master's business; I don't know. I mind my own business.

Jesus continues: "But I have called you friends, because I have made known to you everything that I have heard from my Father." In other words, a friend of Jesus shares in the knowledge of God's operation in the world, what God is doing and how God is doing it. God is creating a community of love that is to embrace everyone. A friend has this love and extends it toward others, but it carries a price. The world that does not know God will hate the friend of Jesus as it hated Jesus for practicing this love. Jesus paid the full price for so loving, laying down his life for those he loves. We have no reason to assume a friend of Jesus would be exempt from the same. Through knowing what Jesus heard from God, the friend of Jesus shares in the responsibility of that knowledge. "What a friend we have in Jesus" is a pleasant and encouraging thought, but "what a friend Jesus has in me" is beginning to feel burdensome. I am beginning to wonder if the move from servant to friend is really a promotion.

It is true the servant does not know what the master is doing, but that has its bright side. The servant doesn't take his work home with him. For him the day ends when he puts aside the shovel and the hoe. But sometimes the master is up all night, pacing and worrying. If the servant becomes the friend of the master, then the master's burdens become the servant's own. It seems friends of Jesus are never completely free of the duty to bear the fruit and to pay the price of love.

"Because I have made known to you everything that I have heard from my Father." But really, who wants to know? Most of us carry within us large areas of deliberate ignorance. From childhood we carry the warm and inspiring image of General George Washington with his troops in the biting snow at Valley Forge. Who wants the picture spoiled by the information that Washington was quartered in a large and comfortable farmhouse nearby? From English literature class we embrace William Wordsworth as the tender and sensitive poet. Why enroll in a graduate course on Wordsworth and be disillusioned by his practice of using a knife already smeared with butter and preserves to cut apart the pages of books newly arrived at the home of his host? Who wants to hear a poor child say, "Mommy, I'm hungry," and to read a marquee announcing "All You Can Eat, $7.95" all on the same evening? Comfort demands avoiding those rallies where passionate and informed speakers assail our ears with the news: 13 million children in America go to bed hungry every night; over 9 million have no health insurance; every 30 minutes a child is shot to death in the United States. There is a lot of information that I prefer not to know.

Is this what it means to be a friend of Jesus, to be told the uncomfortable truth that carries unavoidable duty, the duty to love, to love as God loves, to lay down one's life if need be? The life of the servant is looking better all the time. I recall the first time I saw the inside of a pulpit. The church of my upbringing had a beautiful pulpit with a succession of most attractive tapestries. I admired them every Sunday from my seat near the back pew. The pulpit was awesome. Then I was called to be a minister. On a Christmas break from school, I was asked to preach. It was a trembling experience. Among my memories of that day is the unforgettable image of the contents of the pulpit. Piled inside on two shelves were old bulletins, a scum covered glass of water, a baseball cap, a faded stole, a coverless hymnal, an old Bible, a few sheets of music, pages of handwritten notes, a broken alarm clock, and a burned to the base candle. Needless to say, the view from the pew was much more pleasant. I did not at the time feel I had been given a promotion. In fact, there are plenty of days when being a servant has stronger appeal that being a friend. The old cabin out back looks more attractive than the big house.

I will never forget the first time I was invited as a friend to spend the night in the big house, God's house. I was, of course, excited as a new friend of Jesus and a first-time visitor to the House of Many Rooms. Angels showed me around and answered my endless questions. The food was heavenly and at bedtime I was shown to a room of my own. With a, "Goodnight, sleep well,"

I was left alone. The excitement of the day finally resolved into weariness and weariness into rest. My bed was a cloud. To the soft sound of music coming from everywhere, I drifted into sleep.

Sometime during the night my sleep was interrupted by sounds from the next room. I did not know who was in that room, but somebody was having a bad night. The noise was not snoring, nor did it seem to be sleep talking. I listened more carefully; maybe it was groaning or moaning accompanied by tossing and turning. I thought once to knock on the door, but was afraid to do so. I dared not call out lest I add to that person's discomfort and perhaps wake others. So I tolerated it till morning, catching only snatches of sleep.

At daybreak I heard the person next door move about the room and then step out into the hall. I did the same, wanting to see who it was, and, if appropriate, express regret that the night was so restless.

It was God. I was shocked; God restless and unable to sleep, the God who blesses with peace beyond understanding, the God who hushes even a whimpering child? I was speechless.

God said, "I'm sorry if I disturbed your sleep. I know my groaning was a disturbance, but I couldn't get my mind off all my hurting children down there."

What did that "I don't remember his name" preacher in that "whatever it was" church say to the congregation? "If you find yourself being drawn into the inner circle of the friends of God, blessed are you. But pray for the strength to bear the burden of it."

SERMON _____

Once I Was Blind, But Now...?
John 9:1–41

Thomas G. Long

Compositional Comments

Though this text in John 9 never uses the term *friend* or speaks of the theology of friendship as Gail O'Day does, one can easily read this story through O'Day's lens of friendship. In this sermon, Tom Long shows how the blind man embodies what it means to be a friend of Jesus. After his conversion, the blind man faces all kinds of trouble. The day this blind man meets Jesus is the day major problems arise. The day Jesus gives him sight is the day the blind man truly sees the injustices of the world and the burdens placed on him. His life will never be the same.

Our temptation today is to domesticate Christianity and make it fit our comfortable lifestyles so that we can keep our lives intact. We've taken discipleship out of Christianity and want to believe that once we become Christians Jesus takes on all of our burdens and cares. In the words of Dallas Willard, we've developed "undiscipled disciples."[1] Through this story of the blind man, Long challenges this "Christianity Lite" lifestyle. An earlier version of this sermon was preached in two different contexts—one at the Candler School of Theology chapel and the other at the Festival of Homiletics.

Sermon

Lynna Williams, who teaches creative writing at Emory University, has written a delightful, and in some ways hilarious, short story called "Personal Testimony."[2] The story is about a twelve-year-old girl, the daughter of a west Texas fire-breathing evangelistic preacher, who is compelled every summer to spend a couple of weeks at a fundamentalist Bible camp for children in Oklahoma. During the day this Bible camp is similar to most other summer camps, with hiking, softball, sailing, and arts and crafts. But at night, every night, a "revival meeting" is held for the campers, a high-pressure service of worship where there is sweaty "come to Jesus" preaching and the kids are pressed to surrender their lives to Jesus. The unwritten expectation is that at some time during camp every camper will come forward and give a moving personal testimony.

The problem is these campers are just kids, most of them very normal kids, and a good many of them don't have personal testimonies to give. That's where our twelve-year-old preacher's daughter comes into play. She figured out she could make a little money on the side as a ghostwriter for Jesus, writing personal testimonies for the other campers. For example, for five dollars she wrote a wonderful personal testimony for a boy name Michael, about how in his old and sinful life he used to be very bad and would take the Lord's name in vain at football practice. Now that Jesus has come into his heart, though, his mouth is as pure as a crystal spring.

Michael's "testimony" was a good one, no doubt, but this girl's most dramatic personal testimony, her best piece of work, was written for Tim Bailey. It was about how his life was empty and meaningless until he met Jesus in an almost fatal, and utterly fictitious, pickup truck accident near Galveston, a near catastrophe in which Jesus himself seized the steering wheel and averted disaster. That one took some imagination, and she charged twenty-five dollars for it.

Of course, a lot of the wit of Lynna Williams' short story is derived from the fact that the satire is not too far from the truth. In some church circles, at least, personal testimonies such as these are quite commonplace, and they often seem so canned, so contrived, and so written to formula. They all have the same plot; "Once I was in distress, but now I have triumphed. Once I was lost, but now I am found." As the revival hymn puts it, "I was sinking deep in sin, far from the peaceful shore...but the Master of the sea heard my despairing cry. From the waters lifted me, now safe am I."[3]

Well, these testimonies may seem formulaic, but we should remember where the formula comes from. All of these "once I was lost but now I am found" testimonies actually derive from one of the very first Christian personal testimonies, the one given by the blind man in the ninth chapter of John:[4] "Once I was blind but now I see" (9:25). Ever since this blind man uttered these famous words, Christians have been telling stories of personal transformation, how they have been taken by Jesus from blindness to sight, from trouble to peace.

We need to be careful here, though. When we actually look closely at the whole story of the blind man, the interesting thing to note is that the one person in the world who would not be able honestly to give one of those contrived "once life was bad, but now I'm happy in Jesus" personal testimonies was this blind man. In fact, the day he met Jesus was not the day his troubles ended; it was the day his real troubles began.

This story opens with Jesus and the disciples going into a community in the environs of Jerusalem, a community of moral order and stability. It is at least at rest, and in many ways it is at peace. It has strong institutions, congregations, clergy, neighborhoods, families, and a keen sense of right and wrong. As our politicians often say, "This place has got values, family values."

This community has one more thing. It has a blind man. This is a community with a blind man—in fact, a man who was *born* blind. He has always been blind, always will be blind. Blindness yesterday, blindness today, blindness forever. This blindness is not simply a physical impairment; the man's blindness creates for him a social role. He gets to be *the* "blind man"; and since he gets to be the blind man, all the rest of us get to be the "people who see." This is not just a moral role; it is a theological role, too, because blindness is connected in the minds of the citizens of this community with sinfulness. Blindness is a manifestation of sin, so the blind man is more than just a "blind man"; he is the community's "designated sinner."

That's the way communities maintain moral stability and balance. You get to be the sinner; I get to be righteous. *Those* neighborhoods are bad; *these* neighborhoods are good. *Those* schools are bad; *these* schools are good. You're sinful, and I'm righteous. Even Jesus' disciples accepted this moral world. We can tell that because, when they come into the community, they took one look at the blind man and said, "Rabbi, look, a man born blind! Who sinned? This man or his parents?" (9:2). It had to be one or the other. Was the man the sinner here, or was his blindness the result of his parents' sin?

"Neither," said Jesus, and the world tilted on its axis.

In the moral world that everybody assumed was fixed and immovable, somebody's sin was the cause of this man's blindness. It had to be either the man's sin or his parents' sin. So which was it?

"Neither," said Jesus. "Rather, this blindness is the occasion for the glory of God" (9:3). What Jesus said points not just to a different attitude but to a different moral world, and what happened next is astonishing. Like God in Genesis, Jesus bent down and took mud and created a new world and a new humanity. He spread the mud on the man's eyes and said, "Go, wash in the pool of Siloam" (9:7). When the man did this and came back into the community, he could see. The man born blind, the man who was the designated sinner, came back seeing, came back as a child of the new creation.

And that was when all hell broke loose.

If the man who is supposed to be blind comes back seeing, and the man who is supposed to be the sinner comes back radiating the glory of God, it throws the moral universe off its kilter. All of us are called into question. The only way to respond is to try to make the new world go away, to try to reestablish the world in the safe and stable way it used to be. Sure enough, before this day is over, the man has been accosted by his neighbors, abandoned by his parents, cursed by his ministers, and thrown out of his congregation.

The day he met Jesus was not the day his troubles ended. It was the day his real troubles began.

This man who used to be blind is the last person in the world to be able to chirp, "Once I was blind, but now I see!" In fact, I think what he said was, "Once I was blind, but, oh my God, *now* I see. *Now* I see..."

This is the way it is, isn't it? The more we are drawn into the light of Jesus, the more we have our eyes opened by the gospel. The more we have our eyes opened by the gospel, the more things we see, the more we see how the old world is captive to the powers of darkness and the forces of death, the more ways we see that the shadows fall across us, across that world we assumed was so stable, and the less we can feel at ease in the world as it is. To be given sight by Jesus is to participate in the collision of moral worlds.

One of the best contemporary examples of this I know came in the trial of the Berrigan brothers. In May 1968 two Roman Catholic priests, Daniel and Philip Berrigan, and seven of their Christian friends—two missionaries, a midwife, a nurse, a worker in race relations, and several other companions— walked into the draft board office in Catonsville, Maryland (this was at the height of the Vietnam war). As an act of nonviolent witness for peace, they took some draft files out of a filing cabinet, carried them out into the street, and burned them. They were, of course, arrested and charged with a federal crime.

In October of that year, they were placed on trial in federal court in Baltimore. It was a good court with a good judge. Like the story in John 9, the trial constituted a collision of moral worlds as the defendants tried to explain that what they had done was not so much an attempt to violate the federal law, but an attempt to obey God's law. "Why did you do this?" said the prosecutor to Daniel Berrigan.

"I did it," he said, "because I began to see the cost of being a Christian. When I saw the napalm kill children, my senses were invaded; and I saw the power of death in the modern world."

At this point, the judge interrupted; "Father Berrigan. "This testimony is irrelevant. The war is not on trial, you are."

"Your Honor," replied Daniel Berrigan, "I can only tell you what I see, and what I see is that right now we are standing before the living God."

One of the attorneys said, "Mr. Berrigan, are you saying your religious convictions had something to do with this?"

"Yes, yes, of course, my religious convictions had something to do with this. If it were not for my religious convictions, this would be eviscerated of meaning; and I should be committed for insanity."

Another defendant, Mary Marlin, a nurse, stood up and said, "I did this because I have begun to see things as they are. This is what a Christian does when you see things. You stand up for your beliefs." Then she turned to the judge and said, "Your Honor, you stand well for the law, but what about God's law of peace?"

This confused the judge, who responded, "Uh, I see your point...but you are not my spiritual advisor."[5]

The man in John 9 would recognize all this—the accusations and the fearful confrontations. "How can you, who were utterly born in sin, teach us? You're not our spiritual advisor." The testimony of sight: "I can only tell you what I see. Once I was blind, but *now* I have begun to see."

The more we are drawn into the light of Christ, the less we can rest easy with the world as it is. Which would be fine, if only Jesus would hold our hand through the conflict. If only he would stand right there at our side, like the old hymn says, and hold our hand in the mist of the storm. Then we could bear the inevitable conflict that the faith's seeing evokes. But did you notice in this story that, as soon as he healed the blind man, Jesus disappeared? He stirred up the pot, turned up the heat, and then got out of the kitchen, leaving the man to face the conflict all on his own. Why, why?

Biblical scholars are quick to point out that the original readers of John would have recognized what was happening to the blind man. One of the reasons Jesus is pictured as absent, then, is perhaps to sharpen this sense of recognition. Their own faith in Jesus caused them to be shunned by their neighbors, abandoned by their parents, accursed by their ministers, and thrown out of their congregations. Their relationship to Jesus did not protect them from the rough and tumble of these experiences.

A deeper theological reason explains why Jesus is absent right at the moment that the conflict becomes intense. The reason Jesus does not hover around in the midst of the conflict is that the conflict is necessary if we are really going to see and really going to become people of faith. Opening our eyes to see is not like some "before and after" contrast in a diet ad: one minute we were blind, and now the next minute we see everything clearly. Opening our eyes happens as a process, a process that occurs in and through conflict. It is as people who belong to the light engage in moral conflict in the world that their faith becomes shaped and their vision becomes focused.

Thomas Merton said that whenever a new monk came to the monastery, to the community, the monks held an entrance ritual. This ritual did not involve patting the new monk on the back and saying, "Welcome brother; we're glad to have you." Instead, the new monk would be placed in the middle of the circle of brothers, and the Abbot would say in Latin, "What are you seeking?" In other words, "What do you really want?"

The answer was not, "I seek a happy life," or, "I seek freedom from my anxiety," or, "I seek union with God, and contemplation." The answer was, "I seek mercy, mercy, mercy." "All of the monks," said Merton, "would know that this mercy was to be achieved only in a struggle. In a struggle with blindness, the blindness in the world as it is, and the blindness in us. Those who give up the struggle," said Merton, "are those who are truly blind."[6]

The day we meet Jesus is not the day our troubles are ended; it's when our troubles begin.

Some time ago, I had the privilege of preaching at a Lenten service at Fifth Avenue Presbyterian Church in New York City. I learned about their own experience of being given new sight by Jesus. Fifth Avenue Church is what the New Yorkers call one of the "Avenue Churches." They're on Madison Avenue, Park Avenue, and Fifth Avenue. These churches were built in the nineteenth century for silk-stocking Christians pulling up in fine carriages. Fifth Avenue Church's neighbors are quite impressive. Across the corner is the Saint Regis Hotel, and down the street are Saks and Tiffany's. Right across the street is the Trump Tower. The day I preached there, a banner hung across the street with a photo of "The Donald" himself pointing a finger and saying, "You're fired!"

The entrance to Fifth Avenue Church is a magnificent stone Romanesque arch. For years and years some of the homeless in New York City have taken refuge on the porch of the church under that arch. Members of the church had to step over them to get into evening services and night meetings. Then, several years ago, by the grace of God, the eyes of the congregation were opened. How were they opened? Courageous preaching? Powerful worship? Prayer and Bible study? Maybe by the grace of God, Jesus works through all of the above. I don't know which it was, but suddenly the members at Fifth Avenue church began to see, really see, who was on their front porch and what they were up against in society. "Once we were blind to the plight of these people," the church could say, "but *now, now* we see."

The first thing the church did was to apply to the city for the right to establish a night shelter. "Ten beds," said the city, "only ten beds." They built them, but there were more than ten homeless. So, they tried to get them into other shelters, but they found quickly that the people on their front porch were what social workers sometimes call "service resistant" homeless. They are people who are fearful of institutions and leery of authority. They don't want to be placed in a shelter; they want to be on the porch of the church. So with eyes wide open, the church said, "All right, we will make this porch a place of hospitality. Everyone who sleeps here, we will know by name. We will try to know the story of everyone who comes within the boundaries of our church. We will to the best of our ability protect you. When morning comes, we will have hot coffee and showers if you want."

That was when the trouble started. But this should come as no surprise. The day you meet Jesus is not the day your troubles with the world end; it is the day your real troubles begin.

First the neighbors: "Isn't that the church that used to be blind?"

"It must be a different congregation."

"No, it's the same congregation. I liked them better when they were blind."

Then the authorities were brought into it. On a cold, rainy night in December, the New York City Police Department came with billy sticks and knocked down the cardboard shelters and rousted the homeless off the church porch. The church responded in outrage and protested to the city.

The city said, "You're running an illegal shelter out there, and you can't do it." It ended up in court. The city said; "Your charter is as a house of worship, and this is not your mission."

The church said. "You ask Isaiah about our mission; you ask Jesus about our mission."

The judge said to the church, "You're right," and ruled for the church. The city appealed. The church won again, and the city appealed again–four times.

It's not over yet, but on the fourth occasion, members of the church gathered under the stone arch with their guests, their homeless guests, for a service of thanksgiving. After a prayer of thanksgiving, one of the homeless, who said she wanted to be a gospel singer, spontaneously begin to sing "Amazing Grace." You may remember one of the lines: "was blind, but now I see."

When the hymn was over, one of the members of the church gasped, "Look up," she said. When they looked up, she said, "This is a sign that those who built this church knew all along we would be out here." In the roof of the arch they saw something they had never seen before: an absolutely beautiful mosaic of the angels of God keeping watch and of the eye of God keeping protection. The members of that church had walked under that arch a thousand times and had never seen it. One of the homeless people, however, said, "Yeah, we see it every night when we are flat on our backs."

When they threw the (formerly) blind man out of the congregation, and he was flat on his back, he, too, saw the watchful eye of God. Jesus, who keeps watch over his flock, found him. "Do you believe in the Son of Man?" asked Jesus.

"I want to. Who is he?"

"Good news," said Jesus. "I am he; I am he" (9:35–36).

In a few minutes, we are going to gather at the Lord's table. We will meet this Jesus there at the table. He is the host of this feast, and he invites us to join him. Come eagerly, but also beware. Jesus will open your eyes. When you begin to see, you will never rest easy again, because once you were blind, but *now, now* you see.

3

The Paraclete as Friend

Hope for the Future

GAIL R. O'DAY

According to the hymn "What a Friend We Have in Jesus," all that is
required for the believer to share in friendship with Jesus is to take/carry/bring
all griefs to Jesus in prayer. Jesus will take care of everything else. According
to this understanding of friendship, it is relatively easy to be Jesus' friend. Yet
our earlier discussion of friendship in John suggests that such an understanding
greatly reduces the full theological, ethical, and pastoral content and import
of friendship. As we have seen, friendship in John is not primarily an affective
category or relationship; it is not primarily about what or how we feel, and so
is different from much contemporary discourse about friendship. Friendship
in John is the enactment of the love of God that is incarnate in Jesus and that
Jesus boldly makes available to the world.

Discipleship as Friendship

In this second essay, I want to turn the focus from Jesus as friend to the
future that Jesus' friendship creates for the believing community. A review of
John 15:12–17 is the best place to begin the turn toward this future:

> This is my commandment, that you love one another as I have loved
> you. No one has greater love than this, to lay down one's life for one's
> friends. You are my friends if you do what I command you. I do not
> call you servants any longer, because the servant does not know what
> the master is doing; but I have called you friends, because I have made

known to you everything that I have heard from my Father. You did
not choose me but I chose you. And I appointed you to go and bear
fruit, fruit that will last, so that the Father will give you whatever you
ask in my name. I am giving you these commands so that you may
love one another.

This passage is shaped rhetorically by the concentration and repetition
of the vocabulary of love and friendship. This vocabulary highlights the two
friendship motifs of laying down one's life and speaking boldly and openly.
Key to the use of these motifs here is that attributes that have characterized
Jesus as friend are now transferred to his disciples. The first motif, laying down
one's life as an act of friendship, functions for the disciples just as it does for
Jesus: the ideal (v. 13) is transformed into a commandment and an expectation
about the conduct of one's life (vv. 12, 14, 17). The enactment of love that is
of the same extent as Jesus' love is not simply a philosophical truism for the
disciples, but it is a commandment. The disciples are enjoined to enact the love
that Jesus enacts. The second motif, speaking openly, is central to Jesus' words
in verse 15, as was noted at the end of the preceding chapter. As a result of the
openness and boldness of Jesus' speech to them ("I have made known to you
everything"), the disciples have a complete awareness of what God and Jesus
are doing, and so can be called friends, no longer servants.

Verse 16 is also pivotal in understanding what it means for the disciples
to be Jesus' friends. This verse emphasizes that Jesus chose the disciples, not
the other way around. Friendship with Jesus is not affective or elective on the
community's part. Rather, friendship with Jesus derives from Jesus' own initial
act of friendship–his enacted love in his life and death creates friendship.
Anything that the disciples do subsequently is a response to Jesus' initiating
act of friendship. As a result of Jesus' choosing them as friends, the disciples
are appointed by Jesus to bear fruit.

"Bearing fruit" introduces a new metaphor into the language of love and
friendship. In John 12:24–25 Jesus says, "Very truly, I tell you, unless a grain
of wheat falls into the earth and dies, it remains just a single grain; but if it dies,
it bears much fruit. Those who love their life lose it, and those who hate their
life in this world will keep it for eternal life." This passage suggests that bearing
fruit is the outcome of laying down one's life in love. Jesus' gift of his life in
love bore the fruit of friendship for the disciples; the disciples are enjoined to
bear fruit in the same way.

"Bear fruit" is also prominent in Jesus' teaching about the true vine
(15:1–11). Importantly, this passage links the vocabulary of abiding and bearing
fruit (vv. 4–5) with the vocabulary of love (vv. 9–10). These verses, along with
12:25–26, provide the immediate context for Jesus' commission to bear fruit
in 15:16. The bearing of fruit to which the disciples are enjoined is linked to
Jesus' love for them, God's love for Jesus, and their mutual indwelling with one
another and the community. Bearing fruit is only possible when the community

abides in love. When they bear the fruit of love, they make visible the mutuality of relationship and responsibility that characterizes friends of Jesus. When the injunction to bear fruit in 15:16 is read alongside these earlier occurrences of the phrase, one recognizes that "bear fruit" is metaphorical language for "love one another as I have loved you."

In speaking of his disciples' future lives in 15:12–17, Jesus makes explicit the connection between his life of love and the conduct of friends. Jesus calls the disciples his "friends" (*philoi*), if they enact his commandment (15:14)–to love one another as Jesus has loved them (v. 12), to lay down their lives for their friends (v. 13). They will also be his "friends" if they are able and willing to speak as boldly and openly as he has done. Jesus' gift of his life for others embodies friendship's highest attribute and defines the meaning and extent of "love." Jesus' boldness and courageous speech charts a way of courage for the present and future lives of his disciples.

The name "friend" and the relationship of friendship is a gift from Jesus to the disciples,[1] just as his life is a gift to them. The disciples begin their future with the explicit appellation, "friend." The challenge for them is to enact and embody friendship as Jesus has done. The disciples know how Jesus has been a friend; they are called to see what kind of friends they can become.

Jesus' invitation to friendship in John 15:12–17 is followed immediately by a section of the Farewell Discourse (15:18–16:4) in which Jesus describes the adversity and suffering that the disciples may experience "on account of my name" (15:21). In this section, Jesus exhorts his disciples to boldness of speech ("You also are to testify because you have been with me from the beginning" [15:27]) and names his own boldness of speech as grounds for the disciples' boldness ("I have said these things to you to keep you from stumbling" [16:1]). The conventional way to approach John 15:18–16:4 (often called, for example, "the world's hatred") is to assume that the teachings on friendship at the beginning of chapter 15 are distinct from the teachings on persecution with which the chapter ends. In many John commentaries, the last half of John 15 is read as containing two discrete units: the first that focuses on the community's love for one another, the second on the world's hatred of the community.[2]

Our study of the friendship motifs of laying down one's life and boldness of speech suggests another possibility for understanding these two important sections of the Farewell Discourse. Read in the light of friendship conventions, John 15:12–17 and 15:18–16:4 may not be as discrete or contrasting as Johannine scholarship traditionally maintains. Instead, it is possible to understand these two sections as one continuous teaching about friendship. In 15:12–17, the friendship convention of love and the giving of one's life as embodied in the life and death of Jesus is at the center of Jesus' teaching. Jesus challenges his disciples to love one another as Jesus loved them. In 15:18–16:4, the friendship convention of boldness of speech and action, regardless of the risk, is at the center of Jesus' teaching. This convention, too, as we have seen, has been embodied in Jesus' own practice of friendship. In his words in 15:18–16:4, Jesus continues to challenge the disciples to do what he does–to live their faith boldly and unafraid, regardless of the situation in which they find themselves. Read in this way, 15:12–16:4 is one continuous teaching on the life of friendship: to be a friend by loving as Jesus has loved; to be a friend by witnessing boldly to one's faith.

The life of friendship as depicted in John 15 is a life of challenge. The disciples are enjoined to love and witness in their own lives as fully as Jesus did in his. How is it possible for the disciples–disciples in the story of the gospel of John and disciples throughout the story of the Christian faithful–to accept and enact this challenge? How is it possible for disciples to live fully as friends? God recognizes the difficulty of this challenge and knows that the disciples cannot love as Jesus loved without some help. The Fourth Evangelist's theological and pastoral genius is evident, as he is the only New Testament writer to report Jesus' promise of help in form of the Paraclete.

The Paraclete as Friend

[T]he friend is always found on the better side as counsel and advocate, trying, after the manner of the physician, to foster the growth of what is sound and to preserve it.[3]

This quote from Plutarch, which we looked at in the preceding chapter, is a good beginning point for a study of the Paraclete as friend. Much is made of the difficulty of translating the Greek word *paraklētos,* the noun that John uses to speak of the Spirit. Paraclete can mean advocate, comforter, counselor, helper–and all of these options are represented in the range of English language translations. Yet because *paraklētos* can contain all of these aspects, and not simply one of them, any English noun that is chosen is not sufficient to convey the full range of meaning available to the gospel's original hearers. The transliteration Paraclete is preferable to any single English noun because it does not foreclose on any of the possibilities evoked by John's use of *paraklētos.*

In that regard, Plutarch's identification of a friend as counsel and advocate is suggestive in understanding the Paraclete's role for the post-resurrection community. A friend, as counsel and advocate, tries to foster "the growth of what is sound"; and this is, indeed, one of the main roles of the Paraclete–to continue the growth ("bearing fruit") that Jesus began during his life and ministry. The community needed a friend after Jesus' death, because of the theological and pastoral dilemma that resulted from his death. It is difficult for contemporary Christian communities, who know the history of the development of the church and know the resolution of this dilemma, to imagine the genuine theological crisis that Jesus' death caused for the earliest disciples who were convicted by the claims of the Incarnation. Yet the Christian theological claim that the Incarnation is the central theological distinctive for the revelation of God–that in the life of Jesus one sees God, as the Fourth Gospel repeatedly asserts–carries this dilemma with it intrinsically.

The Incarnation, the Word-become-flesh, entails both life *and* death, because to be human is to die. Human life is finite, and for Jesus to be human means that Jesus will live *and* die. To assert the truth of the Incarnation is to assert that this particular revelation of God in Jesus is time-limited and historically bound. It is also nonrepeatable. Jesus lived at one particular moment in time, and the fullness of the claim of the Incarnation includes the particularity of that one moment.

At the same time, however, the revelatory claim of the Incarnation also transcends time, otherwise the revelation of God in Jesus would have been available only to that small group of followers who knew Jesus in his lifetime. The gospel of John takes great pains to make clear that this was not the case. At the end of the Thomas story, the risen Jesus says, "Blessed are those who have not seen and yet have come to believe" (20:29). This teaching is directed toward the very crisis we have been discussing: How does a community whose central conviction about God is that the Word became flesh—that God is incarnate in Jesus—continue after the Incarnation, continue without "seeing"?

John's answer is the gift of the Paraclete, who continues the work of Jesus for the post-Incarnation community. A theology of the Spirit is also found in other parts of early Christian tradition, most notably in Acts and in Paul, but what is distinctive about John's theology of the Spirit is that he constructs this theology in narrative form. The Paraclete is incorporated into the gospel story and is presented in the gospel itself as the mode of continuity between the Incarnation and the post-Incarnation community. The Incarnation per se cannot be repeated—that would vitiate the very claim of the Incarnation—but the love of God that was embodied in the Incarnation can be continued through the work and presence of the Paraclete. As we will see below, there is a regular linkage in the Fourth Gospel between Jesus' absence and the Paraclete's presence. Indeed, Jesus even says that it is a good thing that he is going away, because unless he goes away, the Paraclete cannot come (16:7).

In the Paraclete, there is continuity of presence and consistency of revelation. The Paraclete is the community's friend in Jesus' absence. The Paraclete empowers the community's acts of friendship and makes it possible for the community to move into its post-Incarnation future. The Paraclete continues Jesus' friendship for those "who have not seen," so that they may come to believe.

Five central teachings on the Paraclete appear in John: 14:15–17; 14:25–26; 15:26–27; 16:7–8; 16:12–15. We will now review these teachings, looking for attributes of friendship, so that we can see more clearly the ways in which the friendship that Jesus embodied is continued in the Paraclete.

John 14:15–17

If you love me, you will keep my commandments. And I will ask the Father, and he will give you another *Paraclete* to be with you forever. This is the Spirit of truth, whom the world cannot receive, because it neither sees him nor knows him. You know him, because he abides with you, and he will be with you.

The first item to note in these verses is the reference to the Paraclete as "another" Paraclete. If we remember that the range of meanings for Paraclete includes advocate, comforter, counselor, helper—and that Paraclete is not simply a synonym for "Spirit"—then it becomes easier to recognize that the first Paraclete is Jesus himself. As we read through the five Paraclete teachings, the ways in which the Paraclete continues the ministry of friendship initiated by Jesus will become increasingly apparent. In this teaching, for example, verse 17 describes the Paraclete in language almost identical to the way the gospel describes Jesus. Just as the world did not receive Jesus (1:10–13), so, too, it will not receive the Paraclete. Just as the world does not see or know Jesus (7:28; 8:19), so, too, it will not see or know the Paraclete. Just as Jesus abides with the community (15:4), so, too, does the Paraclete abide with them. The continuity and commonality of ministry between Jesus and the Paraclete is quite clear.

Other attributes of the Paraclete in this teaching recall Jesus' ministry in general and the ministry of friendship in particular:

1. The Paraclete will be with the community forever. This description contrasts with the time-bound nature of the Incarnation. The incarnate Jesus will and must leave the community, but the promise of the Paraclete is that it will transcend the limits of time.
2. The expression "Spirit of truth" names the Paraclete as one who will be and speak the truth. This is important in terms of friendship motifs, because it links the Paraclete with the motif of speaking openly. A friend will always speak the truth.
3. The verb "abide" (*menō*) is used to describe the quality of the Paraclete's ongoing presence. It is the same verb used regularly of Jesus and God and so affirms that the work of the Paraclete is one with the work of Jesus and God.
4. This first teaching on the Paraclete is introduced by a teaching on love and the linkage of love and keeping Jesus' commandments. The gift of the Paraclete to the community arises directly out of the enacted love that is the hallmark of friendship.

John 14:25–26

I have said these things to you while I am still with you. But the *Paraclete,* the Holy Spirit, whom the Father will send in my name, will teach you everything, and remind you of all that I said to you.

This second teaching also presents the Paraclete in ways that identify the Paraclete as the community's friend:

1. The time-limitedness of Jesus' own incarnate revelation is underscored by the phrase, "while I am still with you." The permanence of the Paraclete's

presence is a direct answer to the time-bound nature of the Incarnation. The continuity between the ministry of Jesus and the presence of the Paraclete is highlighted in the reference to the Father sending the Paraclete in Jesus' name.

2. The description of the Paraclete as one who will "teach you everything" is consistent with Jesus' description of his own ministry to the disciples. ("I have made known to you everything that I have heard from my Father" [15:15].)

3. Continuity between Jesus' ministry and the teaching of the Paraclete is also highlighted by the use of "remind," since the Paraclete will remind the disciples of all that Jesus has said to them. This, too, is an act of friendship, because the Paraclete's full witness will lead the community into fuller understanding of Jesus. The Paraclete will cause the community to remember the incarnational ministry of Jesus.

The genius of the Farewell Discourse is that in it, Jesus offers words of assurance to the community *before* the moment of adversity. Jesus speaks the words that the disciples will need in his absence while he is still with them, so that in the moment of crisis, the resources are already available. It is the Paraclete's work as friend to help the community recover and remember these words of assurance.

John 15:26–27

When the *Paraclete* comes, whom I will send to you from the Father, the Spirit of truth who comes from the Father, he will testify on my behalf. You also are to testify because you have been with me from the beginning.

This teaching repeats some elements from earlier teachings (continuity of the Paraclete's work with that of Jesus and God; the Spirit of truth). New friendship attributes include:

1. The Paraclete enacts the friendship motif of speaking openly and plainly. The Paraclete is portrayed in the role of Jesus' defense counsel, testifying on Jesus' behalf. Testifying, bearing witness, is an important act of plain speaking for the community, and the Paraclete's role as witness is a clear example of how the Paraclete enacts friendship.

2. Importantly, the Paraclete's witness provides a model for the community's own witness. Through the model and presence of the Paraclete, the community will also testify, speaking boldly and plainly as friends of Jesus.

John 16:7–8

Nevertheless I tell you the truth; it is to your advantage that I go away, for if I do not go away, the *Paraclete* will not come to you; but if I go,

I will send him to you. And when he comes, he will *expose the world* [NRSV, "prove the world wrong"] about sin and righteousness and judgment...[4]

This Paraclete teaching highlights the friendship motif of plain speaking:

1. As noted earlier, verse 7 identifies Jesus' departure as the prerequisite for the advent of the Paraclete. The Paraclete's ministry is to make Jesus and his work present and available for the community in Jesus' absence. Verse 7 defines the relationship between Jesus and the Paraclete. The Paraclete's work as friend cannot begin until Jesus' work is completed in the gift of his life for his friends.
2. Verse 8 introduces a vivid picture of the Paraclete's activity in the world. To say that the Paraclete will expose the world regarding sin, righteousness, and judgment means that he will bring out into the open the true meaning of sin, righteousness, and judgment, and hold the world accountable to those standards. The Paraclete, like Jesus before him, speaks openly and plainly, exposing, or bringing to the light, the impact of Jesus' ministry for the world.

In these verses (and especially as the scene continues in vv. 9–11), the Paraclete has the role of prosecuting attorney. The world is the defendant, standing before the believing community. It is important to note the distinction between the juridical roles of the Paraclete in 15:26–27 and 16:8–11.[5] In 15:26–27, the Paraclete's role is that of the defense counsel, bearing witness with and for the community in the world's case against it. In both roles, the Paraclete is cast as one who speaks openly and plainly, without attending to the cost of such plain speech.

John 16:12–15

I still have many things to say to you, but you cannot bear them now. When the Spirit of truth comes, he will guide you into all the truth; for he will not speak on his own, but will speak whatever he hears, and he will declare to you the things that are to come. He will glorify me, because he will take what is mine and declare it to you. All that the Father has is mine. For this reason I said to you that he will take what is mine and declare it to you.

This fifth and final teaching contains themes with which we are now familiar: the time-limitedness of Jesus' own ministry (v. 12); continuity of the Paraclete's work with that of God and Jesus (vv. 14–15); the Spirit of truth (v. 13). In fact, this last Paraclete teaching is more important for the way it deepens familiar motifs than for introducing new ones. In these verses Jesus makes explicit how the Paraclete will guide the disciples into their own futures.

In verse 12, Jesus confronts the disciples with the constraints that time imposes on his teaching to them and points them toward their own futures.

The verb "bear" (*bastadzō*) is normally used to refer to the physical act of supporting or bearing a heavy load (Mt. 3:11; 20:12; Mk. 14:13). Here it is used metaphorically to point to the burden of the disciples' future. The future will test them in ways that they cannot now anticipate; Jesus, therefore, cannot teach the disciples anything more about the future in the present moment. This is a new perspective on the time-limitedness of Jesus' own work. The limits of his own life span placed constraints on Jesus. So did the realities of the disciples' present and future. The disciples will be living into a succession of ever-changing present moments, for which they will need a continuing revelation at those times, to meet those needs and demands. Rudolf Bultmann moves to the heart of Jesus' words in verse 12 when he writes, "The believer can only measure the significance and claims of what he has to undergo when he actually meets it. He anticipates the future in faith, not foreknowledge."[6]

Jesus' words encourage the disciples to approach the future as he does—with faith. We have no certitude when it comes to facing the future, because the future cannot be planned or charted. This lack of certitude—combined with the confidence of faith—is what Jesus is talking about in 16:12. If the disciples knew all the crises that they would face, that their communities would face, they could not bear it. Nor could they bear the gospel revelation from Jesus that they will need to move with faith and confidence into those crises. The simplest way to illustrate the heart of Jesus' teaching is to think about the human life span.

If a person received at the beginning of one's life all of the gospel that one would need for all that life has in store in the future, that gospel would be simultaneously unbearable and incomprehensible. The gospel that one will need to face life at forty years of age would be unbearable at the age of fifteen, just as the gospel that one will need to face life at seventy years of age would be unbearable at the age of forty.

Jesus' promise of the Paraclete in this passage, and perhaps John's most powerful image of the Paraclete as friend, is that, because of the Paraclete, the Christian community will never find itself in this situation of knowing and experiencing too much of the gospel. The promise of the Paraclete is that the Paraclete will carry the promises of Jesus forward into the ever-changing realities that lie in store for people of faith. This means that as life changes, as new sufferings and new hopes emerge, you will receive a fresh promise and word from Jesus, conveyed to the community through the presence and work of the Paraclete. The functions of the Paraclete spelled out in verses 13–15—"guide you into all the truth," "speak whatever he hears," "declare to you the things that are to come," "take what is mine and declare it to you"—are all acts of open and bold speaking in the highest degree. The bold witness of the Paraclete, in which he carries Jesus' teachings into the future, will ensure that the disciples do not face the future alone (cf. 14:18), unequipped with the necessary words of Jesus.

The Paraclete is the community's friend because the Paraclete will proclaim the teachings of Jesus to people of faith in the new and changing circumstances of their lives. Jesus' words are not locked away in the disciples' past, restricted to a particular historic moment. Nor does Jesus' death rob future believers of the chance to receive the word of Jesus in the changing circumstances of their lives. Jesus' promise here is that the ongoing, continuous presence of the Paraclete in the life of the community will ensure that all believers' futures are open to fresh proclamations of Jesus' words. The friendship of the Paraclete, who keeps the revelation of God in Jesus fresh and present for all succeeding generations of believers, empowers the community to live out its own vocation as Jesus' friends.

Friendship Incarnate, Again

The teachings about the Paraclete in the Farewell Discourse are matched in John 20 and 21 with stories that show how the friendship of the Paraclete empowers the friendship of the disciples. The reader of the Fourth Gospel is not left to wonder if the teachings about the Paraclete are true, because John incorporates stories into the gospel narrative that show the truth of these teachings.

John 20:19–23

The opening of this story could not be more removed from the promises of the Paraclete—the disciples huddle behind closed doors in fear. The portrait of the disciples here is the opposite of a community of friends who will live and speak boldly and openly. Yet the risen Jesus makes an appearance to this fear-filled group and gives them a gift that will change their lives and confirm the truth of the promises of the Paraclete: "Jesus said to them again, 'Peace be with you. As the Father has sent me, so I send you.' When he had said this, he breathed on them and said to them, 'Receive the Holy Spirit. If you forgive the sins of any, they are forgiven them; if you retain the sins of any, they are retained'" (20:21–23). Jesus bestows upon his fear-filled disciples his peace and gives them the Holy Spirit, so that they are now accompanied by the friend who will make their own work of friendship and reconciliation possible.

In this brief scene, the reader sees the hope and promise of the Paraclete enacted in the gospel story itself. The gift of the Spirit is not reserved for some distant moment; it is given to the disciples at the very moment of Jesus' departure from the world (cf. 16:7). Everything that was said about the Paraclete in the Farewell Discourse is now part of the gospel narrative. The reader can now see what it looks like to live with the gift of the Paraclete.

John 21:15–19

The portrait of Peter in John 21 is a compelling narrative embodiment of the transformative power of the Paraclete's friendship. Peter's story, well-documented in the gospel narrative, offers no evidence of boldness of speech or action prior to the gift of the Spirit. This is demonstrated most clearly and painfully in Peter's three-fold denial of Jesus (18:15–27). When Peter is asked directly whether he is a disciple of Jesus and thus is afforded an opportunity to testify on Jesus' behalf (cf. 15:27), Peter explicitly denies his discipleship (18:17). John's way of narrating Peter's denial further underscores Peter's lack of boldness of speech because he alternates narration of Peter's denial with narration of Jesus' bold testimony before the high priest. ("I have spoken openly [*parrēsia*] to the world" [18:20].) While Jesus embodies friendship, Peter demonstrates how he is a failure as Jesus' friend.

After the gift of the Spirit, however, Peter redeems that failure. In Jesus' post-breakfast conversation with Peter, Peter responds to Jesus' questioning of him with boldness of speech. Jesus' three-fold questioning of Peter clearly corresponds to Peter's three-fold denial of Jesus, but the point of this questioning is not so that Jesus can learn about Peter. Throughout the gospel of John, Jesus has known everything (1:48; 2:24–25; 13:1), and that has not changed after the resurrection (note that Jn. 21 begins with Jesus knowing exactly where the disciples can cast their nets to catch fish). Jesus questions Peter not because Jesus needs to know, but because Peter needs to *say*. Peter even indicates as much when he begins each affirmation by saying, "Yes, Lord, you know…," and begins his concluding affirmation, "Lord, you know everything." In this three-fold questioning, Peter is given the opportunity to speak boldly, to enact the friendship motif of open speech. This time, empowered by the gift of the Spirit, Peter shows himself to be a true friend.

Equally important to the portrait of Peter as friend are Jesus' words in 21:18–19. These words, as verse 19a makes explicit, are a prediction of Peter's martyrdom. Even though Peter's actual death will occur outside the bounds of the gospel narrative, its prediction is part of the narrative, so that the gospel reader can see that Peter will also embody the other friendship motif of laying down one's life. Peter will follow Jesus completely and will love exactly as Jesus loved—by laying down his life for the sheep. Peter becomes the ultimate friend.

John 21:20–25

Yet the scene with Peter, with its bold demonstration of Peter's friendship, is not the end of the gospel narrative. Instead, the gospel ends with a much quieter scene that focuses on "the disciple whom Jesus loved." Peter and the beloved disciple have played key roles throughout the stories of Jesus' death and resurrection (13:23–26; 18:15–16; 20:3–10), so it is not surprising that the two disciples are paired again at the gospel's conclusion. The beloved disciple is always referred to by his relationship with Jesus and never given a name, a narrative technique that highlights Jesus' love as determinative for this disciple's identity.

Peter, the disciple who will lay down his life in love, asks about the fate of the beloved disciple. Whereas Christian tradition held that Peter died a martyr's death, it held that the beloved disciple lived to be an old man (21:23). Clearly, the beloved disciple did not lay down his life for the sheep as Peter did. Was

Peter, then, to be the model of love and friendship for future communities and not this disciple whom Jesus loved?

The beloved disciple's long life shows another way to be a friend. Whereas Peter's life and death will embody the first friendship motif–laying down one's life in love, the beloved disciple's life and death will embody the second friendship motif–open and honest speech. The beloved disciple's life will be one of full witness, of bold speech, since it is this disciple who is the source of the traditions on which the gospel of John is based (19:35; 21:24). The beloved disciple will embody the second friendship motif as fully as Peter will embody the first, for the beloved disciple's life and legacy is the witness that keeps the gospel story alive. The beloved disciple, too, is the ultimate friend.

Conclusion

In Peter and the beloved disciple, emboldened by the presence of the Paraclete, we see two ways to give authentic witness, two ways to live as a friend of Jesus. The popular question, "What would Jesus do?" misses the point for John. There is no need to ask that question about Jesus–Jesus already gave his life in love for others and always spoke and acted boldly, the ultimate friend. The more relevant question to contemplate is, "What would friends of Jesus do?" because when Jesus called his disciples "friends," he bequeathed a life of love and boldness to all who would follow him.

SERMON _____

Moving beyond Normal Belief
John 11:1–46

CARSON E. REED

Compositional Comments

In her essay on friendship, Gail O'Day suggests that the gospel of John presents Jesus as friend. By taking on the ancient conventions of friendship, Jesus offers to his disciples the gift and blessing of "friend." When asked to write a sermon on John 11 and the raising of Lazarus, I took up this lens as a way of thinking about Jesus and his relationships with Mary, Martha, and Lazarus. In considering the well-known statement of Jesus, "I am the resurrection and the life," I found first-century friendship themes giving rise to a new intensity and passion to Jesus' interest in Martha and Mary's response.

Sermon

It is a normal thing to drop whatever you are doing when word comes that a close friend or family member is suddenly afflicted with a deathly illness. It is normal for a family to send word to close friends with such grim news—in hopes that a true friend would come bringing comfort and some measure of hope.

And so, much of our text is quite understandable. Lazarus, good friend to many, including Jesus, has fallen ill. Concerned about his health, his sisters Mary and Martha send word to Jesus: "Lord, the one you love is ill." No passing acquaintance here. Jesus' good friend, "the one you love," is sick. Indeed, these three siblings are quite attached to Jesus. Mary will later take a costly jar of perfume, anoint Jesus' feet, and wipe them clean with her hair.

Jesus does not do the normal thing. He delays going to his friend. He waits, reasoning that Lazarus' illness is not heading toward death but toward making God's power known. Even though Jesus loves Mary and Martha and Lazarus, he lingers, so that a deathly illness will bring glory to God.

That is not normal. Just last Sunday, a man in our congregation with a heart condition fainted and fell. Three physicians in attendance, along with a couple of nurses, did not linger. The man was quickly taken to a quiet room, the emergency response bag opened up, and in a matter of minutes his condition was assessed and treatment offered.

Jesus hangs back for two days before he announces his intent to go to Judea to see about Lazarus. For his disciples this announcement raises big issues. "Rabbi," they say, "those folks have been trying to stone you—and you want to go back?" It is as if they were saying that to go back to Judea would mean the death of Jesus. Indeed, such a concern is prophetically real.

Jesus does not take stock in their fear. Rather, with yet another allusion to light, which this gospel is famous for, Jesus says that he knows what he is doing. Like Gandalf, who replies to Frodo, "A wizard arrives precisely when he means to," Jesus knows exactly where he is placing his feet when he heads into Judea.

Still, it is not normal. Why place yourself in danger, Jesus? Especially when Jesus notes that Lazarus is sleeping—which the disciples take as a positive sign of health! But danger is not an operational idea for Jesus, plus, the disciples have misinterpreted Jesus' description of Lazarus' condition.

Lazarus is now dead; the sleep Jesus speaks of is an eternal one. In the moment of this news the gospel text makes a comment that deliberately sets in motion another line of thinking: "Jesus, however, had been speaking about his death, but they thought that he was referring merely to sleep" (11:13). So Jesus is speaking about "his" death. Whose death? Well, Lazarus' death, of course. But is something else being foreshadowed here?

Is the gospel writer telegraphing another theme, a theme that echoes throughout this story? That Jesus' own death is being acted out in the contours of this story of Lazarus? We know how the Jesus' story ends, even if we don't know what happens with Lazarus.

Lazarus is the focus at the moment. Jesus declares plainly, "Lazarus is dead." Jesus says more non-normal things. He says he is glad that he was not there at Lazarus' passing so that the people may believe (11:15).

What are we to believe? That Lazarus is dead? Or perhaps, as we have already seen in the gospel of John, the quest is about belief—really embracing Jesus and the way he offers. It is, at least for one of the disciples, a way characterized by facing the reality of death. For Thomas is even willing to embrace death. Good Thomas, with loyalty laced with fatalism he speaks in the tones of Eeyore in A. A. Milne's Winnie the Pooh Bear stories: "Let us also go, that we may die with him" (11:16b).

I suppose the disciples do go with Jesus, but the disciples do not figure in the rest of the story. The attention, of course, is still on Jesus. Jesus' attention is on this matter of death. It takes him some time to arrive in Bethany, a little village two miles distant from the walls of Jerusalem. The word he receives as he enters the village is that Lazarus has been dead for four days. Plenty of people are in the village; many have come out from Jerusalem to call on Mary and Martha, practicing the rituals of mourning and grief.

As the word spreads that Jesus is in the village, Martha leaves the family home and finds Jesus. Her first words to Jesus are filled with grief and longing, "Lord, if you had been here, my brother would not have died" (11:21). Then she says words that may only be sweet words of sentimentality, or they may be words that evoke a deep truth that is rattling around inside of Martha's heart: "But even now I know that God will give you whatever you ask" (11:22).

Was Martha fully aware of Jesus' identity and ability? Or was she merely saying nice words—words that preachers hear from people as they exit worship services? "Nice sermon, preacher." "God really spoke to me this morning through your sermon." Or, more to the point, perhaps Martha's statement about Jesus' ability to speak to God reflects her belief that with Jesus some non-normal things can happen? Martha is open to believing something that has not yet occurred, but could—given the fact that Jesus is involved in things.

Whatever the case, Jesus' response begins to work on the theme of death—or, more accurately, the possibility of resurrection: "Your brother will rise again." Martha responds: "I know that we will rise again in the resurrection on the last day" (11:23–24). Martha is a pious Jew; she knows the content of her faith.

Jesus takes the faith of pious Judaism and makes a turn. It is one thing to say you believe in an idea; it is altogether a different thing to believe that an idea is bound up in one's trust in a person.

The turn Jesus takes here reminds me of the distinction that occurs for every parent who spends eighteen years preparing a son or daughter to leave home, head for college, and begin the real work of independence. For eighteen years mothers and fathers work toward the moment that comes when they stand in some undersized dorm room with fresh sheets on a single bed and the clothes neatly hung on hangers (for likely the last time).

In those awkward moments when both parent and student know it is time for Mom and Dad to walk down the hall to the parking lot with the last of the empty boxes, a crisis of anxiety rises. As I experienced this, for a second time, two weeks ago, I realized the crisis as the tension between the *idea* that I have long believed and the *belief in the young man* that my son is becoming.

Likewise, for Martha, it is not about an abstract belief any longer. Rather, as rubber meets the road, the time has come for belief to come to be vested, not in an idea, but in the person of One who seems to be willing to face death himself. So Martha hears her belief take on personhood. Jesus says to her, "I am the resurrection and the life. Those who believe in me, even though they die, will live, and everyone who lives and believes in me will never die. Do you believe this?" (11:25–26).

Martha does what she can. Martha does what I did two weeks ago. She does not know how her belief in the idea of the resurrection and her belief in the person of Jesus connect, nor how it will all work out, but she believes that Jesus is who he claims to be.

I did what I could two weeks ago. Though I could not connect my conviction that mothers and fathers release their sons and daughters at age eighteen and let them fly with the reality that I love my son and trust him, I made the leap toward a new kind of faith. I hugged him on a hot August afternoon, told him that I loved him, and walked away with a few empty boxes. Reconciling faith in the *idea* and faith in the *person* takes time, I tell myself.

So Martha does what she can. She affirms her faith in Jesus: "I believe that you are the Messiah, the Son of God, the one coming into the world" (11:27). She believes in the resurrection. She believes in Jesus. Still, Martha is left in the mystery of how those two convictions are connected.

With this mystery flowing around her, Martha leaves Jesus and returns to the house. There she comes to her sister, Mary, and quietly tells her, "The Teacher is here and is calling for you" (11:28b). At this word, Mary gets up quickly and rushes out of the house. What is meant to be a private meeting turns out otherwise. All of the folk in the house, assuming Mary is heading toward the cemetery, gather up and follow her. No one who wishes Mary well wants her to visit the tomb by herself.

However, Mary's destination is not the tomb; it is Jesus. When she comes to him, she falls at his feet and says just what Martha had said upon greeting Jesus: "Lord, if you had been here, my brother would not have died" (21:32b).

Jesus sees her weeping. Jesus sees all the company weeping. With all the tears that were flowing, Jesus himself becomes emotional. Though some translations say that he was "disturbed in spirit and deeply moved," a more accurate translation says that Jesus "became angry and deeply agitated."[1]

Of course, it is not clear what brings Jesus to this state. Is it because he sees the suffering and anguish of people who care deeply for another in the face of death? Or is Jesus angry because of the intrusion of this group of people into what he had hoped would be a private moment with Mary? Could it be that he sees the grief at death and knows that his own death is looming just ahead? Or is it, in some way, a combination of all of these factors that causes Jesus to weep—his tears flowing with others in the face of death and doubt.

We do know something. Not everyone standing around was grieving in the same way. Some saw Jesus' tears and said, "See how he loved him!" Others were less generous with their comments: "Could not he who opened the eyes of the blind man have kept this man from dying?" (11:36–37). Some were admiring; some were critical. Everyone was curious about Jesus.

So they lead Jesus on to the tomb. Jesus asks those gathered to do something quite out of the ordinary. "Open the tomb." Such action was not normal, because, as Martha, the sister of this very dead man, states quite clearly, "Lord, already there is a stench because he has been dead four days" (11:39b).

Jesus brings us round to the theme of our story. "Do you believe?" Caught between saying things about believing Jesus and really acting on those beliefs, Mary and Martha—along with the disciples, along with the crowd, and along with us—are faced with a rather smelly situation. Jesus says, "Did I not tell you that if you believed, you would see the glory of God?" (11:40).

So they roll back the stone. Either because of the possibility of something remarkable, something life-giving, occurring, or perhaps simply to accommodate this abnormal friend of the family, they open the entrance to the tomb. Certainly something is about to happen. Will Jesus be embarrassed and exposed? Or can the one who heals be capable of something greater?

Jesus does not look into the dark tomb. His interest is in what has been at stake since the first word about Lazarus' illness reached his ears. Gazing into the heavens, he speaks with thanksgiving to the Father and confesses, "I [know] that you always hear me, but I [say] this for the sake of the crowd standing here, so that they may believe that you sent me" (11:42).

Speaking about belief and demonstrating the power of such belief are very different things. Jesus cries out a word of command: "Lazarus, come out!" Out of the darkness of the tomb comes a dead man walking–bound up with burial strips of cloth. Imagine the silence and awe of the crowd broken only by the compassionate command of Jesus: "Unbind him, and let him go" (11:44b).

Now we might imagine the gospel writer lingering over this amazing demonstration of power. What is it that we have witnessed? Or, in what way does this foreshadow Jesus' own death and resurrection? But the story does not turn this way, nor should we. The unfolding story continues its journey along the rail of belief. No detours here.

Do you believe this? Many Jews standing there that day did believe. They saw, and they believed. Others standing in front of that open tomb saw what Jesus did and went to tell the Pharisees. Remarkably, one event evokes two different responses.

Even today in our telling, different responses are likely. Indeed, one might conclude, after all, that such a story is worthy of early Christians eager to get others to believe. And yet, the variety of responses to Jesus' command to Lazarus to come out of the tomb is not the sort of thing early Christians would wish to convey.

No, I think we are forced to engage a moment of crisis not unlike Martha did when she met Jesus at the edge of the village. We are forced to deal with a man walking who should by all counts be dead.

Do you believe?

The verdict on our son's success at college still remains to be seen. Two weeks does not a college career make! But the confidence we have about the future is rooted in the character of our son–not in the collective wisdom of parents who send children off at eighteen years of age.

We all reach a point when all that we know and all that we believe is simply not sufficient for the task of anchoring a life. Here comes Jesus, who challenges us to look beyond the normal to embrace faith. The faith we embrace is not the content of faith. It is Jesus himself. As Gail O'Day says: "Faith, therefore, is not assent to a series of faith statements, but assent to the truth of Jesus' relationship with God and the decisive change that relationship means for the lives of those who believe."[2]

Maybe, just maybe, believing in Jesus, as abnormal as it may seem to some, really is the only real option that presents itself, at least for those who have listened to Jesus long enough to come to trust him.

SERMON _____

A Call to Courage
John 16:33

D'ESTA LOVE

Compositional Comments

This sermon was preached at the Rochester Sermon Seminar on May 22, 2007. At the time I received the invitation, I was working on material for a class at the Abilene Christian University lectureship on the Final Discourse in John's gospel (John 14–16). I decided it would make my work easier if I developed a sermon from those same chapters. The task was far more difficult than I had thought. The Final Discourse is repetitive, contains many themes and topics, and has no narrative thread other than, perhaps, "the hour of Jesus."

My attention was drawn to the final verse of the discourse (16:33). I thought it would easily allow numerous contemporary applications. I immediately began making notes of images of "tribulation" in the world and easily found many from which to choose. As I began seriously reading the gospel afresh, I realized that my contemporary images were actually taking me away from my text and were not allowing me to speak from within the gospel. When I realized that the tribulation about which Jesus was speaking was not from Rome but from Jerusalem, my sermon began to come into focus. I was led into the heart of John's gospel, observing the works of Jesus and listening to the voices of those who hated him because of his works. Frankly, I became afraid of the implications of the message. I wasn't sure I wanted my sermon to be so prophetic, so I tried to find another text. But I kept being drawn to John 16:33.

When I read Gail O'Day's commentary on John's gospel in *The New Interpreter's Bible,* she helped me see that the Final Discourse is not an offer of "cheap grace" but a call to a future that requires courage.[1] I returned to my passage and read it again. This time I heard Jesus' words, "But take courage," and they became a refrain that would not let me go. It was a message both for me and my audience. So I committed myself to my text and let the gospel as a whole interpret it for me.

I was worried about my tone and my motivation as I addressed my audience. I agonized for months about perceived agendas and defensiveness. Again, O'Day was helpful.[2] Her lecture on the evening before I preached gave me peace and the posture I needed to deliver (and it *was* like giving birth) what I believed to be a difficult and prophetic message. In her description of Jesus as friend, as understood in the first-century Mediterranean world, she explained that a friend speaks boldly and truthfully to her friends. That gave me an image

I could carry with me into the pulpit. I hoped my sermon would be perceived as a bold and prophetic message, spoken in love from a friend.

Sermon

Having loved his own who were in the world, he loved them to the end. "Little children, I am with you only a little longer... Where I am going, you cannot follow me now... If you love me, you will keep my commandments... This is my commandment, that you love one another as I have loved you..." (Excerpts from Jn. 13–15)

"Believe in God; believe also in me... If I go,...I will come again and will take you to myself, so that where I am, there you may be also." (14:1b–3)

"Peace I leave with you; my peace I give to you. I do not give to you as the world gives. Do not let your hearts be troubled, and do not let them be afraid." (14:27)

"If the world hates you, be aware that it hated me before it hated you... If they persecuted me, they will persecute you... They will put you out of the synagogues... Indeed,...those who kill you will think...they are offering worship to God." (15:18, 20b; 16:2)

"I have said this to you, so that in me you may have peace. In the world you *have tribulation* (RSV). But take courage; I have conquered the world!" (16:33)

Jesus had some hard things to say to those whom he loved in the world. It is hard to say goodbye.

Recently a student of mine said, "The world is falling apart." We might agree, when a stranger enters a one-room schoolhouse and kills six Amish school girls, or when a student on a college campus kills thirty-two classmates and a beloved faculty member. We might agree, when the names of terrorists are all too familiar and images of genocide, death squads, and suicide bombs daily invade our homes. We might agree, when the war in Iraq seems never to end, and thousands of innocent people continue to die. When we experience strife in our communities and families and when dangers in the world and on the Internet put our children at risk, we would affirm that in the world we have tribulation. When we hear that in the world we have tribulation, but in Jesus we have peace (16:33), our weary hearts are comforted, and we draw courage from his words.

In the narrative world of John's gospel, Jesus is not speaking to the disciples of trouble and woe in the world. He calls the disciples to courage because they will be cast out of their synagogues and those who kill them will think they are bringing worship to God. They will be persecuted by those who persecuted

Jesus. The tribulation of which Jesus speaks is not from Rome, but from Jerusalem. It is not from Caesar's palace, but from the temple, the Sanhedrin. Oh, the world is certainly in Rome, but it is also in Jerusalem.

Jesus is hated by the leaders of his own religious heritage who assume to know the truth of how things should be. They are his own who received him not (1:11). They are of the world because their ideological values put them at odds with the work of God in Jesus. They hate and persecute Jesus, and they will hate and persecute those who follow him. We know who they are; they are the voices of certitude, the guardians of orthodoxy, the keepers of the boundaries.

In John's gospel Jesus is God's incarnate Word of life and love who brings healing and wholeness to the world, particularly to those excluded by the religious authorities. Therefore his works challenge their certitudes and their boundaries. He disregards their purity and social boundaries, violates their Sabbath laws, and challenges their understanding of sin and who is the sinner. We know who they are: they are the keepers of the boundaries. They fear Jesus because they are afraid Rome will come and destroy their holy city, so they protect their own self-interests and persecute and kill him.

Jesus calls us to follow him, to go with him, even to Samaria. He calls us to cross a boundary into a borderland, a village across the tracks. Among the outsiders, the ostracized, the defiled, Jesus finds true worshipers. He offers the gift of God to a woman who has been excluded and judged permanently unclean under the purity system, simply because she was born a Samaritan female. He gives to this defiled woman—and, through her, to her village—access to the life of God. The boundaries of race, religion, gender, and social expectation are of no consequence to Jesus. They separate her from him; and they engender fear, hatred, and prejudice. Jesus *must* cross the boundary into Samaria. Not because it is the way to Galilee, but the way to the cross. He calls us to follow him.

I don't know if there were priests and Levites at the border or lurking in the shadows, but they took note of Jesus' stay in this village. Later, they claim Jesus has a demon, and they call him a Samaritan (8:48). He went to a neighborhood beyond their boundary and was labeled by the keepers of the purity system. Jesus is calling us to courage.

We love the story of the man born blind. We tell our children how Jesus put mud on the man's eyes, sent him to wash in the Pool of Siloam, and he came back seeing. We love to quote the blind man, "I was blind, now I see" (9:25). But we miss the conversation about, "Who sinned so that this man was born blind?" When Jesus heals the man, the keepers of orthodoxy don't know what to do with him. Jesus challenges their certitude. Now that the blind man sees, things are not so black and white. These religious leaders determine that the man was born in utter sin, so they throw him out of their holy place and leave him at the side of the road to beg. We are not surprised that Jesus is also judged a sinner. He has violated their sabbath laws, but he has also crossed a purity boundary and challenged their presuppositions about who is the sinner.

The religious leaders have excluded the "sinners," the "unclean," the marginal. Jesus disregards their boundaries and the fears and prejudices associated with them. The keepers of the sabbath quickly respond, "We know that this man is a sinner" (9:24). "This man is not from God, for he does not observe the sabbath" (9:16). Jesus is calling us to courage, to take our stand with Jesus and the blind man.

We love to tell our children the story of the good shepherd who knows his sheep by name. But in our bedtime stories we do not include Jesus' words: "I have other sheep that do not belong to this fold. I must bring them also, and they will listen to my voice. So there will be one flock, one shepherd" (10:16). The shepherds who are called to guard the sheep have become the guardians of the gate instead. And they say, "He has a demon and is out of his mind" (10:20), and they took up stones to stone him (10:31).

The call to courage means following the incarnate Word, who came not to condemn but to give life. Following Jesus takes us across the boundaries that separate and exclude. Following Jesus takes us beyond the four walls of our sanctuaries to seek those who have been shunned, silenced, declared unclean, pronounced sinners. Following Jesus takes us to the margins, into borderlands and to the side of the road. When we follow him, we will experience tribulation.

Before we hasten to Samaria, we must not overlook the boundaries that are also in our churches, our holy places. Permit me to illustrate one such boundary out of the particularity of my own experience. If you don't know where the boundaries are, just ask a little girl in your congregation who has been told she cannot take up the attendance cards because she is a girl. Or ask the women who for years have set the table, baked the bread, poured the wine, prepared the meal, but have never served it. Ask the women who, at this seminar, have called us to worship and led us in prayer, but return to their silent places in the sanctuaries of their home congregations.

If we answer the call to courage, we will go to the margins of our churches, hear the voices of women, and receive their gifts. We will claim Joel's prophesy, "I will pour out my spirit on all flesh; / your sons and your daughters shall prophesy" (Joel 2:28; Acts 2:17). We will embrace our estranged brothers and sisters of our own religious heritage from whom we have been separated too long. We will expand our own understanding of the fold and open the gate to all who hear the shepherd's voice. We will seek those who languish in the borderlands and at the side of the road outside our holy places. We will call our children home, those who have been broken and wounded by the boundary keepers because of divorce, addiction, substance abuse, sexual identity, and neglect. We will reclaim those who left us because of our certitudes. We will speak God's word of life and love to our churches and to the world; and when we do, we will know tribulation.

These are hard things to say, and they present complex challenges to us. I know that we are all boundary keepers. We all have something to protect. But let us be clear. Boundary keeping invites the world into the church. It fosters separation, exclusion, judgment, fear, prejudice, and hatred—all of which belong to the darkness. While we have been called to courage, we are also called to grace and truth and to be God's word of life and love to the boundary keepers in our churches. A delicate and complex balance hovers between caring for and tending the flock, and guarding the boundaries to the exclusion of others. We have work to do, and we need courageous leaders who will be as God was in the world and lead us out of darkness into light.

Courageous voices among us are crossing the boundaries of arrogance and prejudice. They are boldly proclaiming messages of inclusion and are challenging the hierarchy of patriarchy and the paternalism of our legalistic past and present. They have seen the necessity of going to Samaria, crossing the boundaries and opening the door to the fold, and they are experiencing tribulation from the guardians of the faith, the keepers of doctrinal purity.

But there is good news tonight. We have a friend in Jesus, who, against the backdrop of tribulation and fear, has washed our feet and welcomed us into the Father's house, in which there are many abiding places. He has drawn us into the mutual abiding of the Father, the Son, and the Spirit.

We have a friend in Jesus tonight who has breathed sweet peace into our hearts and lives. He does not give to us as the world gives. It is not a false security that draws behind boundaries for fear of Jerusalem or the world contaminated by sin or the keepers of the boundaries. It is not the peace that takes us to war and that is won when all conflict has ceased, and our enemies are subdued into submission. It is the peace that calls us to be courageous in the face of persecution, knowing that we have an abiding place in the sanctity of the Father's love, the comforting and consoling presence of the Holy Spirit, and the reassurance that Jesus has overcome the world.

We have a friend in Jesus who has loved us to the end and laid down his life for us. "In the world you have tribulation...But take courage; I have overcome the world."

4

The Word as Sign

THOMAS H. OLBRICHT

After years of reflecting upon and teaching the theology of the gospel of John, I have come to believe that a focal point permeates the gospel and is introduced in the prologue, "In the beginning was the Word" (1:1). The importance of Jesus' words and those of his disciples persists all the way through the gospel into the epilogue in which the disciples are to "feed the Sheep." It is through the word that the Son who is the Word brings eternal life to those who believe through his word and by the word of his "feeding" disciples.[1]

The gospel of John may or may not be made up of component parts and sources. I am inclined to think not.[2] Nevertheless, the thread running through the gospel is clearly present in the final form we have received. I agree with Robert Kysar who, at the close of his recent collection of essays on John, reveals his movement away from a historical-critical approach. He writes, "I think that the time may come in the near future when the modern method of biblical study will of necessity be revised in significant ways in favor of attending to the text as it is before us and how we respond to it."[3]

Works and words go hand in hand in the gospel of John and are central to John's theology. In fact, the works of Jesus come about as the result of his words. Just as Jesus worked though his words, so will his disciples: "Very truly, I tell you, the one who believes in me will also do the works that I do and, in fact, will do greater works than these, because I am going to the Father" (14:12).

Through the proclamation—that is, through the words describing the works or the signs of Jesus—believers gain eternal life: "Now Jesus did many other signs in the presence of his disciples, which are not written in this book. But these are written so that you may come to believe that Jesus is the Messiah, the Son of God, and that through believing you may have life in his name" (20:30–31).

83

Rudolf Bultmann, in his magisterial New Testament theology, made an identical point regarding the significance of the words:

> That is the fact—the *works of Jesus* (or, seen collectively as a whole: his work) *are his words.* Numerous formulations indicate that to John deed and word are identical. *The identity of work and word* can be further seen in what is said of the effect of the word. "The words that I have spoken to you are spirit and life" (6:68). This is followed by Peter's confession: "You have the words of eternal life."[4]

In a chapter on "Faith as the Hearing of the Word," Bultmann wrote, "Thus it becomes clear that in the proclaimed word the Proclaimer himself is present, acting."[5]

The works and words of Jesus are signs that Jesus "had come from God and was going to God" (13:3). For too long, some scholars have limited the signs of Jesus in the gospel to the works of Jesus. Both the words *and* works of Jesus are signs.[6] Raymond Brown, in his benchmark two-volume commentary on John, recognized as much when he wrote, "Yet even words may be signs, e.g. in xii 33 (xvii 32) and xxi 19 there is a statement which serves as a sign (*sēmainein*) of how Jesus or Peter is to die."[7] Earlier in his commentary, Brown wrote, "Not only are Jesus' miracles works; his words are works, too (xiv 10)."[8] Yet Brown did not recognize the specific instances in which words are clearly signs in Jesus' comments, for example, to Nathanael or the Samaritan woman at the well.

When the Jews asked Jesus for a sign he gave them words, not action. The words referred to action to transpire at a future time:

> The Jews then said to him, "What sign can you show us for doing this?" Jesus answered them, "Destroy this temple, and in three days I will raise it up." The Jews then said, "This temple has been under construction for forty-six years, and will you raise it up in three days?" But he was speaking of the temple of his body. (2:18–21)

Rudolph Schnackenburg recognizes the sign in this case as a different sort, but still does not perceive that in the gospel of John the words are as revealing of who Jesus is as are the "action" signs.[9]

The words that Jesus spoke to Nathanael: "I saw you under the fig tree before Philip called you" (1:48) are indeed a sign that Jesus was from God. Gail O'Day captures the significance of Jesus' statement: "Nathanael correctly perceives Jesus' knowledge as an act of self-revelation and so comes to faith (vv. 49–50)."[10] In effect this is the first sign that John reports in his gospel. The sign of the water changed into wine at the wedding celebration was the first sign in Cana of Galilee (2:11). The next was also in Cana of Galilee (4:54), suggesting that John was not launching a catalog of signs for some reason, but bestowing special significance to Cana. Jesus' declaration to the woman at the well in Samaria, "For you have had five husbands, and the one you have now is not your husband" (4:18), was also a sign that Jesus was from God. This statement was as much a sign as those statements concerning the destruction of the temple, the healing of the royal official's son (4:46–54), and the cure of the paralytic (5:1–9).

The theological thread running through the gospel of John is that the words proclaiming the signs of Jesus (words translated into actions) result in life in his name. In effect, the focus of the gospel of John is on proclamation. The signs must be portrayed in order that belief follows. When the signs are believed, life in his name results.

Hearing the words that reiterate the action leads to faith as readily as does *beholding the action* firsthand. Before Thomas stood face to face with Jesus he had declared that he would not believe, "Unless I see the mark of the nails in [Jesus'] hands, and put my finger in the mark of the nails and my hand in his side" (20:25). A week later Jesus stood before Thomas and invited him to do just that. But Thomas was so overawed he simply burst out, "My Lord and my God!" (20:28) without putting forth his hand. Thomas believed because he was in the presence of his living Lord. Jesus then declared, "Have you believed because you have seen me? Blessed are those who have not seen and yet have come to believe" (20:29).

On what grounds is it possible for those who did not see to believe? John answers immediately that they believe because they read or heard of the signs that Jesus did (20:30–31). The proclamation of the signs produces faith in those who hear, even many years removed from the original occurrences. The words declaring the actions produce belief. When Jesus asked the disciples, "Do you also wish to go away?" (6:67), Peter responded, "Lord, to whom can we go? You have the words of eternal life. We have come to believe and know that you are the Holy One of God" (6:68–69). George Beasley-Murray captured the essence of Jesus' declaration to Thomas:

> They have not had the privilege of the disciples in seeing Jesus alive from the dead, nor of having their faith quickened in the extraordinary manner granted to Thomas. Theirs is a faith called forth by the word of the Gospel; but it is none the worse for that, for their trust in the Lord revealed through the Word is of special worth in his eyes.[11]

Jesus is in himself the very word of God. Not only does the word setting forth the signs produce faith in Jesus; Jesus is in himself the Word, the revelation of God par excellence. Jesus is not so much the ontological foundation or life-producing *Logos* or principle in the universe as affirmed by middle Platonism or Stoicism. Rather he is the revelatory Word through whom all things were spoken into existence (Jn. 1:3, Gen. 1:3). He is life, and by that life discloses an actuality that throws light upon all things and at the same time forces darkness to recede, thereby revealing all (Jn. 1:4–9). The Word (the revelatory utterance) took on human concretion—that is, flesh (Jn. 1:14). As a result, God himself is disclosed to humans in their fleshly state.

No one has ever seen God the father. It is God the only Son, who is close to the Father's heart, who has made him known (Jn. 1:18). Jesus himself is the Word. His words and works declare that he came from God and is returning to God. Everything about the Son of Man discloses who he is and the character of his ministry in the world. It is not surprising therefore that from John 1 to John 21 Jesus is placarded as the *Logos,* the revelatory word of God.

In the gospel of John, Jesus clearly produces his mighty works through his words. In turn, the words announcing and often generating these works or signs produce faith. If we take up the specific instances of the mighty actions of Jesus, we discover that these come about through the very words of Jesus. When the water is changed to wine, Jesus only speaks, with no action on his own part. "Fill the jars with water" (2:7), he *says.* When the royal official from Capernaum comes to Jesus at Cana of Galilee and reports that his son is at the point of death, the lad is healed because of the *words* of Jesus, "Go; your son will live" (4:50).

Later Jesus travels to Jerusalem for a Jewish festival. A man lies by the pool of Bethzatha who has been ill for thirty-eight years. Friends normally carried those incapacitated into the pool for healing. But this man has no one to pick him up. Jesus does not carry the man to the pool. He *speaks* to him: "Stand up, take your mat and walk" (5:8). On a later occasion the people follow Jesus up onto a mountain. Sensing they are hungry, Jesus has compassion and decides to feed them. He does so without any physical activity except that he takes from a lad five barley loaves and two fish. "Then Jesus took the loaves, and when he had given thanks, he distributed them to those who were seated; so also the fish, as much as they wanted" (6:11). The multiplication of the loaves and fishes came about as the result of the *words* of Jesus in the prayer. Jesus stills the fears of the disciples on the stormy sea—and, by implication, the sea itself—with his *words,* "It is I; do not be afraid" (6:20).

When Jesus heals the man blind from birth, he spits on the ground, makes mud with his saliva, and puts it on the man's eyes. He then tells the man, "Go, wash in the pool of Siloam" (9:7). It is only after the *word* that Jesus speaks, however, that the blind man washes in the pool and is healed.

For some of Jesus' acquaintances, the great challenge to Jesus was the death of his friend Lazarus. Lazarus' sisters Mary and Martha were distraught, yet reconciled to their brother's death. Jesus heralds the demise as a means of glorifying God (11:4). Jesus declares himself "the resurrection and the life" (11:25). When Jesus approaches Lazarus' tomb, a stone blocks the entrance. The healing actions of Jesus come about through his *words.* He says to those weeping, "Take away the stone" (11:39). Thereupon, Jesus prays to God, thanking God that God hears his prayers. Then Jesus cries with a loud voice, "Lazarus, come out!" (11:43). The *words produce the action.* Lazarus walks out of the tomb wrapped in strips of burial cloth. Jesus has unlimited credibility. Whenever he speaks, something happens. After Jesus' resurrection, seven disciples go fishing on the Sea of Tiberias in Galilee. They fish all night without success. Their luck changes at the *words* of Jesus, who comes along on the beach nearby, and directs them: "Cast the net to the right side of the boat, and you will find some" (21:6).

Whenever Jesus *changes the course of human life,* he does so by *speaking.* He charges the disciples to transform the world through teaching: "Feed my sheep" (21:17). Those who follow Jesus are to confront a dark world with descriptions of the works (signs) of Jesus, which he produces through his words. The disciples, like their master, are to be proclaimers and do even greater works. How will they produce their works? "For the words that you gave to me I have given to them, and they have received them" (17:8). "Sanctify them in the truth; your word is truth. As you have sent me into the world, so I have sent them into the world" (17:17–18). "I ask not only on behalf of these, but also on behalf of those who will believe in me through their word" (17:20). *Words have the power to highlight the actions of Jesus and in turn produce faith.* "But these are written so that you may come to believe that Jesus is the Messiah, the Son of God, and that through believing you may have life in his name" (20:31).

What are the works by which the disciples will excel even beyond Jesus? In John's gospel, the disciples are never sent out by Jesus to "cure the sick, raise the dead, cleanse the lepers, cast out demons," as in the synoptics (Mt. 10:8). Another telling observation is that Jesus immediately brings up the Holy Spirit (the *Paracletos*) following the affirmation that they "will do greater works than these" (Jn. 14:12).[12] In the whole section on the Paraclete (John 14–17) there is never any mention that the disciples, because they are filled with the *Spirit,* will cure the sick or cleanse the lepers. The Paraclete (the Holy Spirit) is to replace Jesus. "And I will ask the Father, and he will give you another Advocate [Paraclete], to be with you forever" (Jn. 14:16).

The work of the Spirit is to "teach you everything, and remind you of all that I have said to you" (Jn. 14:26, compare also 16:8–15). The Spirit will enable the disciples to testify on behalf of Jesus: "You also are to testify because you have been with me from the beginning" (15:27). The Holy Spirit will enable the disciples as they multiply to speak the words of truth about Jesus the Word. They will go forth after his resurrection to depict his belief-producing signs. We can further observe that no mention is made of the believers healing people and casting out demons in the Johannine letters. Just as the work of Jesus is in his words, so is the work of the disciples. They will produce far more words than Jesus ever does because many will come to believe and the disciples will multiply.

Bultmann perceives that the greater works have to do with words in John. On John 14:10 he comments, "In Jesus' word, the work of the Father is brought to fruition; on his own, and for himself, Jesus is nothing: he is simply and without exception the revelation of the Father."[13] In contrast, Beasley-Murray strenuously objects to Bultmann's identification of the works with the word.[14] His observations are instructive in regard to highlighting the death and resurrection through which Jesus takes away the sins of the world. Nevertheless, the means by which the believers disseminate this power of the death and resurrection to future generations is through their life-producing words depicting these mighty salvific acts.

Finally, many aspects of the discussions of Jesus with the crowds who seek him out after the feeding of the 5,000 highlight the importance of the words of Jesus. The focus is now on the bread that Jesus says he can supply that will lead to eternal life (6:27). This bread seems to have metaphorical, though also actual, ramifications—just as does the water that Jesus promises the woman at the well in Samaria. The water that Jesus can supply will "become...a spring of water gushing up to eternal life" (4:14). Jesus promises to give completely filling bread to those who came to him (6:27). What is this bread he will give? Jesus continues speaking metaphorically: "For the bread of God is that which comes down from heaven and gives life to the world" (6:33). Again, what is this bread? Jesus makes it clear that *he* is the one who has come down from heaven: "I am the bread of life. Whoever comes to me will never be hungry, and whoever believes in me will never be thirsty" (6:35). Furthermore, the bread that came down from heaven in the days of Moses, the manna, did not continue to satisfy, for those who ate of it hungered the next day. Jesus states, "I am the living bread that came down from heaven. Whoever eats of this bread will live forever; and the bread that I will give for the life of the world is my flesh" (6:51).

At this point Jesus makes a controversial and alienating assertion: "Very truly, I tell you, unless you eat the flesh of the Son of Man and drink his blood, you have no life in you" (6:53). Almost immediately, Jesus makes an even more astounding claim, unless we understand it in the light of the theme of the gospel— that is, that Jesus is the Word and that he heals and saves by his word. Jesus declares, after the disciples complain about the difficulty of accepting his statement about eating his flesh and drinking his blood, "It is the spirit that gives life; the flesh is useless" (6:63a). This is to say, as I understand it, that the everlasting life he gives is not as a result of a literal eating of his body and drinking his blood. Rather, it is the proclamation of his death and resurrection and the celebrating of his body and blood that brings about eternal life. His mighty salvific acts in his death and resurrection are appropriated through the words declared about them, not through the eating of the fleshly body and the drinking of the literal blood. Jesus makes it clear that it is the words that he has spoken that bring eternal life. "The words that I have spoken to you are spirit and life" (6:63b). Salvation comes through pronouncing the words of the one who is the Word! "But these are written so that you may come to believe that Jesus is the Messiah, the Son of God, and that through believing you may have life in his name" (20:31). O'Day correctly observes:

> The protesting disciples (like the "Jews" of v. 52) do not rightly perceive the flesh of which Jesus speaks. They see only Jesus' flesh; they do not see "the Word become flesh" (John 1:14). Jesus' words in v. 63 expose

this misperception. The flesh as flesh *is* useless; only the Spirit gives life to the flesh, and the Spirit dwells in the Son of Man (cf. 1:33) and in the words that Jesus speaks.[15]

"Simon Peter answered him, 'Lord, to whom can we go? You have the words of eternal life'" (6:68).

What are the implications of the theology of John for Christian ministry in this time? We who proclaim Jesus as Lord and Christ are to feed the flock of the living God through words heralding the one who is the Word. Our most compelling task is to "tell the old, old story of Jesus and his love."[16] It matters not so much that we tell our story, though that sometimes may be worthy. It matters even less that we tell stories we have garnered from our experiences and reading. What ultimately matters is that we proclaim year in and year out what Jesus said and did. For, "these are written so that you may come to believe that Jesus is the Messiah, the Son of God, and that through believing you may have life in his name" (20:31).

I will here offer two examples of the manner in which the signs of Jesus may be preached.

The first one has to do with Nathanael.

How did Nathanael come to faith that Jesus was from God? He came to faith in four steps.

First, one who was already a believer contacted him. The day after Jesus met Andrew, possibly John, and Peter (Jn. 1:40–42), he went to Galilee where he found Philip. Jesus said to him "Follow me," and Philip complied (1:43). Philip in turn sought out Nathanael and said to him, "We have found him about whom Moses in the law and also the prophets wrote, Jesus son of Joseph from Nazareth" (1:45). We might identify Philip as a catalyst in the steps to faith.

Second, Nathanael was not immediately impressed and expressed his doubts. "Can anything good come out of Nazareth?" Philip did not push the case at that time. He simply responded, "Come and see" (1:46).

Third, Nathanael went from being a doubter to a believer because of a sign. Seeing Nathanael, Jesus declared, "Here is truly an Israelite in whom there is no deceit" (1:47). A puzzle was introduced. Nathanael burst out amazed, "Where did you get to know me?" (1:48). Jesus' answer compounded the puzzle, "I saw you under the fig tree before Philip called you" (1:48). Nathanael was not closed off completely to the suggestion that Philip had previously planted. Now he was impressed because Jesus exhibited extraordinary abilities. Through some sort of prescience, Jesus knew Nathanael's whereabouts though separated at a considerable distance. Jesus, it appeared, must have God connections of some sort.

Fourth, Nathanael believed. The sign overrode his doubts: "Rabbi, you are the Son of God! You are the King of Israel!" (1:49). Jesus then assures him that signs to follow will be even more convincing: "Very truly, I tell you, you will see heaven opened and the angels of God ascending and descending upon the Son of Man" (1:51). The sign Jesus exhibited by his words led Nathanael to faith. We need to note, however, that the signs were not significant in themselves. They were significant only because they pointed to Jesus.[17]

The sign is not the thing. Jesus' announcement to Nathanael that he saw him in advance was not itself God's Messiah, rather the one uttering it was. As one drives west on Interstate 90 past the famous Wall Drug Store and approaches Rapid City, South Dakota, one sees a large sign on the right, proclaiming, "Mt. Rushmore National Monument, next exit." But the sign is not the monument. The monument has the faces of George Washington, Thomas Jefferson, Abraham Lincoln, and Theodore Roosevelt carved on Mt. Rushmore some twenty miles to the southwest. The sign is not the monument, but it points one in the right direction. The signs in John are not the Messiah, the Son of God. They, however, declare that what Jesus says and does is so unlike the words and deeds of mere humans that they proclaim that *in him*–indeed in a man–is God!

The second sermon to be preached from a sign is developed from the wedding in Cana. The sign in this case begins in an empirical word or action. Signs often are inaugurated from something on and of the earth. But the signs point beyond their earthly origin to those from above. The sign at the Cana wedding centers upon the depleted then replenished wine. Before the replenishment, however, the declaration of a true believer–in this case Mary– provides a catalyst. "Do whatever he tells you" (2:5). In the second stage the disciples of Jesus who were inclined to believe observe what transpires. The disciples are open to the prospect that Jesus could achieve the implausible. In the third stage the water is changed to unbelievably good-tasting wine. The water isn't just any water. It is six large containers of water employed in Jewish rites in which the water is sprinkled on the one who seeks purification. That Jesus changes this ritual water into wine anticipates the purification that is soon to replace Jewish sprinkling. It is a new purification that results from the baptism of the water and the Spirit (3:5) based upon belief that Jesus is the Messiah (3:16) and through the drinking of the fruit of the vine–his blood (6:53). The disciples have been prepared for this openness by their rapprochement with Jesus and the confidence of Mary. Fourth, because of this revelation of Jesus' glory (2:11)–that he creates the good wine by his Word–the disciples believe in him.

The coming to faith in which signs are involved continues according to these same four stages even into the present. Often a believing parent first points to Jesus. Second, there is an openness on the part of the growing youth that a divine source is the most likely explanation of Jesus' unusual words and actions. In the third stage on the way to faith the child next hears of Jesus' uncommon feats. Fourth, as a result, the young adult receives Christ in faith–born of water and Spirit.

Some years ago, an evangelistic team, "Good News Northeast," was campaigning in New England. The leader was from the Northeast, but the team was centered at Abilene Christian University, and a number of the students were from Texas. Their regular routine was going from door to door volunteering to help people or study the Scriptures with them. One day, Wayne Barnard, now an administrator at Abilene Christian, was walking along the sidewalk when he saw a woman weeding her flowerbed. Without saying anything, he walked over and started weeding, too. After a bit of time she straightened up, looked at him, and said, "What do you think you're doing?" He responded, "I'm helping you weed your flowers." Hearing his voice, she responded, "You aren't from here, are you?" He said, "I'm from San Antonio, Texas." That was a puzzle a sign. "What are you doing here in Chelmsford?" He proceeded to tell her about their mission. She invited him to come into the house. They sat at the kitchen table. He opened his Bible and read and commented. After an hour or so she said, "I'm not really interested in this, but I know a woman who is." She gave Wayne the woman's name and address, and later that day he went to see her. She was interested indeed! After a period of study she was baptized into Jesus Christ and has remained a faithful disciple ever since. Puzzling actions of the people of God are still involved in the initiating stages on the way to faith.

"These are written so that you may come to believe that Jesus is the Messiah, the Son of God, and that through believing you may have life in his name" (20:31).

The proclaimer of the word of God is committed to telling of the signs Jesus wrought.

SERMON ─────────────────────────────────────

Nathanael, a Disciple by Water and the Word

John 1:43–51

THOMAS H. OLBRICHT

Sermon

The story is told that a seventeenth-century German prince was intrigued by the question, "What is the first human language?" Those with whom he associated assumed that Hebrew was the first—indeed the very words spoken by God to Adam and Eve! But how can this be proven? The prince, after several restless nights, decided that the way to resolve the matter was to isolate two babies from ever hearing spoken words. As the two grew, they would eventually speak. Whatever language they spoke would obviously be the first. As the story goes, the prince never found out. Why? The children did not survive isolated upbringing. Babies grow into adulthood through loving words! My suspicion is that this story is what we now call an urban legend. What it alleges, however, is a profound truth. Human worlds are created by words!

Nathanael is special in the gospel of John. In fact, by that name he is mentioned only in the gospel of John. And he does not simply show up, for a time occupy the center of attention, and then disappear. At the end of the gospel he is grouped with six others from among the twelve as they fish in the Sea of Galilee. Nathanael is special in John because he was the first person about whom the details are spelled out as to why he became a disciple of Jesus Christ. He was astounded by Jesus' response after the puzzled Nathanael asked him, "Where did you get to know me?"

Jesus answered, "I saw you under the fig tree before Philip called you" (1:48). Jesus won Nathanael for his growing circle of disciples by his unprecedented words. Jesus himself was the Word. He laid the foundation for his church, the community of faith, by his word. We sing of this remarkable creation in the majestic hymn, "The church's one foundation is Jesus Christ her Lord. She is his new creation by water and the word."[1] Nathanael entered into God's kingdom by *water and the word!*

Jesus is the maker of all things in heaven and on earth: "All things came into being through him, and without him not one thing came into being" (Jn.1:3). When we think of Jesus as creator, we likely think of the cosmos—the mountains and glaciers, the distant galaxies, the black holes, and the resplendent stars. Jesus the Word indeed made the mighty universe by his word. But he made more than the universe by the word. It is by his word that Jesus created the church.

It is also by his word that he created the twelve. Jesus the Christ continues to this very day to make disciples by the word.

> Now Jesus did many other signs in the presence of his disciples, which are not written in this book. But these are written so that you may come to believe that Jesus is the Messiah, the Son of God, and that through believing you may have life in his name. (Jn. 20:30–31)

Jesus' response to Nathanael's query, "Where did you get to know me?" was a sign of Jesus' incredible power. That it was possible for him to say, "I saw you under the fig tree before Philip called you" was a sign that Jesus was someone else again.

Jesus Gathered Disciples

We turn now to this surprising story of how Nathanael became a disciple of Jesus. However special Nathanael may have been, he was not the first disciple! In the early days of his ministry, Jesus gathered disciples as the result of John the Baptist's testimony. John was apprised of Jesus' unique role in the plans of God when Jesus presented himself to John for baptism at the Jordan near Bethany.

> I myself did not know him, but the one who sent me to baptize with water said to me, "He on whom you see the Spirit descend and remain is the one who baptizes with the Holy Spirit." And I myself have seen and have testified that this is the Son of God. (Jn. 1:33–34)

John the Baptist had been preaching for some time when Jesus arrived for baptism. John had impressed several along the Jordan with his ministry and message. He gathered supporters as the result of his call for repentance. For months John taught and baptized while his followers assisted him. Jesus milled among the crowds on the banks of the Jordan two days after he was baptized. Once as Jesus passed by, John stood with two of his disciples. Pointing out Jesus to them, he announced, "Look, here is the Lamb of God!" (1:36). The two took special notice and followed Jesus, eventually spending the day conversing with him. One of the two was Andrew, who fished for a living in partnership with his brother Simon (Peter). Andrew was so taken with Jesus that he sought out Peter. Finding him, he took him to meet Jesus. After that meeting Andrew and Peter determined to leave their nets and follow this incredible one from Nazareth.

The day afterward, Jesus left the Jordan for Galilee. On arrival he sought out Philip. We don't know why he sought out Philip. How did he know him to begin with? A likely possibility is that Philip was the unnamed disciple of John the Baptist who on the previous day had gone with Andrew to talk with Jesus. Philip is crucial in the account of Nathanael's conversion. He introduced Nathanael to Jesus. John the Baptist, spellbound by the descent of the Spirit upon Jesus, pointed him out to Philip. Philip, in turn, because of John's testimony and his own conversations with Jesus, persuaded Nathanael to meet Jesus.

People who knew Jesus because of a prior faith commitment have made that same connection down through the ages. Sometimes these people are parents. Sometimes they are friends. Sometimes the followers are special proclaimers of the word.

The Discipling of Nathanael

Nathanael was not readily impressible or easily taken in. He had his opinion of those gullible persons who believed almost everything. Philip, however, was so captivated by Jesus that he could not restrain himself. He just had to share his discovery with someone! He, therefore, hurried to locate his friend Nathanael. After exchanging the conventional pleasantries, Philip blurted out, "We have found him about whom Moses in the law and also the prophets wrote, Jesus son of Joseph from Nazareth" (1:45). Nathanael knew about the predicted messiah, as did many of his compatriots. He eagerly anticipated the day in which a new king after the archetype of David and Solomon would appear on the horizon. When that came about, this newly anointed one would overthrow the repugnant Romans and restore the rule of God to his beloved country.

Nathanael's first thought was disbelief. How could his good friend Philip, otherwise such a sensible man, be so easily deceived? *You say he is from Nazareth? My word!* "Can anything good come out of Nazareth?" (1:46). In his opinion, Nazareth was a place without merit, an insignificant village. Wasn't the messiah to come from some place of past importance—Bethlehem, for example, where David himself was born? Or Jerusalem might be another obvious choice. David and Solomon put Jerusalem on the map so that it compared favorably with other major cities in the ancient world. The queen of that distant affluent country on the Arabian coast—Sheba—paid Solomon a visit. She was so overawed that she spread it abroad that in respect to his wisdom and wealth the half had never been told. How could the messiah come from such a paltry hamlet as Nazareth? Nazareth was nothing more than a little village off the beaten track in the hill country.

Interestingly, Ann Rice, who reports that she has turned her back on writing vampire novels and has rediscovered her religious roots, is reading books by scholars on the life of Jesus, and is refocusing her publishing career with books about him. In her recent book *Jesus the Christ,* she depicts daily life in Jesus' Nazareth. She envisions Nazareth as a stagnant wayside with little opportunity for employment for a family of carpenters such as were Joseph, his extended family, and Jesus. She suggests that the family enhanced their skills by working alongside Egyptian craftsmen during their stay there.

The up-and-coming cosmopolitan city of the region around Nazareth was Sepphoris. At one time it housed a palace of Herod the Great, though later the city was decimated. During Jesus' early manhood, Sepphoris was impressively rebuilt by Herod Antipas and became the showcase metropolis for all of Galilee. Rice envisions Joseph, his other sons, and relatives, along with Jesus, traveling north five miles from Nazareth so as to employ Joseph's recently acquired wood-working skills. Had Philip connected Jesus with Sepphoris, Nathanael's opinion may have been different.

Harry Truman, born in Lamar, Missouri, ran for president against the sophisticated easterner Thomas Dewey, Governor of New York, in 1948. Few people gave Truman a chance. He was essentially a ne'er-do-well from a small Missouri town. Now Truman had climbed the ladder a bit by moving to Independence, Missouri, and owning a haberdashery. He was elected to the United States Senate, but it was widely reported that he was indebted politically to the Pendergast machine of Kansas City. Truman's opponents asked, in view of the corrupt Kansas City politics, can anything good come out of Kansas City? *The Chicago Tribune* headline even declared Thomas Dewey the winner the morning after the election. However, as we know, Truman had the last laugh. The place of one's upbringing may not tell the whole story. Despite Truman's frequent squabbles, his presidency has stood the test of time in the view of biographer James McCullough.

How is it possible that the messiah could grow up in so contemptible a town as Nazareth? Philip didn't quarrel with Nathanael's assessment of Nazareth. He wasn't interested in defending the town. He was deeply impressed with Jesus, who just happened to be from Nazareth. Philip responded simply, "Come and see." What was Nathanael to do? He saw that Philip was deadly serious. So out of friendship for Philip and likely to humor him, Nathanael reluctantly agreed to meet this man from Nazareth. He got ready, and they set out.

Nathanael may have been dubious of Philip's claims, but he was convinced that God's messiah would one day appear and lead the Jews out of bondage. He was a good prospect in view of his interests and convictions. It's just that Jesus did not seem a likely candidate. But all of that was to change. Jesus caught Nathanael completely off guard. Jesus did not wait until Philip and Nathanael arrived. As they approached, Jesus immediately centered his attention on Nathanael. "When Jesus saw Nathanael coming toward him, he said of him, "Here is truly an Israelite in whom there is no deceit!" (1:47). Nathanael, flabbergasted, exclaimed, "Where did you get to know me?" Not only did Jesus address him directly, he also worded a compliment so explicit that no one in his right mind would say this without prior detailed knowledge. Jesus did not exactly answer Nathanael's question. He responded in such a manner that Nathanael knew for sure that here was no ordinary human being: "I saw you under the fig tree before Philip called you" (1:48), Jesus replied. Such powers as Jesus exhibited must somehow be connected with God.

Despite his earlier skepticism, Nathanael made an immediate decision. He exclaimed, "Rabbi, you are the Son of God! You are the King of Israel!" (1:49). He went to meet Jesus fully convinced that he could not possibly be the promised messiah. What Jesus said so took him by surprise that all doubt disappeared. What Jesus did did not make the difference. What he said made all the difference. Jesus' declaration was clearly a sign that he had come from

God. John, the writer of the gospel, was convinced that signs are the means through which men and women come to believe that Jesus is the Messiah, the Son of God (20:31).

Words as Signs

What, in John's opinion is a sign? A sign is an event or statement that points beyond the human scene to God. A sign cannot possibly have any other explanation other than that divinity is involved. When the Pharisees demanded that Jesus give them a sign after he drove the money changers out of the temple, he replied, "Destroy this temple, and in three days I will raise it up" (2:19). Jesus responded with words. The proof that the words came from above would be evident when Jesus rose from the tomb. The sign in this case was first the words of Jesus, then later his action signified by the empty grave. The sign Jesus gave the woman at Jacob's well was his statement about her married condition: "You are right in saying, 'I have no husband'; for you have had five husbands, and the one you have now is not your husband. What you have said is true!" (4:17b–18).

The Samaritan woman was well aware that Jesus could not have known her situation from any human source, so she attributed his words to input from beyond: "Sir, I see that you are a prophet" (4:19). The source of the action or of the word is from beyond. The sign directs ones mind heavenward!

The sign points beyond the deed or word. The sign itself is not the reality, but points to it. As one drives west of Boston on route 2, about 20 miles out a sign announces that the next exit is the road to Thoreau's celebrated Walden Pond. The sign is not the Pond. It points one in that direction. For John the sign embedded in the word or action was not the reality. The reality was the beyond to which the sign pointed. In our world sometimes believers tout speaking in tongues or an alleged cancer cure rather that the Lord who is the source. Nathanael heard the words, and now he believed beyond a shadow of a doubt that Jesus was the Son of God—that is, the king or promised Messiah of Israel. The sign brought about the gospel's declared purpose—faith in Jesus as the Son of God, Messiah.

Jesus acknowledged Nathanael's newly achieved faith but de-emphasized what Nathanael had experienced as the ultimate sign:

> Jesus answered, "Do you believe because I told you that I saw you under the fig tree? You will see greater things than these." And he said to him, "Very truly, I tell you, you will see heaven opened and the angels of God ascending and descending upon the Son of Man." (1:50–51)

It is not certain what Jesus had in mind, but we are immediately reminded of Jacob's dream as he slept with his head on a stone at Bethel: "And he dreamed that there was a ladder set up on the earth, the top of it reaching to heaven; and the angels of God were ascending and descending on it" (Gen. 28:12). In that dream God promised Jacob that his progeny would populate a mighty nation. The implication may therefore well be that people who believe in Jesus will see his disciples multiply like the dust of the earth. New communities of faith will spring up around the globe and extend from shore to shore. These communities are the Lord's "new creation by water and the word." "All things came into being through him, and without him not one thing came into being" (Jn. 1:3).

Conclusion

Jesus called the twelve one by one in order to form the inner nucleus of a new community of God's people, the church of the Lord Jesus Christ. Nathanael was inducted into the select circle of the twelve by Jesus' unprecedented words. Even today the procession continues. The Philips are still out there eager to introduce candidates to Jesus as the Messiah, the Son of God. Wherever Nathanaels acknowledge the prospect of God breaking into the world so as to introduce God's kingdom, then the recital of Jesus' signs creates disciples: "If the light of his presence has brightened your way / O will you not tell it today?"[2] Whenever that occurs, Jesus creates an additional disciple by the power of his word.

SERMON _____

He Always Had Some Mighty Fine Wine
John 2:1–11

MARK FROST

Compositional Comments

In this sermon, I have attempted to attend to Thomas Olbricht's insights regarding the essential unity of Jesus' words and works and how both serve as signs pointing to his identity as God. At the heart of the sermon is a basic contrast between our impotent works and the powerfully effective words of Jesus. Our works–even our well-intentioned religious activities–cannot bring us the joy that is so aptly symbolized by the wine at the wedding in Cana. On the other hand, for those who hear and obey the words of Jesus, everything is changed. There is new life, and a joy that can only come as a gift from God.

As Olbricht points out, the miracle at Cana is effected by words. Mary tells the servants, "Do whatever he tells you" (Jn. 2:5). The reader is thus primed to listen for whatever words Jesus says next. What follows are two simple instructions: "Fill the jars with water," and, "Draw some out." Both instructions are followed by a brief mention that the servants complied with Jesus' words. The result was an abundance of the very best wine. What had been done many times before in obedience to the Law of Moses had a radically different result when done in response to the words of Jesus!

At several places in the sermon, I have tried to illustrate the power of words to create a new reality in Christ. One instance involved my longing for the joy of the Spirit during a time of depression. While I was looking for some kind of internal experience, God was instead sending people to me with words that were intended to minister to me. Another instance is the story at the end of the sermon about a faithful vacation Bible school teacher, who penned a few simple words inside a Bible. These words lay dormant for decades, but eventually set in motion a chain of events that led to hundreds of people coming to faith in Jesus.

Sermon

Church is a beehive of religious activity. Some folks teach Bible classes. Others take care of the church building and grounds. Still others greet visitors, lead worship, hand out bulletins, pass baskets, stock the pantry, take prayer requests, count the contribution, staff the welcome center, and change diapers in the nursery.

Our church is a hotbed of religious activity in a special way this morning, because vacation Bible school begins tonight. A lot of energy has been spent this week moving furniture, building sets for drama productions, decorating everything in sight, baking cookies, preparing lessons, and sewing costumes.

Religious activity is what we do. And it's what we reward. Take a look at our heroes, the people we celebrate publicly:

- The good sister who has taught Sunday school for forty-seven years straight
- The gentleman who keeps the baptistery cleaned and filled
- The Bible class that faithfully supports orphans in Honduras
- The teenager who collects soda cans and gives the money to the benevolence fund
- The kids who brought back a trophy from the area Bible Bowl competition

We major in religious activity. But come with me to the wedding at Cana, and I think you'll see a very different emphasis. You can't miss it. Jesus values celebration and fine wine above religious goings-on. Jesus produces a deluge of fine wine: one hundred fifty gallons![1] It's just a hunch, but I suspect that we might increase our attendance a bit if we hauled in 150 gallons of wine and put out the word, "The party's at the Church of Christ on Sunday!"

Outrageous! Unthinkable! The truth is that we—followers of Jesus—are embarrassed and frightened at the thought of doing anything like what Jesus did on this occasion. Maybe it's time for us to face the fact that—our WWJD bracelets notwithstanding—we fail to do a lot of things that Jesus did. Just take a look at two of the early miracles in the book of John: here he produces six huge jars full of wine. Later, he takes five loaves of bread and throws a feast for 5,000 people, with enough left over to fill twelve baskets.[2]

"Well," you say, "we have bread and wine at church, too. It's something we call the Lord's supper."

But is it the same as what Jesus did? A little pinch of cracker and a thimbleful, not of wine, but grape juice? Who would ever equate that with the staggering surplus Jesus produced? You see, somewhere a few centuries back, a philosophy called minimalism infected our practice of the Lord's supper. The scholars of that day asked, "If bread and wine are the essential elements, what is the minimum amount of each necessary to meet the requirements?" The paltry portions we serve on Sunday bear witness to how they answered that one.

Ironically, many of us apply that kind of minimalist thinking to the activity that usually follows the Lord's supper: the collection. Although we're urged to give generously, abundantly, and outrageously, we ask, "What's the smallest amount I can give to meet the requirement?" Unfortunately, we're trained to think in minimalist fashion. We've lost our grip on Jesus' penchant for profusion.

John's gospel keeps reminding us that Jesus is all about abundance. In the place of a bucket of well water, Jesus promises a spring welling up from within, a never-ending stream of living water.[3] Even the miraculous flood of wine is superseded later by his promise to those who remain connected to him. He says they will bear a continual, abundant harvest of the fruit of the vine.[4]

So why do churches skimp on the bread and wine, choosing instead to serve up an abundance of religious hustle and bustle, along with a heaping helping of duty and responsibility? Where's the wine? Where's the party? Is religious activity all we have to offer?

This is not to say that Jesus disparages all religious activity. In fact, it plays a central role at the wedding in Cana. The story itself is brief. The author is sparing in detail...except when he describes the water jars. He focuses our attention on the jars long enough to point out considerable detail. Six—count them—six jars. Made of stone, not clay. The twenty-to-thirty-gallon jumbo size. Most significantly, we're told that they were the kind the Jews used for ceremonial washing. These jars were all about religious activity—exclusively so. Thus, the story implicitly poses the question, "What if someone could transform our religious activity into the exquisite joy of fine wine?"

Jesus doesn't condemn the religious activity the jars represent; he doesn't abolish it. But he holds out the possibility that there's more to be gained from it than blisters, sore backs, and general weariness. In fact, he shows us that it can be a source of joy and celebration. So don't reject all religious activity. But don't forget the celebration either. Having spent a lifetime in church, I have to tell you that it's hard for me to see the Cana wedding without feeling that we're missing something. But what?

We Miss the Point

The wedding at Cana didn't take place in a vacuum. It occurred in the context of considerable dialogue and debate about ceremonial washings. There are hints about the intensity of that discussion in the book of John. Right after the account of the water turned to wine, we find John the Baptist doing a lot of...well...baptizing, which is, of course, a kind of ceremonial cleansing. And "a certain Jew" instigated an argument with John's disciples over it.[5] Before long, there was great concern and commotion over who was doing the most baptizing, John or Jesus.[6]

We can get some idea of the parameters of the debate about ritual washing from the Mishnah, a written record of Jewish oral law. Although the Mishnah came along a couple of centuries later, its laws were forged from rabbinical debates that were ongoing in Jesus' day. The Mishnah has no less than 186 pages on the subject of ceremonial washings! It specifies, among other things, who must wash, when to wash, what kind of water to use, the amount of water required (yes, the rabbis were into minimalism, too), the kind of container to be used, how to hold the hands when washing, how to dry the hands after washing, etc. The granddaddy of all of these ritual washings was the *mikvah,* which involved immersing the whole body. Maybe it's just a coincidence, but the Mishnah specifies a minimum of 150 gallons for a *mikvah.* Hmmm...the capacity of the jars in Cana.

What was the point of all this washing? It appears to have been a sincere attempt on the part of the Jews to make themselves acceptable to God. The idea was that if you could get the rituals done just right, with just the right kind of water, and following just the right procedure, God would stop frowning and say, "I guess you're OK."

I know that we often imagine that this is the point of our religious activity as well. So we continually busy ourselves with the ecclesiastical equivalent of drawing and hauling water. We wear ourselves out in our religious activities. If you don't believe it, just walk into any church and look for the busy people. When you find them, you will see weary souls, longing for rest, but hanging in there because they want to "please God," which usually means "earn God's approval."

If I understand what Jesus did at the wedding, it sounds like really good news to our bone-weary church workers. The point of religious activity is not to gain God's stamp of approval, but rather to position oneself to receive an abundance of God's wine! Whether it's drawing water and hauling it in stone jars, or scrubbing the fellowship hall floor, or teaching the toddlers' class, or devoting oneself to the discipline of prayer and fasting, there's really only one point to it: giving Jesus the opportunity to inundate us with his abundance. While 150 gallons of water is the bare minimum for a *miknah*, 150 gallons of wine is a jaw-dropping surplus of delicious delight. Here's a profound reality: after we've worn ourselves out trying to meet a minimum requirement, Jesus can transform that minimum into over the top blessings.

Our acceptability to God does not hinge on the quantity or quality of our religious activities. John settled that in the very first chapter: "To all who received him, to those who believed in his name, he gave the right to become children of God—children born not of natural descent, nor of human decision or a husband's will, but born of God."[7] We are acceptable to God not because of what we do but because of who we are. We are God's beloved children by faith in Jesus. God loves to lavish blessings on his kids!

We Miss the Call

Where do the servants at the wedding get the notion to draw all this water and lug these heavy stone jars around? It's certainly not their idea. It begins when Mary says, "Do whatever he tells you."[8] She alerts the servants to listen for Jesus' words. They have no mission; they have no task to perform until Jesus speaks. Their first and most important job is to listen for his voice.

That's why I'm amazed that so much of our religious activity takes place without really listening for the Lord's voice. Because actions are *religious*, we assume, "If we do it, God will come." How could God *not* bless us in the doing of spiritual things? Do you realize that nearly all of the church's activities originate in committee meetings that begin with a perfunctory prayer: meetings of well-intentioned people, who want to do good things for God and his people, but who spend little time listening for God's voice. It's a rare church that gathers in humility and brokenness before God and says, "We have no plan; we have no agenda; we have no purpose until we receive a word from you. We will wait to act until we are certain of your call."

Have we forgotten how John's gospel begins? "In the beginning was the Word."[9] That's where it starts. There's no value in filling stone water jars simply because it's a religious thing to do. But there is great value in filling those same jars in response to the Word.

"But we do listen to the word," you say. "We are a rootin' tootin', Bible-totin', Bible-quotin', give 'em book, chapter and verse church." That's not contested. But our pursuit of biblical knowledge doesn't guarantee that we hear Jesus. Later in his ministry, Jesus has a scathing indictment for some folks who studied their Bibles...well...religiously: "You diligently study the Scriptures because you think that by them you possess eternal life. These are the Scriptures that testify about me, yet you refuse to come to me to have life."[10]

I'm afraid that we come to the word with a faulty understanding of our task. We think our purpose is to discover principles for righteous living, which we can then apply in our everyday activities. That concept sounds familiar. Isn't it the paradigm used by the rabbis of Jesus' day—the ones whose legalistic wrangling eventually yielded 186 pages of principles for ritual cleansing?

The purpose of Bible study is not to discover principles, but to know a person—Jesus—and to train ourselves to listen for his voice. One indication of our deafness to his voice is that we seek his instructions only with regard to religious activities. But his call is much broader than that. It cuts across all of life, leaving no area untouched. His call has to do with how we earn and spend our money; how we treat employees, bosses, coworkers, and street bums; how we act in front of church people; and how we act when we think no one is watching.

Here's the challenge: hear his call, and do whatever he says. Of course, that means paring back other activities to make room for obeying his call. There are some things I wish Jesus had called me to do because they seem to be intriguing and exotic, but I can only waste time and energy by filling my schedule with them. There are other activities at which I'm quite competent, but not particularly called to do. I'm tempted to fill my schedule with them, because that's comfortable and usually rewarding. But I will tell you that the greatest reward—the taste of wine—is reserved for those who slow down and listen carefully for the call of Jesus, and then "do whatever he says."

We Miss the Intended Recipients

I hate it when I come to a familiar passage such as the wedding at Cana, thinking that I know what it says, only to discover something glaringly obvious in the text that I'd never seen before. Well, here's something I had always missed: the guys who busted their guts hauling all that water didn't get the first taste of wine. Jesus didn't tell them, "Draw some out and drink your fill!" He said, "Draw some out and give it to the master of the banquet," so he could then share it with the wedding guests. Were the servants allowed to share in the bounty? We aren't told. It seems that the considerable effort of the servants was not for their personal benefit, but so that others could enjoy fine wine.

This week, I've felt dry and thirsty. That's not terribly unusual. I come from a long line of depressed people. If you wanted to prove that depression is genetic, you could use my family tree as a key piece of evidence. This past week, my depression genes were expressing themselves with abandon. All week long, I read, reread, studied, and meditated on the wedding at Cana. I knew that the wine represented joy, but as I studied, my depression simply wouldn't lift. Then I started getting angry. "God," I complained, "On Sunday, I'm supposed to tell folks about how you provide superabundant joy, but here I am as dry as a dust bunny. Where's this wonderful wine of gladness that I'm supposed to experience?"

That's when it hit me. The wine Jesus provides is not likely to come to me as a result of my own efforts. It will come if and when Jesus blesses the work of others, changes it into wine, and bids them serve it to me. Then it dawned on me that Jesus had been doing just that all week long. Almost every day last week, someone who is not part of my normal circle of acquaintances has approached me in love and concern. Some reported that they had been thinking of me and wanted me to know of their appreciation. Another simply observed that I looked troubled and offered prayer and support. One man felt a prompting to move me to the top of his prayer list, although he didn't know why. One sister woke up at 5:30 a.m. one morning with a sense that she should pray for me. Afterward, she sent me a beautiful message of encouragement and comfort. Her activity in response to the call of God became wine to me, but it wasn't really wine to her. After all, how much do you appreciate being awakened at 5:30 a.m.? I was humbled to realize what God had been doing on my behalf through the conscientious service of others. I was convicted of my blindness to the fact that Jesus was seeking to use my own labors to bless others and not myself. When our activity—religious or otherwise—is a response to the call of Jesus, he most often uses that activity for the benefit of the other guests at the feast.

The Week Ahead

There will be much ado at our church building this week. That's the way VBS is. But will there be wine? It depends on whether or not we allow Jesus to transform our frenzied water hauling into his special vintage. Vacation Bible school can be about herding kids to and fro, getting a headache from all the screaming urchins, singing "Booster" *ad nauseam,* and going home exhausted. Or it can be about something altogether different.

A few years ago, I was sitting in a lecture hall at the Pepperdine Bible Lectures. My wife and I, chatting as we waited for the session to begin, mentioned something about living in metropolitan Detroit. The man sitting in front of us spun around to face us. "You're from Detroit?" he asked. Then he explained that he owed his spiritual life to a church in Detroit. I'll let you listen to his story in his own words:[11]

> I grew up in East Los Angeles, CA. My neighborhood was gang-infested, and the only hope we had was to get out. We moved to the suburbs where gangs were fewer, but drugs and trouble were just as plentiful. I eventually married, but a life of drugs continued.
>
> One evening as my friends and I were getting "drugged out," our newborn daughter began to cry. My wife Cheryl had already gone to bed so I went into the nursery to comfort our daughter. Standing in the darkness, I came to the realization that she deserved more than I was providing. She deserved a chance. I quit the drugs but needed something more—something to fill the void. We needed God in our lives.
>
> So I asked Cheryl if she had attended any particular church when she was young. She replied that she did remember one church from her childhood in Detroit. She couldn't recall its name, but she knew that they had given her a Bible for perfect attendance at VBS.
>
> The Bible was in her hope chest. We opened it up and there on the "Dedication Page" were these words: Presented to Cheryl Fuller. From Mrs. Butler, Hayes Avenue Church of Christ, Detroit, Michigan.
>
> We immediately began to seek out one of those "Church of Christs." We were taught and baptized by Russell Wilson. I attended the Southern California School of Evangelism. Cheryl and I have been serving the Lord since December 1974. We have two daughters, now grown, who are faithful Christians.
>
> None of this would have been possible had it not been for Mrs. Butler, who cared enough to teach vacation Bible school to a freckled, red-headed little second grader. Every life we have touched with the gospel, every congregation we have labored with, every country we have taken the message to…Mrs. Butler was beside us.
>
> —Steve Orduño

Had you been able to observe that VBS at the Hayes Avenue Church of Christ in the mid-1950s, I'm sure you would have seen a lot of religious activity. Had you observed Mrs. Butler dutifully filling out the presentation pages on all those "perfect attendance" Bibles, you might have concluded that it was just so much busywork. But I think Mrs. Butler knew better. I think she knew the One who had called her to the task. Of course, now we know that she wasn't merely engaging in some tedious and tiresome religious activity. She was serving up wine: gallons and gallons and gallons of mighty fine wine from Chateau Cana.

SERMON _____

Signs and Wonders and Faith
John 4:46–54

DAVE BLAND

Compositional Comments

This sermon takes its cue from Thomas Olbricht's essay on "The Word as Sign." Olbricht's essay persuasively argues that the signs in the gospel of John include not only the works and miracles of Jesus, but also his words. The two, words and works, operate in tandem; one does not and cannot exist without the other. The healing of the official's son in John 4 combines both the word and the work of Jesus as sign. Jesus heals this father's child simply by speaking words, "Go; your son will live" (4:50). The result is the miracle of healing; word and work function together. Olbricht maintains that we've focused on the end result, the miracle, and not on that which produced the miracle, the word of Jesus. In addition, as one reads the gospel of John, one discovers that while miracles serve a purpose, their purpose is limited because of human limitations.

Often the crowds follow Jesus to see a miracle. They view him, as the official in this story initially does, as a miracle worker. While Jesus intended his miracles to lead people to believe in him, often that did not happen. At the conclusion of the first half of the gospel, John laments, "Although he had performed so many signs in their presence, they did not believe in him" (12:37).

Though, as contemporary North American Christians, we tend not to believe in miracles or miraculous healings, we still find ourselves wishing for them, longing to have just one more bit of evidence to confirm our belief in Christ. Ultimately, however, all that we need, all that the official in this story needed, is to hear the words of Jesus, the word of God—nothing more, nothing less. This sermon emphasizes the power of Jesus' words and the word of God to produce belief and change lives.

Sermon

Christianity in North America in general dismisses the experiences of miraculous healings. They just don't happen anymore. If miracles do occur, we attribute them to the sophisticated medical technology we possess. In the Old Testament signs and wonders cluster around God's deliverance of Israel from the land of Egypt. God performs miracles so Egypt will know that Yahweh is the true God. In the New Testament, signs and wonders are often associated with Jesus and the coming of the Kingdom and with the spreading of the gospel in Acts by Paul and others who did mission work among the Gentiles. They perform miraculous works to lead people to faith in Christ.

Yet miracles don't seem to cease with the final missionary journeys of the early disciples. Scripture implies that God continues to perform miracles. James says to his congregations and to us, "Is anyone among you sick? Call for the elders and have them pray for you and anoint you with oil in the name of the Lord. The Lord will heal you…The prayer of the righteous is powerful and effective" (Jas. 5:14–16). I believe that. I believe that God continues to perform miraculous healings in our world today.

A colleague of mine, Theresa Jordan, tells of the time in her family's life when her Mom was about five months pregnant with her. It was a winter day in South Bend, Indiana. Snow covered the ground. Her Mom, out driving, lost control of the car going down a hill and crashed into a telephone poll. The ambulance rushed her to the hospital in critical condition, where they told Theresa's Dad that surgery was necessary to stop the internal bleeding. But the surgery was very risky and could kill both mother and baby. However, if they didn't do surgery both mother and baby could die. Facing this life-threatening predicament, her Dad had to decide what to do by morning. The family alerted the church where they worshiped. The church immediately entered into an all-night prayer vigil (something this church was often known to do).

The next morning the doctors, shaking their heads in disbelief, contacted Theresa's father, "This is amazing. We can't explain it, but your wife and baby are going to be just fine. The bleeding has stopped. Mom and child will recover nicely on their own." God performed a miracle that day. God continues to perform miracles in his own way and for his own purposes.

John records Jesus performing miraculous healings in his gospel account. John refers to them as "signs" and mentions several instances. He tells of Jesus' healing a lame man by the pool of Bethzatha, giving sight to a blind man, and raising Lazarus from the dead. Jesus does not heal them because he loves them more than others. Jesus has a larger purpose: to lead people to belief in God. Jesus performs many miraculous signs in the course of his ministry, but John includes just a few so that we might come to believe that Jesus is God's Son and, as a result, receive abundant life. Signs fulfilled an important purpose beyond just the immediate healing of a person.

Yet, here's the real rub. Scripture expresses reservations about the role miraculous signs play in leading people to belief. Signs carry limitations primarily because of human misperception, immaturity, and abuse. For one, God's not the only one who can perform miracles. Others are capable as well. For example, Pharaoh's magicians whom Moses encounters in Egypt can perform a level of pretty impressive miraculous activities. Paul tells the Thessalonians that Satan uses signs and wonders to delude people into following him (2 Thess. 2:9–10). Simply because one witnesses a miracle does not mean it's from God.

Another limitation of performing miracles is that they can become a façade. Christians can become so focused on miracles that they avoid the real work of Christ in serving and caring and loving others. Jesus warns his disciples at the end of the Sermon on the Mount, "Many will say on the last day, 'Lord we performed miraculous deeds in your name.' But I will announce to them depart from me, I never knew you" (Mt. 7:22–23).[1] These disciples give the appearance through their impressive miraculous powers that they are true followers of Christ. However, they live a lie; as far as disciples, they are frauds.

Still another reservation about miraculous signs is that a person can focus exclusively on the miracle and view Jesus as nothing more than a wonder worker, similar to being awed at watching a performer execute an amazing feat in the center ring of a circus. Jesus continually faces this problem. Often the crowds follow him only for the purpose of seeing him perform a sign (Jn. 2:23–25; 3:2–3; 4:45–48; 7:3–7). And this angers Jesus.

That is why in this story in John 4 the crowds and the official follow Jesus. Once again, Jesus comes to Cana in Galilee. A respected civil official, a VIP, travels fifteen miles up from Capernaum to see Jesus. He's distraught. His son is near death. In desperation this official seeks a cure. He's heard of the powerful healings this miracle worker performed in Judea. Maybe he could take advantage of Jesus' powers to save his son. He pleads with Jesus, "Sir, come down before my little boy dies!"

Surprisingly, the official's petition perturbs Jesus. Jesus turns and addresses not only the official but also the whole crowd following him, "All of you Galileans have to be dazzled by signs and wonders before you will believe!" Amazingly, Jesus' rebuke doesn't deter the official in the least. The desperate father continues to implore Jesus, "I beg you to come; it's a matter of life and death for my son!!"

Despite the official's lack of understanding of who Jesus is, the father's imploring request touches Jesus. Jesus then speaks a brief but powerful word to the dad, "Go on back home. Your son lives."

Most amazingly, the official believes! Why? I don't know! But he believes right there on the spot. The official doesn't question; he doesn't have to see his son to believe. He just hears the words of Jesus, and that's sufficient for him! Jesus' words produce faith, not the miracle. The man believes the bare word Jesus spoke. The official moves from seeing Jesus for *what he does* to seeing Jesus for *who he is*.[2] And he believes. Not only that, his whole household comes to believe. This VIP demonstrates a faith that moves from seeing Jesus as wonder worker (v. 48), to possessing an individual faith (v. 50), to finally receiving a collective faith with his whole family (v. 53). In the end, the official receives not only the gift of his son's life but also the gift of faith in Jesus.

Even though North American Christians remain quite skeptical about miracles, we still wish for them; we desire to experience them. We want just a little more proof to confirm our belief in Jesus. So we scour the land looking for that bit of evidence that will clinch the case for Jesus. We chase after esoteric lost books of the Bible such as the recently found *Gospel of Judas,* or we rummage through the *Gospel of Thomas.* Millions read *The Da Vinci Code* in search of some clue. We get all giddy when some archeologists claim to discover a new artifact from the time of Christ such as the "Holy Grail." Or some scientists investigate the Shroud of Turin, and claim it could possibly be the burial cloth of Jesus, and we are ecstatic! Or researchers discover an ossuary from the first century with the inscription, "James, son of Joseph, brother of Jesus" and we say, "Yes! Evidence!" We want that final bit of proof that will push us over the top and convince us that Jesus is who he says he is. We want at least some sign that our faith is really true.

We reason, "If I could just witness a miracle, wouldn't that be awesome? If I did, then I know I could lay it all on the line for Christ. I'd give him my all." That again is the deceptive nature of our human desire. John reveals that though Jesus performed numerous signs in the presence of others, still many did not believe (12:37). Jesus raises Lazarus from the dead. Yet immediately afterward, Caiaphas counsels the Pharisees to kill Jesus because of it (11:47–53)!

Yet we so desire visual, or experiential, or some sensory confirmation of our faith. *If we just had a little more proof.* Some time ago, a young woman became critically ill.[3] Her prognosis was grim; she would likely die within the year. She and her family had a nominal commitment to the church. The woman asked the minister, "If Jesus healed in the Bible, then surely he could heal me today. If not, what use is he?" So she prayed. The church prayed. Her family pleaded and begged God, "Lord, if you will restore her health, our whole family will recommit ourselves to you. We'll be faithful, and we'll show that faithfulness in coming every week to church." The minister also prayed with all his heart believing that God could and would heal her. To everyone's amazement and joy, she was healed. It baffled the doctors; they couldn't explain what happened.

Next Sunday the whole family was in church. The young woman gave her testimony, praising God for God's goodness. The following Sunday, the family was there again. A few Sundays down the road only the woman and her husband came. Still later their attendance became sporadic, until finally they completely stopped coming to church. The woman began to rationalize her experience and ultimately dismissed it as nothing more than a work of medical science. Here she had experienced the most dramatic sign God could give her: healing through the prayers of righteous people. But after a few months the whole experience faded into nothing.

In John, miracles are "signs." They point beyond themselves to something or someone else. Signs are like training wheels parents put on a child's first bicycle. It's all right for the child to depend on those extra little wheels to hold the bike up for a time. But eventually the child must abandon those helper wheels and learn to ride the bike without them. Training wheels on a mountain bike, for example, do not help, but hinder travel! They may, however, be a necessary step toward learning the skill. John says the signs that Jesus performed produced embryonic faith. But that faith must grow beyond a dependence on the signs.[4]

Miraculous healings do occur. Praise God! Contrary to what we might think, though, they are not necessary to believe in God. We don't need proof to validate our faith: "For those who will not believe, final proof is never quite enough; for those who will believe, final proof is not necessary."[5] All that is necessary are the words of Jesus. It's all this official needed. All that is necessary is to hear the words of Scripture.

That's all the two disciples on the road to Emmaus need. As the two disciples walk beside Jesus, they do not know it is Jesus. Jesus opens Scripture and reads and interprets it to them and they believe. Jesus performs no miracle; he does not reveal the scars in his hands. He just reads and interprets Scripture. And they believe. When Philip, the first evangelist, goes forth in Acts, the Holy Spirit catches him up and places him in the context of an Ethiopian who is searching. Philip opens Scripture, reads, and explains. The Ethiopian believes! No miracles were performed, just the Word read.

In Luke's gospel, the rich man in Hades looks up and sees Lazarus in the bosom of Abraham. He cries out to Abraham, "Send Lazarus back from the grave to warn my brothers about this awful place so they can avoid it."

Abraham replies, "If they don't believe Scripture, which speaks about God and Christ, neither will they believe if they see someone raised from the dead" (Lk. 16:27–31). The word of God is adequate for generating and sustaining faith. No training wheel faith is necessary.

John is not just offering a model of strong faith displayed by the official. He underscores the power of Jesus' word. God's word is sufficient. Near the conclusion of the gospel of John, Jesus says to Thomas, "Have you believed because you have seen me? Blessed are those who have not seen and yet believe" (Jn. 20:29). How are they going to believe without seeing? By hearing God's word. Faith comes by hearing. God's word takes those who are open and receptive to it and changes their lives. We believe God's word, and God's word continues to transform us into God's likeness.

Believing Is Seeing

The Dynamics of Faith in the Gospel of John

GREGORY STEVENSON

No gospel is more capable of making its readers uncomfortable than the gospel of John. Luke challenges us to care more about people on the margins. Mark calls for a more radical form of discipleship. Matthew demands that we rethink some of our notions of Christian identity. John strikes at the very nature of our faith, where belief is a slippery concept and where one repeatedly meets characters who profess belief in Jesus, but then have an encounter with him that exposes the shallowness, emptiness, or misguidedness of that faith. For example, Jesus encounters a group of Jews who profess belief in him, yet he then calls them children of Satan (8:31, 44). Encounters with Jesus are fraught with danger in this gospel. Reading the gospel creates a tension between the belief we profess and the belief Jesus demands. Those who hear this gospel with their ears open are constantly prodded to ask, "Do I believe?"

Theological Orientation

John's purpose for writing is "so that you may believe that Jesus is the Christ" (20:31).[1] By this he means not the mere intellectual acceptance of Jesus' identity but a certain theological orientation. John raises the question of why some believe in Jesus while others do not (1:10–12). To describe this dualistic response to Jesus, John employs the metaphors of darkness and light: the world is darkness, and Jesus has entered it shining as the light (1:4–5). Yet why do some see the light, while others remain blind to it?

John the Baptist provides a clue when he explains, "The one who comes from above is above all; the one who is out of the earth is out of the earth and speaks out of the earth. The one who comes out of heaven is above all" (Jn. 3:31).[2] John here identifies two different ways of speaking and being in the world. The one who is "from above" and "out of heaven" contrasts with the one who is "from below" and "out of the earth." These categories are not about divine versus human, but about one's theological orientation in the world. Is one theologically oriented "from below" or "from above"?

Recently, I turned on the television in our basement and could not find any channels. I could see nothing except snow and hear nothing except static. I puzzled over this awhile until realizing that one of my children had hit the button on the remote that switched the frequency from cable to analog. I was on the wrong frequency. As long as I stayed on that frequency, I was never going to see or hear anything comprehendible. Once I made the switch over to the cable frequency, however, everything came clear. Belief, in the gospel of John, is very much like this. People struggle to see Jesus for who he really is and to hear what he says because they are operating on different frequencies. The following chart lays out the dualistic language John uses to identify these two different frequencies, or theological orientations.

Heavenly Frequency: from above – out of heaven – spirit – light – day
Earthly Frequency: from below – out of earth – flesh – darkness – night

When Jesus says in John 5:37b–38, "You have never heard his voice or seen his form...because you do not believe him whom he has sent," he reveals a kind of belief prerequisite to seeing and hearing. Belief in the gospel of John is about learning to operate "from above" as opposed to "from below," "out of heaven" as opposed to "out of earth." On one level, this dualism between heaven and earth in John's gospel finds unity in the person of Jesus. He is the Word become flesh (1:14); in him heaven and earth coexist. Yet John 1:14 is a statement of identification with humanity and not one of theological orientation. Jesus comes to earth, but does not operate "out of earth." He lives below, but is not oriented "from below." Theologically speaking, Jesus operates on a higher frequency. Belief involves learning how to operate on that same frequency. Throughout his gospel, John parades before the readers a host of characters who have difficulty seeing and hearing Jesus because they operate from below. They inhabit the darkness and the night.

Cast of Characters

Nicodemus (John 3)

John introduces Nicodemus as a "leader of the Jews" and a "Pharisee" who comes to Jesus "by night" (3:2). "By night" is not merely John's attempt at historical accuracy or narrative ambience, nor is it simply a reference to Nicodemus' fear of discovery. Given John's fondness for the metaphorical dualism of light/dark and day/night, the designation "by night" most likely functions to direct the readers towards a preliminary evaluation of Nicodemus. Does Nicodemus belong to the darkness? That initial suggestion, however, appears overturned when Nicodemus speaks: "Rabbi, we know that you are a teacher who has come from God." Nicodemus speaks like one who believes, but he is not done speaking. He adds, "for no one can do these signs that you do apart from the presence of God." (3:2) This, too, sounds like faith, until one recalls that the Nicodemus story follows immediately after John writes that many believed in Jesus because of the miraculous signs that they saw, "but Jesus on his part would not entrust himself to them" (2:23–24).

Jesus is suspicious of a faith based on signs. The proper function of signs in the gospel of John is as an aid that facilitates the transition from the earthly frequency to the heavenly frequency. As an aid, signs work differently for different people. Some see a sign and use it as a catalyst to begin operating "from above." Others, however, see the same signs but continue to operate "from below"—and Jesus will not entrust himself to them. With Nicodemus the question then becomes: Of which type is he? Is he "out of heaven" or "out of earth"? Does he belong to the "day" or to the "night"?

Jesus engages Nicodemus in conversation—a dangerous endeavor in the gospel of John. Jesus is the light, and so his conversations tend to be enlightening. They function to expose the darkness, to cut through all of the claims of "belief," and reveal the true nature of a person's faith. This occurs through the use of metaphor and irony. Jesus typically speaks to people with figurative and metaphorical language, language that can be easily misunderstood if one does not have the ears to hear. Jesus speaks "out of heaven." Those who listen "out of earth" misunderstand what he says. They cannot hear what he says or see him for who he is because they are on the wrong frequency.

Jesus begins his conversation with Nicodemus by stating, "No one can see the kingdom of God without being born *anothen*" (3:3). The Greek word *anothen* can mean either "again" or "from above." This poses a problem for translators who must choose one of the options. I suggest the use of this term here in John is deliberately vague. *Anothen* can be construed as having both a heavenly meaning ("from above") and an earthly meaning ("again"). Modern evangelicalism has turned "born again" into a spiritual phrase; yet, here it has a decidedly earthly connotation, and that is exactly how Nicodemus hears it. I suggest that Jesus, however, means "from above" when he uses this term. He essentially says to Nicodemus, "Unless one is born from above, one cannot *see* the kingdom of God."

Without changing frequencies, without learning to operate "out of heaven," one cannot see the light that Jesus brings into the world and so that person remains in the darkness and is blind. In fact, Nicodemus appears to reveal himself as just such a person when he misunderstands Jesus to say that one must be born "again" and so comments on the impossibility of reentering the womb (3:4). Jesus speaks "from above." Nicodemus listens "from below." So Jesus says to Nicodemus in 3:10, "Are you a teacher of Israel, and yet you do

not understand these things?" When Jesus concludes his conversation with
Nicodemus by commenting that "the light has come into the world, and people
loved darkness rather than light" (3:19), he appears to provide a final note on
this man's faith. Nicodemus cannot see or hear clearly because there is too
much interference. As a "leader of the Jews" and a "Pharisee," Nicodemus is
distracted by his religious position. He has something to protect in this world.
His connection to what is "from below" blinds him to what is "from above."

The final verdict on Nicodemus, however, is not so clear. He shows up
twice more in this gospel. In the first scene, he stands up for Jesus at a meeting
of the Pharisees, but will not go so far as to confess faith in him (7:45–52). In the
second, he helps Joseph of Arimathea bury Jesus. John tempers this apparent
act of faith by describing Joseph as one who follows Jesus secretly "because
of his fear of the Jews" and Nicodemus as the one who had previously "come
to Jesus by night" (19:38–39). That John connects Nicodemus once again to
secrecy and night may indicate that Nicodemus still has not fully escaped the
darkness.

Ultimately, Nicodemus is an ambiguous figure.[3] He is not blind, but his
vision is not so great either. He remains distracted by his religious position.
Nicodemus sees enough to come to Jesus, to stand up for him, and to help with
burial preparations, but not enough to come fully into the light. He exists in
the twilight, caught between the day and the night.

The Samaritan Woman (John 4)

In contrast with Nicodemus, Jesus encounters the Samaritan woman at
the sixth hour–in the middle of the day. Does her association with the day
foreshadow a different result? Will she make the full transition to the light?
As with Nicodemus, conversation with Jesus begins with static (4:7–15). Jesus
asks her for a drink, yet she comments on the ethnic barrier that divides Jew
and Samaritan. Jesus says he can give her "living water," yet she replies that
the well is too deep to draw living water (a phrase that she may understand
to mean running water). Jesus adds that he can give her water that will never
make her thirsty, yet she asks for that water so as not to have to draw from
the well anymore. Throughout this conversation, the Samaritan woman has
difficulty seeing Jesus for who he is because earthly concerns have distracted
her. Societal and ethnic expectations keep her focused on the physical and
blind to the spiritual.

Jesus, however, seems to recognize in her one who is primed to switch
frequencies from the earthly to the heavenly, so he gives her a sign (4:16–18).
When she replies with, "You are a prophet" (4:19), it looks as if she can now
see–except that she then allows herself to become distracted by a contemporary
worship debate (4:20). Jesus, however, puts that debate to rest when he tells
her that the time has come to stop talking about worship and to start talking
about the *worshiper* (4:21–24). The true worshiper, he says, is the one who
worships from above, who worships in spirit. The true worshiper is the one
able to transition from the darkness to the light.

That Jesus suddenly becomes uncharacteristically clear in his language with her ("I am he, the one who is speaking to you" [4:26]) suggests that he recognizes in her the potential to be such a worshiper. Indeed, following this encounter, she returns to the city and preaches to all who will listen (4:28–29, 39). The Samaritan woman ultimately makes the transition into the light—though with much effort.

The Crowd (John 6)

In John 6, one encounters a crowd of people who have been following Jesus because they saw the signs he had been doing for the sick (6:2). Have these signs led them to transition to a genuine belief that operates "from above?" Or are they blinded to Jesus by their focus on his ability to remedy physical need? That the feeding miracle Jesus performs for this crowd is based on physical need (hunger) is instructive. After Jesus meets their physical need just as he did with the sick, the crowd proclaims him as "the prophet who is to come into the world" (6:14). They believe, but theirs is a misguided faith. Rather than allowing the sign to open their eyes to Jesus, they allow the sign to distract their vision. They want to make Jesus king by force, thus remedying another of their physical needs (6:15). Jesus identifies the source of their blindness: "Very truly, I tell you, you are looking for me...because you ate your fill of the loaves" (6:26). The sign failed to help them achieve genuine belief because their physical needs—sickness, hunger, political subservience—were creating interference. Their belief was operating "out of earth."

In the subsequent conversation between Jesus and crowd, Jesus challenges them to switch frequencies, to operate "from above" rather than "from below." His method of accomplishing this is to speak to the crowd "out of heaven" by communicating spiritual concepts in figurative language. When the crowd listens "out of earth" by interpreting everything in physical and literal terms, Jesus responds by becoming increasingly more figurative. This only ratchets up the tension. Jesus talks of the bread that has come down "out of heaven," but the crowd interprets this as physical bread—bread that is "out of earth" (6:32–34). Jesus says he is this bread "out of heaven," but they say that is impossible because he is the son of Joseph (6:35–42). Jesus not only says he is the bread; he also insists they must eat it. They interpret that to mean cannibalism (6:48–52). Jesus then ratchets up the tension to the breaking point when he says, "Unless you eat the flesh of the Son of Man and drink his blood, you have no life in you" (6:53). When the crowd has difficulty accepting this, Jesus says, "Does this offend you?...The spirit is what gives life; the flesh counts for nothing. The words that I have spoken to you are spirit" (6:61–63).[4] Jesus speaks "out of heaven," but as long as they listen "out of earth" they will never hear him. Jesus is the Word become flesh (1:14), but the crowd is so focused on the flesh that they fail to see or hear the Word. The result is that they leave and no longer follow him (6:66).

Jesus turns to the Twelve and asks, "Do you also wish to go away?" a question addressed as much to the readers as to the Twelve. The crowd couldn't handle the tension between the call to live "from above" and the distractions "from below" that were pulling them in different directions. The question for the Twelve, and by extension the readers as well, is, "How much interference can you handle before you either walk away or remove the distractions 'from below?'"

The Jews (John 8)

In his encounter with the Jews of John 8, Jesus accuses them of failing to believe and then defines why: "You are from below, I am from above; you are of this world, I am not of this world" (8:23). By this he defines not a human versus divine distinction but a distinction in theological orientation. They operate "from below" and have shown no ability to change frequencies. Until they do, they will never have the kind of belief Jesus requires.

In fact, John notes that some heard his words and "believed in him" (8:30). But what does this mean? In a later verse, Jesus identifies these very same Jews who had "believed in him" as children of the devil (8:44). They believed in him, but it was not the kind of belief Jesus demands. They fail to see or hear Jesus because they are distracted by their religious and ethnic heritage as children of Abraham (8:31–39). Despite their belief, their theological orientation remained "from below," so that Jesus can say, "Why do you not understand my language? It is because you are not able to hear my word" (8:43).[5] They remain spiritually deaf and blind. Consequently, these very same Jews who "believed in him" try to kill him (8:59).

The Blind Man (John 9)

The first eight chapters of the gospel of John contain stories of people who struggle to come out of the darkness, who are blinded to Jesus by earthly distractions. These stories reach a climax in chapter 9–in the story of a blind man.

John 9 sets up two themes from the beginning: blindness and sin (9:1–3). Jesus encounters a man blind from birth which prompts the disciples to ask, "Rabbi, who sinned, this man or his parents, that he was born blind?" By stating that the man's physical condition has nothing to do with sin, Jesus highlights the point that sin is not about physical blindness but spiritual blindness. Sin is equivalent to unbelief in the gospel of John, to an embracing of the darkness.[6] Note that Jesus' reply to their question about sin sets it in the context of light and darkness: "We must work the works of him who sent me while it is day; night is coming when no one can work. As long as I am in the world, I am the light of the world" (9:4–5).

Jesus restores sight to the blind man, an act described in only two of the chapter's forty-one verses. As with the feeding story, the miracle itself is of less interest to John than the subsequent conversations. References to the blind man's healing throughout the narrative are telling. The phrase "opened his eyes" occurs seven times in this chapter (9:10, 14, 17, 21, 26, 30, 32). Given the tenor of the passage as a whole and the opening reference to light and darkness, this repetition points toward a central theme of this chapter and of the gospel as a whole: the transition from darkness to light. What does it mean to have one's eyes opened? Whose eyes are opened, and whose remain closed?

The initial conversations center around the man born blind, his parents, and the Pharisees. Both the parents and the Pharisees reveal themselves to have eyes that are closed. The Pharisees cannot see Jesus because they are distracted by the fact that he performed this miracle on the sabbath (9:16). The man's parents cannot see Jesus because they are distracted by a desire to protect their social position and to avoid getting thrown out of the synagogue (9:22). As readers, we begin to wonder, "Who are the real blind people?" The Pharisees and the man's parents are stumbling around in the dark. Confronted with this sign, they still fail to see because they are blinded by worldly concerns.

In stark contrast to these convoluted conversations involving the Pharisees is the stunning simplicity of the final conversation between Jesus and the man born blind (9:35–38).

> JESUS: Do you believe in the Son of Man?
> BLIND MAN: And who is he, sir? Tell me, so that I may believe in him.
> JESUS: You have *seen* him, and the one speaking with you is he.
>   (italics added)
> BLIND MAN: Lord, I believe.

Given what has come before in this gospel, the simplicity and ease with which this man makes the transition to the heavenly frequency is astounding. More than anyone else in this gospel, he is immediately able to see Jesus for who he is. The irony is that it is a (formerly) blind man who is best able to see.

Jesus then explains why: "For judgment I came into this world so that those who are blind might see and those who see might become blind" (9:39).[7] In this story, those who can see physically (Pharisees, the parents) are blind spiritually, while the one who was blind physically is the only one to see spiritually. In essence, what Jesus says is that those who are blind to physical things can see spiritually, while those who are focused on the physical are spiritually blind. Those who can see physically are distracted by what they see, by all the worldly things demanding their attention. When they become focused on those things, they become blind to spiritual things and live in the darkness. But those blind to physical, worldly things thus do not allow themselves to be distracted. They are able to see. The man in this story was blind from birth. All his life, he was blind to the things of this world. Without such interference, when Jesus stands before him, he above all is able to say, "Lord, I believe."

John 9 clarifies the nature of belief in the gospel of John. Those who see Jesus clearly, who see "from above," do so because they are not distracted by the things "from below." The disciples' earlier question ("Who sinned?") derives from a belief that blindness points toward sin. So it does—but not physical blindness. Sin is a state of spiritual blindness.

Belief and the Passion Narrative

Preparations (John 11–12)

Although scholars find good reason for locating the start of the passion narrative in John 12, John 11 provides an important theological foundation for the death and resurrection of Jesus. When the disciples question Jesus' decision to return to Judea following the news of Lazarus' illness, Jesus once again raises the theme of darkness and light. He says, "Are there not twelve hours of daylight? Those who walk during the day do not stumble, because they see the light of this world. But those who walk at night stumble, because the light is not in them" (11:9–10). Jesus is the light of the world, and so the death of Jesus will bring darkness. Night is coming (9:4). There are twelve hours of daylight, but Jesus is now approaching the time of twilight. Although the night approaches, important work must be done first.

After Jesus informs the disciples that Lazarus has died, he adds: "For your sake I am glad I was not there, so that you may believe" (11:15). Those following the gospel account may have thought the disciples already believed, but the belief of which Jesus speaks here has a particular content. They must believe that *Jesus can raise the dead.* Believing such a thing is vital to the disciples' faith because Jesus himself, like Lazarus, will soon be in a tomb. When Martha acknowledges to Jesus that her brother will arise in the hereafter, Jesus corrects her. "I am the resurrection and the life," he says. "Do you believe *this*?" (11:25–26; italics mine). What Martha and the disciples needed to believe was that Jesus has power over death in *this* life because, in the raising of Lazarus, he will be setting the stage for his own resurrection.[8]

Preparations for the passion begin in earnest in John 12. Six days before the Passover, Jesus returns to Bethany, "the home of Lazarus, whom he had raised from the dead" (12:1). This reference to Lazarus sets this chapter in the context of death and resurrection. Indeed, the three primary events of this chapter are Mary's anointing of Jesus for burial (12:1–8), the triumphal entry into Jerusalem (12:12–19), and Jesus' prediction of his death (12:23–36). In 12:23, Jesus states: "The hour has come for the Son of Man to be glorified." Night is fast approaching, so Jesus informs the crowd: "The light is with you for a little longer. Walk while you have the light, so that the darkness may not overtake you" (12:35). This language hearkens back to John 1, in which John says that the light came into the world, but the world did not perceive it. John here adds an editorial comment that highlights this phenomenon. He says that many did not believe in Jesus because their eyes were blinded, and that many who did believe would not confess him "for fear that they would be put out of the synagogue; for they loved human glory more than the glory that comes from God" (12:37–43). Once again, the need to protect something "from below" leads to blindness.

Foot Washing and the Faith of the Disciples (John 13–16)

The story of Jesus washing the disciples' feet (13:1–20) is all about the cross. Consider the context. Preceding this story is Jesus' anointing for burial, triumphal entry, and prediction of his death. Immediately following it are predictions of Judas' betrayal (13:21–30) and Peter's denial (13:36–38). The opening verses of chapter 13 relate that immediately prior to the Passover, the devil prompts Judas to betray Jesus and that Jesus knows he is leaving this world and returning to the Father. Jesus, *therefore*, gets up from the table, wraps a towel around his waist, and begins washing feet (13:1–5). The pallor of death, the shadow of the cross, looms over this event. John has constructed his gospel so that one cannot help but read this story in the light of the cross.

The importance of the foot-washing story centers on the faith of the disciples. Throughout the gospel, the disciples have struggled with seeing and hearing clearly. That becomes a crucial issue when standing in the shadow of the cross. If the disciples are unable to see the cross clearly, to view it "from above," then they will not get it. If they view the cross "from below," from an earthly perspective, all they will see is the death of their master and the dissolution of their hopes. Jesus needs for them to learn how to operate "from above," to view the cross from a spiritual perspective. This is his last chance to accomplish that. Shortly following the foot washing, John says that Judas went out to betray Jesus. Given the prevalent theme of "day" versus "night" in this gospel, John adds the telling statement: "And it was night" (13:30).[9] Night is descending, and it is vital that the disciples not be left in darkness. Thus, Jesus washes their feet.

Placing the story in this context makes sense of the odd encounter between Jesus and Peter. Peter refuses to allow Jesus to wash his feet because he cannot accept the violation of social convention. Washing feet was typically the role of a slave. Having Jesus behave as their slave is unacceptable to Peter. Jesus' reply is instructive: "You do not know what I am doing, but later you will understand" (13:7). Other times in the gospel, John makes statements to the effect that the disciples in a particular instance failed to understand what Jesus was doing or saying, but eventually came to comprehend (2:22; 12:16). In each instance, that later comprehension came after the resurrection. Jesus here tells Peter that, because what he is doing is all about the cross, Peter does not possess the ability to understand it now. Peter, however, becomes emphatic in his denial. He says, "You will never wash my feet, ever" (13:8a).[10] Jesus responds with equal emphasis: "Unless I wash you, you have no share with me" (13:8b). This response appears unduly harsh, unless read in the context of the cross. If Peter cannot accept Jesus washing his feet, then Peter has no hope of comprehending the cross and, therefore, can have no part with him. If Peter cannot accept the lesser act of Jesus washing his feet, then he could never accept the greater act of Jesus dying for him.

This event is about Peter and the other disciples learning to view the cross "from above." So when Jesus concludes by asking them, "Do you know what

I have done to you?" his question points to more than just the washing of feet. He has given them an interpretive model for the cross. After the resurrection, they are to look back on this event with a new perspective, a perspective that views the cross as an example of humility and self-sacrificing service in love. The cross is about the Lord of the Universe, the Word through whom all things were made, coming down to earth and serving humans in love. Jesus says to the disciples, "So if I, your Lord and Teacher, have washed your feet, you also ought to wash one another's feet" (13:14). He is calling them to more than just service. He is calling them to embody the *pattern* of the cross. He calls them to love each other to the extent that they are willing to lay down their lives for one another–just as their Lord is about to do.[11]

The foot-washing scene takes place prior to the cross. As Jesus notes, it is only "later" that the disciples will understand. On this side of the cross, they continue to struggle with their belief. For instance, Peter boldly proclaims he will die with Jesus, but then Jesus predicts that Peter will disown him three times (13:36–38). Philip asks Jesus to show them the Father, prompting Jesus to reply, "Have I been with you all this time, Philip, and you still do not know me?…Do you not believe that I am in the Father and the Father is in me?" (14:8–10). In John 16, Jesus speaks to his disciples in characteristically figurative language, and they characteristically misunderstand. When he finally informs them that he is leaving the world to go back to the Father, they reply, "Yes, now you are speaking plainly, not in any figure of speech! Now we know that you know all things, and do not need to have anyone question you; by this we believe that you came from God" (16:29–30).

"By this we believe," the disciples claim; yet Jesus is not so quick to accept the validity of that belief. He responds, "Do you now believe? The hour is coming, indeed it has come, when you will be scattered…and you will leave me alone" (16:31–32).[12] The disciples claimed to believe, but then learned their own actions were about to call that belief into question. The disciples are among those in this gospel who wrestle with trying to comprehend Jesus. They are trying to get on the right frequency, but keep encountering interference. Part of their problem is that they are standing on the "before" side of the cross.

The Resurrection and Belief (John 20)

John's post-resurrection narrative reveals a shift in the disciples' belief. The resurrection cuts through the interference, removes the distractions, and opens their eyes. In John 20, four different individuals or groups encounter the resurrection with differing levels of response. What unites each response, however, is the language of sight. First, the beloved disciple runs to the tomb and enters it. John then tells us that "he *saw* and believed" (20:8). John does not provide the specifics of his belief; in fact, he says that the disciples at this point did not realize that the Scripture foretold the resurrection (20:9). Nevertheless, although he may not understand the scriptural connections, this disciple is able to look at the empty tomb and the burial clothes and, like the blind man of John 9, see something that others miss.

Next comes Mary Magdalene. She has a more difficult time with her belief because she continues to be distracted by earthly things. She sees the tomb, yet concludes someone took the body. She sees two angels, yet still fails to put the pieces together. Then, she sees Jesus himself, but mistakes him for a gardener (20:11–15). Only when Jesus calls her name does she recognize him, like the sheep who know the voice of their shepherd (10:3–4). She runs back to the other disciples proclaiming, "I have *seen* the Lord" (20:16–18). It is not so much seeing that leads Mary to believe as it is her belief in the word of Jesus that allows her to see.[13]

Third are the apostles, minus Thomas. They are hiding out of fear of the Jews (20:19), distracted by concerns for their physical well-being. When Jesus appears to them, however, that distraction disappears. They become overjoyed "when they *saw* the Lord" (20:20). This connection between sight and belief climaxes in the story of Thomas. The disciples report to him, "We have *seen* the Lord." Thomas responds, "Unless I *see* the mark of the nails in his hands,...I will not believe" (20:25). Thomas is distracted by a desire for the same physical evidence the other disciples received.[14] Jesus accommodates this request when he appears before him and states, "Put your finger here and *see* my hands" (20:27). Thomas replies, "My Lord and my God!" The disciples now stand on the other side of the cross and resurrection. They have learned to remove worldly distractions and to see clearly.

When John records the final statement of Jesus in this chapter, it reads as one directed as much to the readers as to Thomas: "Have you believed because you have *seen* me? Blessed are those who have *not seen* and yet have come to believe" (20:29). Thomas and the disciples believed because they saw with their physical eyes, but a greater level of faith is the ability to see spiritually. Those who hear and read the words of John are not in a position to see Jesus and his signs physically. They must rely on the testimony of others. Consequently, John then writes, "These are written so that you may come to believe" (20:31). These things are written so that those who read them may learn to remove the interference from their lives and switch from the earthly to the heavenly frequency. John's goal is that all learn to operate "from above."

Implications for Preaching

For all its grammatical simplicity, the language of the gospel of John is rich with metaphors, wordplays, and dual meanings. The Jesus of this gospel challenges his hearers with language that is highly metaphorical. Jesus resists explaining these metaphors to his hearers—even at the risk of being misunderstood. In his encounter with the crowd of John 6, Jesus allows the crowd to walk away from him when they fail to grasp the significance of his metaphors. It's a stunning evangelistic method. Rather than dilute his language for the benefit of the crowd, Jesus demands that they wrestle with the metaphors.

Clarity is important in the act of preaching, yet clarity should not be achieved at the expense of being challenging. The contemporary church has too often shied away from language that is metaphorical or symbolic out of fear that the audience may become confused and miss the message. Yet, if the Jesus of John is to be our model, we must reclaim the power of metaphor for our preaching. We must reclaim language that both inspires and forces us to wrestle with the object of our proclamation. The Jesus of John constantly uses metaphors and symbolic language to challenge his hearers to operate on a higher frequency, to operate "from above." We, as preachers, can do no less than to employ language that challenges our hearers to open their eyes and to see the imprint of the one who came "out of heaven" all around them.

Conclusion

Belief in the gospel of John is closely tied to sight. Do we see "from above" or "from below?" Do we walk in the light where all is clear or stumble around in the darkness where all is shadow? This gospel provides numerous examples of people at different stages of belief, people who see with varying levels of clarity. These examples offer models of belief that resonate with twenty-first–century Christianity.

Some are like the disciples: quick to profess belief, but then just as quickly to have their actions contradict those words. Some are like Nicodemus and the other Jews who believe in Jesus but will not confess him openly because they have their status to protect. Some are like the Samaritan woman, distracted by social and religious debate. Their eyes are so focused on the form of worship that they miss the one they are worshiping. Some are distracted by physical needs, such as the crowd in John 6. They are hungry and tired and therefore so focused on going to their comfortable homes, eating a fine meal, and laying down in their plush beds that they blind themselves to all those around them who are hungry and tired and have no place to lay their heads. Others are like Martha: confident in what Jesus can do on the last day, but not so confident in what he can do in their lives today. Some are like Mary. They can look into an empty tomb and not be convicted. They need a more personal connection; they need Jesus to speak their names. Others are like Thomas. They want to believe but require evidence. Then, some are like the blind man, so unencumbered by worldly concerns that, when Jesus asks them, "Do you believe?" they are able to say immediately, "Lord, I believe."

If these examples are any indication, belief in John is not a product, but a process. It is not as simple as either believing or not believing. The disciples themselves seem to believe one minute and not the next. Belief is the process of constantly struggling to rid ourselves of what distracts us and keeps us in the darkness. It is the lifelong process of embodying Jesus' call to "love one another as I have loved you" (15:12), to live out the pattern of the cross.

SERMON

I've Always Liked Nicodemus
John 3:1–15

DAVID FLEER

Compositional Comments

In preparing for the following sermon, I had access to the essays by Gregory Stevenson and Tom Olbricht, now included in this volume, as well as Gail O'Day's larger corpus, notably her commentary in the *New Interpreter's Bible*. Evidences of their work are apparent throughout the sermon.

In developing the sermon's plot, I was initially convinced by Stevenson's argument that Nicodemus remains a shadowy figure, staying "in the twilight between the day and the night," and for supportive reading carefully consulted his source.[1] O'Day's counter-argument (deftly complemented by a graduate student's unpublished essay) tipped the scale to a more optimistic reading of Nicodemus. The tipping point came from this powerful image: "At the very moment you would expect Nicodemus to sneak in at night, when his disciples were denying and betraying him at this frightful time, Nicodemus hauls a hundred pounds of spices to give exposed honor to Jesus."[2] As Stevenson notes, John retains Nicodemus' moniker (night) in the closing scene. But this man risks his life for another man his peers have just convicted, a symbolism that reconstructs, for this reader and preacher, Nicodemus' character. This optimistic reading finds expression in the sermon's final move, symbolized in the reconstructed *Florentine Pieta*.

This sermon was preached during the opening of the tenth and concluding Rochester Sermon Seminar and was meant for an audience of preachers, many of whom had a shared history with the conference. Thus, overt references to persons and events from previous seminars were chock full of meaning to this audience. At the sermon's conclusion, the image of Michelangelo's *Florentine Pieta* appeared on the screen, an effort at an effective and tasteful closing reflection for the sermon.

Sermon

I've always liked Nicodemus, admired him and looked up to him. I picture Nicodemus as a religious leader wearing his black gown with the appropriate colors, framed degrees on the wall, mahogany shelves—so distinguished.

I've always liked Nicodemus, a man of infectious confidence.

Listen to him. "We know," he says. He uses phrases such as, "we understand" or "we can say with assurance." Assurance. No soft-pedaling with Nicodemus. No gray areas.

I've always liked the thoughtful, intelligent, and politically savvy Nicodemus.

Opportunity comes along, falls from the sky. He investigates. He's careful, considerate, and cool under pressure. Nicodemus represents a wide range of constituents and responds appropriately, away from the limelight, when darkness allows him to enact his "don't ask, don't tell" policy. He knows how to play the game. He's calculated and calibrated.

I've always liked Nicodemus' vitality. It's night. He's not home watching *American Idol.* He's out, investigating and inquiring, looking into new things—such as when a new teacher arrives, and he's the first person there.

I've always liked Nicodemus. If he hadn't gone into religion, I imagine him an engineer or an accountant, asking,

"How much weight will this beam bear?"

"What will this cost?"

"To whom does she report?"

He knows how things work, how things fit.

I've always liked Nicodemus—his pedigree, his stature. The Reverend, Doctor, Bishop, M.Div., D.Min., Ph.D. When the governor and presidential candidates come to town, he is at the first table, among the first served, with waiters in watchful attendance. He offers the invocation, and the anthropologists of status take note.

I've always liked Nicodemus, because he represents the fringe benefits that should come to one who has given his or her life to the patient nurturing of the sacred institution we call the church.

You will not be surprised to hear that Michelangelo's last work, a majestic marble sculpture, included Nicodemus. The *Florentine Pieta,* or *Lamentation over the Dead Christ,* depicts Jesus' body just removed from the cross, arms limp, one leg at an odd angle, head fallen back upon his shoulder, body slumped against his kneeling mother, both supported by Nicodemus. Like a weight lifter, Nicodemus towers over and enfolds Mary with his sinewy arms. Michelangelo's Nicodemus is hooded, bearded with age, looking down on the Christ and his mother.

Art historians think Nicodemus is Michelangelo's self-portrait. He began the sculpture when he was in his mid-70s, intending to give the work to a church and requesting that he be buried at the foot of the altar.

Which is why I am so pleased to hear that Nicodemus intends to visit Jesus, because I look forward to their dialogue.

One evening I happen upon a conversation of great interest, the night Nicodemus visits Jesus of Nazareth. Initially, my presuppositions are confirmed and enhanced, when I hear him say, "Rabbi, we know that You have come from God as a teacher; for no one can do these signs that You do unless God is with him" (Jn. 3:2, NASB).

These words, frozen like Michelangelo's statue, sit there for us to consider.

So impressive, don't you think? Nicodemus "seeking" Jesus, taking the initiative, coming to Jesus. How does John's five-finger exercise work? "Seek, believe, repent, confess, be baptized."

Then, listen to the first words out his mouth. "Rabbi," he says to Jesus. Echoes and allusions of Nathanael and Andrew, "Rabbi..." And the inquiring disciples of John 9, "Rabbi, who sinned?..." And Mary at the tomb—the moment she realizes that he *isn't* the gardener, but the resurrected Jesus—"Rabbouni" she says, which translated means, "Rabbi." Add to Nicodemus' character list "respectful" and "in very good company." Then Nicodemus adds the clincher, "We know that you have *come from God.*"

Look at Nicodemus' face when the words "*come from God*" leave his mouth. Whom does he look like?

"Why," you say, "He looks just like John the evangelist: 'In the beginning... the Word was God.'"

Look again: whom does he look like when he says, "*come from God*"?

"Why," you say, "He looks like Jesus..." You're right! Jesus later says, "I am from God, and God sent me" (7:29).[3] Nicodemus looks like a statement of faith!

Which makes his phrase, "*We* know," especially attractive. Now we're hearing more than confidence and understanding. Nicodemus represents the community: "*We* know." He's the people's leader. Nicodemus has a host of folks behind him. Let's embrace Nicodemus, bring him into the fold. Skip the steps after "seek." Let's baptize this man right now!

Consider the Detroit Lions, "Rebuilding since 1957," and with a recent history of disastrous first-round picks in the NFL draft. At last month's draft, the Lions' turn comes up, and the consensus best player in the draft is *still available.* One long-suffering Lions fan says, "For...the...love...of...God...pick the best player."

Nicodemus is a great pick.

Eight-year-old Caleb, barely visible, stands in the baptistery next to Daddy, who is in his waders choking back sobs, "Do you believe that Jesus is the Christ, the Son of God?" Like a deer in the headlights, Caleb squeaks out a high-pitched "yes." We applaud this baptism!

Into the room walks Nicodemus! "For the love of God, baptize *this* man."

Which is *why* I find Jesus' interaction with Nicodemus so troubling, so hard to believe. The pattern of the dialogue isn't hard to follow: Nicodemus says..., Jesus says..., Nicodemus says..., Jesus says..., Nicodemus says..., Jesus says...

What's hard to follow is why Jesus doesn't recognize that Nicodemus is the "catch of the day." Why doesn't Jesus embrace this man? Why does Jesus quickly reduce Nicodemus to a series of questions?

Nicodemus: "How can a man...? He can't enter, can he...? How can this be...? What...?" Until Nicodemus disappears. Test for fingerprints at the end of this scene. Nicodemus doesn't get there. He's left the stage.

This causes us to ask, "What's troubling Jesus?"

Indeed—What is troubling Jesus?

Once we start looking around, we don't have to go far before we discover a problem. Suspicions rise when we hear Nicodemus say, "No one can do these *signs* that You do unless God is with him." That shoots up a red flag: *signs*. Nicodemus' belief is based on *signs*. Even after the curtain has risen for this scene, the narrator's voice still reverberates from the previous scene, "Jesus didn't trust himself to people whose trust was based on signs...Jesus didn't believe in people whose belief was based on signs."

That's what's troubling Jesus; Nicodemus' belief is based on *signs*.

Something's troubling John too. John says Nicodemus came at *night*. The red flag is *night*. All through John's story he uses this image, *night*. He's *not* talking of an exact time (1:00 a.m.). He's *not* talking of a cover to prevent recognition. He has more in mind than a parent asking, "Where were you so late? What good happens after midnight? Only trouble brews after hours."

When *John* says *night,* he has something worse in mind. Jesus says, "You can't work at night... You stumble at night." Judas betrays Jesus...at night. When Nicodemus walks off stage, Jesus says, "People love *darkness* because their deeds are *evil*" (3:19, italics added).[4]

Nicodemus comes at night. Who is he? A wolf in sheep's clothing? Now we have a problem with Nicodemus.

Nicodemus tells Jesus, "No one can do these signs that you do, *unless* God is with him." That sounds a little presumptuous, don't you think? Telling Jesus what God can and can't do, as if Nicodemus has the upper hand, "no one can...*unless.*" Making pronouncements: "God doesn't answer the prayers of sinners...God doesn't perform miracles today." Expecting Jesus to fit his preconceived notions: "We know that God blesses *our* troops."

Who does he think he is, "God's agent"? This should make us all a little nervous.

Which reminds me... Did you know that Michelangelo destroyed the Florentine Pieta before he completed it? Broke it up. Smashed it. Really! Art historians speculate why. Some think the block of marble was defective. Some think a foot or hand broke off. So he abandoned the sculpture. Didn't finish it.

I wonder... Maybe Michelangelo decided he didn't want to be Nicodemus anymore, because Nicodemus is an *ambiguous* man, with one foot in each world.

I think I've seen him around, seen him in Scripture. Nicodemus looks like the elder brother out in the field standing at the end of Jesus' parable; will he go in to the party? He looks like Jonah listening to God, "and should I not have mercy on Nineveh, who doesn't know its left hand from its right? " (Jon. 4:11).[5] What will this angry man do with his nationalism?

I've seen Nicodemus at your church! He is fifteen years old, at the very margins of your peripheral vision, not part of your church's culture. He stands at the door after church waiting for conversation with you.

Nicodemus is the elderly non-Christian who occasions church, at arm's length, in the back pew. But his occasional post-sermon comments make you think he listens more carefully than almost every baptized member.

Nicodemus is every person you know with one foot in each world, wrestling with the shape and depth of faith.

Then Jesus says, "Are you a teacher of Israel, and yet you do not understand these things?" (Jn. 3:10). Something very unexpected happens. Jesus' words carom off Nicodemus and strike us in the heart, all of us who are the teachers of Israel. Because, I have to confess, this isn't the first time I've been to this conversation.

Back in the mid-70s when Jimmy Carter, Gerald Ford, and everyone was "born again," yellow bumper stickers asked, "Born Again?" I once stood next to a Baptist, in front of this bumper sticker. I said, "Do you know what this means?"

The Baptist said, "Yes, do *you* know what this means?"

I said, "Yes, it means baptism. He who believes and is baptized shall be saved."

The Baptist said, "No. It means you must accept Jesus as your personal Lord and Savior."

At that moment someone shoved me into the Baptist, who pushed me back, which I thought rude. So I grabbed his arms to prevent further assault, which he interpreted as an offensive gesture. Pretty soon we were both on the ground kicking and gouging and calling names.

He called me a Campbellite. I called him "hard-shelled" and "unteachable." We butted heads and butted certitudes.

That was my first ecumenical experience with this text, and it was ugly. So, I'd like to go back and try again. This time, just us, looking at the words that caromed off Nicodemus, when Jesus says, "Are you a teacher of Israel, and yet you do not understand these things?" This time, all of us together, listening to Jesus with Nicodemus, trying to understand.

But Jesus isn't easy to understand. He's hard to hear. It sounds like he says,

"You must be born *againfromabove.*"

We turn up our hearing aids, lean in, and ask, "Would you please repeat that?"

Jesus says, "You must be born *againfromabove.*"

We turn to someone who knows the language, "What did he say?"

She says, "He said you must be born *anothen.*"

We say, "What's that?"

She explains, "It means, '*again from above.*' The word has a double meaning, both space and time…" As she explains, we realize that *Jesus* is creating ambiguity, creating mystery.

Right when the light comes on, Jesus turns to us and says, "Here is what I mean. The wind or spirit moves where it wills. You can see and feel its presence, but can say nothing more than, 'that's a westerly wind.' The new birth is like the wind; A mystery beyond your understanding, beyond your control" (Jn. 3.8).[6]

A movement from certitude, to ambiguity, to discipleship.

After Jesus has been lifted up in the final scene, Nicodemus comes –again– this time to bury Jesus with a hundred pounds of spices, an excess of anointing love. In that act, Nicodemus abandons his neutrality and secrecy and moves from ambiguity to discipleship. From certitude to ambiguity to discipleship.

We enter this seminar–the next 48 hours–praying that God will work again amongst us, perhaps as God did two years ago. After seven years of my begging and cajoling a conservative Church of Christ minister to attend, he finally came to the seminar the year of Mark's gospel, with Fred Craddock, Morna Hooker, and that liberal from Illif who "performed Scripture," Richard Ward. "What will happen?" I worried. When the conference concluded, the first evaluation I read was the conservative minister's. "Richard Ward," he said, "re-introduced me to my Lord." From certitude to ambiguity to discipleship. Or I think of the small group discussion immediately following last year's incredibly challenging look at living in the world imagined in the Sermon on the Mount, when one minister asked the group, "What are we to do with this? Sell our churches and give the proceeds to the poor?" Someone chortled, and the minister said, "I'm very serious. How do we live with this?" From certitude to ambiguity to discipleship.

Or the year before that, when one minister answered only one question on that year's evaluation. The question was, "Do you plan to attend next year's seminar?" Only two words on the entire page. Next to the query was the affirmation, "Absolutely!" At the top of the page, his name, *Royce* (Dickinson). He was gone days later. From certitude to ambiguity to discipleship.

The shattered *Florentine Pieta*. Michelangelo's assistant asked for the Pieta's broken pieces. Years later artists reconstructed the work, following the master's model. From certitude to ambiguity to discipleship.

SERMONS_____

Do You Want the Living Water?
John 4:1–15
Do You Want to Be Made Well?
John 5:1–9

ALYCE M. MCKENZIE

Compositional Comments

A year or so ago I was asked to preach three sermons at an annual "Renewal Event" at the First United Methodist Church in Stephenville, Texas, a small college town in central Texas that is the home of Tarleton State University. "It's what they used to call a 'revival,'" the pastor told me. "Only now we call them renewal weekends." I agreed to be their *renewal* preacher, a word I was more comfortable with than *revival*.

Why? Because, in many people's minds, a revival preacher is one who relies on guilt and volume. He or she reduces faith to a purely personal decision to accept a purely personal Lord and Savior. I am not that preacher. I do not believe that a preacher can revive a people's faith by appealing to their guilt, individualism, or the strength of their wills. Only God can revive faith. The preacher's role is to invite listeners into an encounter with God in the course of which there is the possibility that they will allow God to revive their faith.

As luck would have it, I was, at the time of this invitation, reading Craig Koester's book *Symbolism in the Fourth Gospel* in connection with a chapter of a book I was writing about preaching the Wisdom themes of the Bible. Koester believes that John's gospel conveys the saving identity of Jesus through the use of symbols. By symbols Koester means the images, actions, and persons that are understood to have transcendent significance in John. The images (seven "I am" metaphors) and actions (miracles and healings) are other sermons for other days. It was the third kind of symbols, the people and groups who Jesus encounters, that caught my attention for my renewal sermons.

Koester believes that these persons and groups, each with their distinctive traits, represent different ways of relating to God. Some relate better than others. The purpose of these encounters, like that of the gospel as a whole, is that they might believe in Jesus and have life in his name. Biblical scholar Gregory Stevenson, in his essay in this volume, offers the insight that when we participate in these encounters, we are led to question our understanding of what it means to believe. To engage in conversation with Jesus is to put our present faith at risk.

People who converse with Jesus in the gospel include Nicodemus, the Samaritan woman, the royal official, the woman at the well, the invalid at the pool, the crowds, the man born blind, Mary, Martha, Lazarus, the disciples, the High Priest, and Pilate. Gail O'Day contrasts the compact stories of the synoptic gospels that report events in Jesus' ministry with John's long dialogues in which event and discourse are intertwined. These dialogues invite us to become participants in the interaction between Jesus and various individuals and, thereby, to be transformed.[1] In John's gospel, says O'Day, theological claims come in a narrative mode.[2] O'Day continues, "to proclaim the biblical texts faithfully, we must first allow ourselves to enter into the texts, to be shaped by the biblical stories, in all their diversity and rough edges, and then move from that participation in the text to proclamation."[3]

The following two sermons were part of a sermon series entitled "Up Close and Personal: Encounters with Jesus in the Gospel of John." In the case of both the woman at the well and the man by the pool, Jesus is speaking at one level, while the other party is speaking and interpreting at another. Jesus is speaking of the water of eternal life, and the woman is thinking of well water. Jesus, standing right next to the invalid at Bethzatha, asks, "Do you want to be made well?" He is speaking of healing through the restoring touch of the Word and Wisdom of God, while the man has his eyes on the bubbling water and all the people between him and it. This is the insight Gregory Stevenson names so well in his metaphor of digital and analog frequencies. People don't believe in Jesus in a profound and life-changing way because they are operating on the literal frequency, not the spiritual. Their "belief" is intellectual assent or fair-weather, self-serving lip service. His application of this insight to the dualities of John's gospel (light and dark; from above, from below; of heaven, of earth; etc.) names the obstacles that prevent people from believing in Jesus at a more profound level.

As a guest preacher from out of town, I sought to identify a concern that would be relevant to a wide spectrum of people. I also listened for themes that, while relevant to people's individual lives, also had communal import. The theme of not accepting the healing that is right next to us surfaced for me in dialogue with John 5. The theme of the identity of Jesus as one who knows all our secrets and still offers us living water surfaced in dialogue with John 4. Gail O'Day's emphasis on Jesus as a friend who, by definition, keeps nothing secret, but who speaks honestly and fearlessly, was influential in my reflection on John 4.

John's gospel is the opposite of the game "Show and Tell." It's "Tell and Show." First in the Prologue (Jn. 1:1–14), he tells us who Jesus is, the Word and Wisdom of God made flesh. Like the Prologue to a Greek tragedy, this information sets the audience up to know things the characters in the story do not.

After this initial "tell," the rest of the gospel is the "show." It shows us what happens when the Wisdom and Word encounters various individuals, each of whom reminds us of an aspect of our own lives. These people include the man by the pool in John 5; the woman at the well in John 4; and Nicodemus, ruler of the Jews, in John 3. My two sermons will focus on the woman at the well and the invalid at Bethzatha, two encounters that prove that, in John's gospel, it is a risky thing to be engaged in conversation by Jesus. It leads to a challenge, and a chance for transformation.

SERMON: *Do You Want the Living Water?*

You can't live for long without water. That's the only reason she makes this tedious, daily journey to the well. It's the last place she wants to come, but the place she needs to come to if she is to live. She is so tired of the smell of dust and sand and sweat. She is repulsed by the taste of the bitter grit in her dry mouth. At least the jar feels cool on her head; but even empty, it's so heavy it causes shooting pains down her neck and into her shoulders. On the trip back home it will be even heavier. She hears her sandals slap-slapping on the sand. She sees the shimmering haze that settles over everything at a distance.

Who is this woman approaching the well? She is a person, like each of us, who has secrets to hide, but who still needs water every day to live. That need is what has drawn her here to this place at this time. She is a person whose inner life is shrouded in darkness but who is walking toward the Light. She is a person whose inner life is parched with thirst who is walking toward Living Water.

Who is this woman approaching the well? As a Samaritan woman, her gender, social status, and ethnic identity would have consigned her to darkness. She is a living, breathing embodiment of the irony that runs through the whole gospel of John: that Jesus was rejected by those we would expect would accept him and accepted by those we would expect would reject him (Jn. 1:11). She is the mirror opposite of Nicodemus, whose story John has just told us in chapter 3. He is a man, a Jew, a religious leader, a respected member of the community. This résumé would seem to cast him in a flattering light. Yet he came to Jesus at night. After their conversation, he remains caught between night and day, in limbo between a skin-deep belief in Jesus because he can turn water into wine, and a soul-stirring belief in Jesus that leads a person to follow him, rejecting both convention and convenience. He is a man who leaves the light of Jesus' presence to live in a perpetual twilight.

That encounter was disappointing to us. But with each step closer to the well this woman takes, we feel heightened hope. We discover a couple of clues that her encounter with Jesus will end better than that of Nicodemus. John tells us Jesus "had to" (4:4) go through Samaria on his journey from Judea back to Galilee. This is not a geographical necessity as much as it is a theological necessity. Jesus needs to come to this well and meet this woman as part of his self-revelation as Savior, not only of the Jews, but of the whole world. Another reason for us to have higher hopes for this encounter is that it happens in broad daylight. Light and day are associated with belief in Jesus throughout John's gospel. And not just skin-deep belief in Jesus because he performs signs that benefit us, but soul-stirring belief in him that leads us to trust him and live for others.

Who is this woman who is approaching the well in broad daylight? She is someone who may just be able to tune into the spiritual frequency on which Jesus is operating. She is someone who may just be able to believe in Jesus, and not just because she sees signs. The conversation to come is just as convoluted and complicated as the ones we ourselves have with Jesus. It signals to us that coming to faith will not be easy for her. She will struggle with Jesus' words, moving back and forth between the literal and spiritual levels of the encounter. Scholar Gail O'Day names the transformation the woman undergoes as a movement "from the comfort of tradition to the risk of experience."[4]

As she draws closer and can see his face, she may even feel relieved that she doesn't recognize him. He wasn't from around there. Her secrets were safe from him. However, we know something this Samaritan woman doesn't: how risky it is to be engaged in conversation with Jesus in John's gospel.

As we gather to worship today, we are taking a risk, because we all have our secrets, too. I'm not talking about the positive ones that are fun to keep. Like what you got someone for Christmas or the surprise party you're planning. I'm talking about the painful secrets that we try so hard to keep hidden from the light of day. Whether it's misconduct in the past or emotions and actions in the present, we don't know what to do with them. Roman Catholics can go to confession and tell the priest. Protestants can hire a therapist or tell their pastor. Or we can all just go on Dr. Phil.

The Puritans kept spiritual journals, aids to confession and repentance. But no matter how good the lock is on your "Dear Diary," your little brother or your spouse may manage to open and read it. No matter how well the celebrity tries to hide that video, it always ends up on YouTube. Our secrets vary, but they have one thing in common: they are wrapped in the fear that, if anyone, or someone in particular, finds out about them, we stand to lose something—a relationship, a job, our reputation, respect.

Do you ever wonder if we are keeping our secrets or if they are keeping us?

Frank Warren, a forty-one-year-old blogger, started his blog PostSecret. com in 2004 as a temporary community art project. He invited people to mail in postcards that had their secrets written on them. The secrets were to be anonymous, and they were to be something the person had never shared with anyone else. Since he began, he has received over 30,000 postcards, many of them decorated by their senders. He reads them all and picks ten to twenty to post on his blog every Sunday. He has published *Postsecret: Extraordinary Confessions from Ordinary Lives,* a compilation of 400 postcards, and he is planning additional volumes.

Secrets range from humorous to heartrending. Here is a sampling from this week:

- Your disgusting spray-on tan hurts my eyes.
- In high school I was so desperate for a boyfriend I dated a guy who went to Star Wars Conventions...and he dumped me.
- Even vegetarians think of meat from time to time. I know I do.
- I suffer from an eating disorder, and I fear my mother's suffering.
- My insomnia is going to get me fired.
- I can't stand my stepmother.
- I was seven years old the first time I attempted suicide.
- Every life I save reminds me of the one I couldn't.
- I had an affair. We stopped before we got caught. I miss her today.

This story from John's gospel suggests a different strategy for what to do with our most closely held secrets. It suggests that we bring them to the one who is sitting by the well. Who is he? As readers of John's gospel, we know who he is before the woman ever meets him. If she had known, our secret-keeping friend would have run in the opposite direction—for he is the one who knows all our secrets. Just before his encounter with Nicodemus in chapter 3, we learn this startling fact about him: "Many believed in his name because they saw the signs that he was doing. But Jesus on his part would not entrust himself to them, because he knew all people and needed no one to testify about anyone; for he himself knew what was in everyone" (Jn. 2:23–25).

Not only is he the one who knows all our secrets, he is also the one who tells us all the secrets of God. He is the premier Secret Teller! We learn just before this encounter that he is the one who "comes from above...from heaven...testifies to what he has seen and heard...speaks the words of God" (3:31–34).

Who is this sitting by the well as this woman, hugging her secret to herself, approaches the well? He is the one who is our Friend, which means, not that he wants to share a cup of coffee with us at the well, but that he will, when the time comes, lay down his life for us and that he always tells us fully, honestly, and fearlessly what we need to hear—the truth about ourselves and about God. That God loves us and sent him to save us and give us the gift of eternal life. That we must cease to love darkness rather than the light, confess and relinquish all obstacles to belief in him, and devote our lives to being friends to those around us. In other words, we must confess our secrets and be cleansed, forgiven, and refreshed by water that is different from drinking water; it is the living water, the presence of Christ at the depths of our lives that will quench our thirst forever, that will become a wellspring within each of us that springs up into eternal life.

When we enter into this story, as John hopes we will, we are, like this woman, all secret keepers approaching the man at the well. He is not going anywhere anytime soon. During the whole thirty-four verses of this story, all kinds of people come and go: the woman, the disciples, and the Samaritan villagers. The man at the well stays put, stable in his identity, and in his intention to transform ours. If our faith is transformed by our participation in this story, and John hopes it will be, it will be by our coming to recognize, with the woman, the identity of this man who waits for us at the well.

That Jesus knows all her secrets is for her a sign—the miraculous power of a prophet. It's like turning the water to wine was for Nicodemus. It is like Jesus' healings and his multiplying loaves were for the crowds in John chapter 6. She is impressed by his supernatural knowledge. That's what she tells the townspeople when she returns to invite them into his presence. "Come and see a man who told me everything I have ever done!" (Jn. 4:29). Already her faith is taking root, spreading from skin-deep to the depths of her soul. People who only believe in Jesus for what he can do for them go home and enjoy their salvation in the privacy of their own homes. They don't put down their water jugs and run to invite others to meet him for themselves. They aren't the catalysts by which others can say, "It is no longer because of what you said that we believe, for we have heard for ourselves, and we know that this is truly the Savior of the world" (Jn. 4:42).

The old saying goes, "You can lead a horse to water, but you can't make him drink." Nicodemus stood at the water's edge and trudged away. This woman made the choice to drink. By the end of her complicated, conflictual conversation with Jesus, she decided to trust Jesus enough to open the door of her inward pain, her deeply held secrets, and invite him in. She allowed herself to be transformed by the identity of this One who waits for each of us at the well. Who is he? He is the one who, though he knows all our secrets, still offers us the Living Water.

SERMON: *Do You Want to Be Made Well?*

"And knowing that he had been lying there a long time, Jesus said to him, 'Do you want to be made well?'" (Jn. 5:6).[1]

Doesn't that strike you as an obvious question?

In our story the man had been suffering for thirty-eight years. This is no temporary thing; it's a hopeless case. Thirty-eight is the number of years Deuteronomy 14 tells us the Israelites wandered in the wilderness. Thirty-eight years signals that, if a miracle is to happen here, it will have to be a big one!

It would make more sense to me if the story opened like this:

"Knowing that the man had been ill for thirty-eight years, Jesus immediately healed him."

Instead, it says, "Knowing that the man had been ill for thirty-eight years, Jesus asked him, 'Do you want to be made well?'"

That doesn't make sense!

Or maybe it does. My friend Jan is an ICU nurse at Presbyterian Hospital in Dallas. She told me of observing a certain scene more than once. A person, usually a man, has just had quadruple bypass surgery. He regains consciousness and almost immediately begins saying to his wife, "I need my cell phone and my blackberry. Bring my mini-printer and my laptop." Jan says she and the other nurses exchange a look that says: "He'll be back soon." Did *he* want to be made well?

Ill for thirty-eight years, and Jesus asks, "Do you want to be made well?" That makes me think of churches that ask, "Why aren't we growing?" A church consultant comes in and analyzes things and tells them, "You need to become a missional church, not just an attractional church. You need to understand the changing neighborhood around you. You need to broaden your spectrum of worship styles. You need to offer an after school program." They write the consultant a check and send him off with their thanks.

At the next meeting someone says, "We shouldn't have to do all that. They should come to us."

At the next meeting the agenda is, "Why aren't we growing?"

I heard of a man we'll call Ed, who got divorced at mid-life and moved back in with his elderly parents. Gradually, he took over their care. He would come to the church on Tuesday mornings, knowing he'd find his pastor in his office working on his sermon. Ed would complain about what a burden his parents were to him, how they kept him from being able to date. How they took up all his time and much of his money. How his life could be so much freer if he didn't have them like an albatross around his neck.

After a number of years, his parents both died within a six-month period. The pastor thought to himself, "Now Ed will finally be happy. He won't come to see me on Tuesday mornings." Sure enough, that was the case for about three weeks. Then Ed returned, rapping on the pastor's office door, "I miss them so much. They were the best parents anyone could wish for. My life is so empty without them."

Biblical scholar Gail O'Day shows how John in his gospel focuses on Jesus as our friend who empowers us to be friends to one another. One thing about a friend is that a friend speaks honestly and without fear, rather than merely telling us what we want to hear. This pastor decided to be a friend to Ed. He said, "No, Ed, your life is not empty. Your glass is full of all your favorite things: discontent, misery, an 'if only' attitude, a 'things will be great when' mind-set. You are a person who enjoys being unhappy. Face it and embrace it. It is your identity. It is who you are."

Knowing that the man had been ill for thirty-eight years, Jesus asked him, "Do you want to be made well?"

What was the man's malady? Apparently some sort of paralysis that left him unable to move his legs, or at least only able to move them with great difficulty.

The man doesn't point out his need for healing himself. Jesus perceives it and takes the initiative.

He was poor—the word used for mat (*krabbatos*) is that used for the rough pallet used by the poor. He was alone.

We would hope in our lives that if we ever suffered a disabling physical condition, there would be others around us we could depend on. At the very least we would hope for a wheelchair and a van with a lift. But this man was paralyzed; he was poor; he was alone.

Let's not minimize his suffering. But let's also consider that he had perhaps gotten into a routine that was familiar and somewhat comforting.

It's possible to build a whole life around our suffering or illness. Consider cases of alcohol abuse. Binging and purging. Domestic abuse followed by rituals of courtship. We can even build our whole life around something that seems like a good thing, such as work. "But I'm doing it all for my family," we tell ourselves.

Jesus asked the man, "Do you want to be made well?"

The legend was that these pools had healing properties. From time to time they would begin to bubble, and the water would swirl. That signaled that you would be healed if you could get into the water first while it was still bubbling.

When Jesus asks the man, "Do you want to be healed?" the man thinks Jesus is asking him, "Why aren't you in the water?" and launches into this explanation: Access to the healing water is limited; too many people stand between me and the water. Even if there weren't, I have no one to help me down the steps in time.

The man here, like the woman at the well in the previous story, regards Jesus as a nosy bystander to whom he has to explain all the reasons his life cannot change.

I want to be healed, but the grocery store is all out of Joel Osteen's book *Your Best Life Now.*

I want to be healed, but I can't afford to attend the "how to make your fortune in real estate" seminar being offered at the Hilton this weekend.

"I want to be healed, but I can't get down into the water in time." We sort of roll our eyes with impatience while the poor guy explains all this. We know that's not what Jesus is asking him. We get the dramatic irony; we can tell the difference between spiritual and literal. We have read the Prologue. Each of these people is distracted by something, some concern or preoccupation that keeps them stuck at the literal level. Biblical scholar Gregory Stevenson compares their preoccupations with snow and static on a TV screen when the TV is tuned to the wrong frequency.

We understand that Jesus is offering this man a direct healing. We would never stand by a pool squinting to see the healing in a bunch of bubbles if Jesus were standing right next to us: Jesus the Light of the World, Jesus the Bread of Life, Jesus the Living Water, Jesus the Vine. We recognize that Jesus is the only person, the only power in this world that has the authority to ask us, "Do you want to be made well?"

Distinction Between Healing and Physical Cure

Jesus is not asking us, "Do you want to be cured?" but rather, "Do you want to be made well?" ("made sound" or "made healthy"). There is a big difference between healing and cure. We all want to be cured of all ailments, all problems, and all negative circumstances in our lives.

I can't explain to you why sometimes today people's healing manifests itself physically and others receive healings that are spiritual and relational and emotional. I can affirm that, even though many of us suffer from ongoing physical ills that may never be cured, God still heals.

A clergywoman who has been blind from birth was once asked, "How can you sing 'Amazing Grace!'?" The questioner was referring to the verse that says, "Amazing Grace! How sweet the sound that saved a wretch like me! / I once was lost, but now am found; was blind, but now I see."[2]

The pastor replied, "When I get to the last phrase, I stand and sing with all faith in the God who never leaves me and who fills me with the joy of the Spirit, 'Amazing Grace! How sweet the sound that saved a wretch like me! / I once was lost, but now am found; was blind, and I still can't see!'"

Maybe *rise, take up your mat and walk* doesn't mean the same thing for every one of us here this morning.

Maybe your healing is to find a way to live with dignity and even joy when a chronic illness is part of your life, either in your own being or that of a loved one.

Maybe your healing is to be at peace and live more positively with some circumstance in your life that is not going to change.

Whatever the case, Jesus stands beside you, asking you, "Do you want to be made well?"

Jesus comes to you where you are, seeking healing from a source of power that has no healing power, ready, at a word from you, to fill your life with the Holy Spirit's peace and joy.

Closing Story

When I first began my ministry almost thirty years ago, I got a call one evening from a parishioner at around 10 p.m. "My nephew is very distraught." She said. "He says he's even willing to talk to a minister. Can you meet with him?"

"Of course," I said. "When is good for him?"

"How about right now?"

Twenty minutes later I was sitting in my living room across from a young man in his late twenties, who began telling me a story I had already heard too many times before. He was pale as a paper towel and had a deep gash in his temple that had just been stitched. He told me of how he and his friend had been at a local bar and had had a few drinks. He was driving them home and ran off the road. As we sat in my living room, his friend was fighting for his life in ICU, and all he had were four stitches in the side of his head.

We had one of those big coffee-table Bibles on our coffee table. It had Sallman's "Head of Christ" on the front cover. As the young man told his sad story, he ran his fingertips over the face of Jesus, tracing the brow, the nose, the lips, the chin,…the brow, the nose, the lips, the chin. As he finished his tale, he looked up at me and said, "Jesus Christ, what am I going to do?"

I wasn't sure if this was a curse or a prayer.

Whichever it was, it called for an honest answer. So I gave it.

"You have two options. You could begin your sentence of suffering now, as, day by day, month by month, you destroy your liver with more alcohol to drown the pain and destroy your spirit with guilt.

"Or, you can hear Jesus standing beside you saying to you, 'Do you want to be made well?' Then you can turn that curse into a prayer and ask him, 'Jesus Christ, what am I going to do?' Jesus will answer your question. His answer is, "Stand up, take your mat and walk. And lo, I will be with you every step of the way.'"

SERMON _____

Seeing and Believing
John 20:1–18

MORNA D. HOOKER

Compositional Comments

In his essay on "The Materiality of John's Symbolic World," Richard Hays highlights the divisions in John's gospel "between darkness and light, above and below, spirit and flesh." All are important for the resurrection narratives in John 20:1–18. Earlier in the gospel, the evangelist tells the story of the raising of Lazarus—an "earthly" sign pointing to the "heavenly" reality of resurrection to a new, spiritual life. Now we have not the sign, but the reality. This new life is not life in the flesh, since flesh is by definition mortal (cf. 1 Cor. 15:2–4); unlike Lazarus, Jesus has not simply been brought back to life, but has been raised to a life that cannot be destroyed.

The opening line of our narrative, in contrast to the way the story begins in the other gospels, stresses the darkness before dawn, and points us back not only to the contrast between darkness and light in 1:1–18, but to the story of Nicodemus in chapter 3. Nicodemus comes to Jesus by night (3:2); he comes to the Light, but the crucial question is: Will he believe in Jesus, or will he be one of those who loves darkness rather than light? (3:17–21.) To enter the Kingdom, Nicodemus must be born from above; he must be born of Spirit, not flesh. Now, in these resurrection narratives, we realize why it is so important to be born "from above": those who operate at this level can see what others miss. We watch the disciples at the tomb, and see how "their preconceived categories prevent them from seeing what is right before their eyes." Mary sees an empty tomb and draws the wrong conclusion. She sees Jesus—and thinks he is the gardener! Peter sees the grave clothes, but doesn't comprehend the significance of the way in which they are lying. Mary and Peter are only repeating the mistakes that have been made many times—by the disciples and others—in the previous pages. To comprehend the truth, they need to move from darkness to light, to be born of the Spirit, to operate from above instead of from below. These things are possible only because, as the evangelist has told us already, Jesus is himself the Light who overcomes the darkness, and because, having descended to the world below, he has now ascended again. The Word was "made flesh," but the signs that we have seen in the flesh point to realities that belong to the Spirit.

All the gospels describe how, during his ministry, men and women found it difficult to grasp the truth about Jesus. Only after his resurrection did they understand the scriptures (John 20:9). With faith in the Risen Lord, things finally clicked into place. As Gregory Stevenson expresses it, comprehension demands that we tune into the correct frequency. The fourth evangelist alone –because of his use of the spatial imagery of "above" and "below" –links this comprehension with the ascension. In so doing, he reminds us that it is a mistake to cling to what seems to be tangible, to the things that come "from below:" to see Jesus we need to turn to the things that come "from above."

Sermon

"In the beginning was the Word, and the Word was with God... In him was life, and the life was the light of all people. The light shines in the darkness, and the darkness did not overcome it." (Jn. 1:1, 4–5).

The striking words with which John opens his gospel point us back to Genesis 1:1 and its version of the creation of the world: "In the beginning...the earth was a formless void and darkness covered the face of the deep... God said, "Let there be light"; and there was light... And there was evening and there was morning, the first day" (1:1–5).

Now John has come to the end of his story, and he reminds us once again of those opening lines of Genesis. For it was "early *on the first day of the week, while it was still dark*" (Jn. 20:1, emphasis added), that Mary Magdalene made her way to the tomb. The darkness has struggled to quench the light, but it has failed. As light returns to earth, it brings with it new life, the dawn of a new creation.

Mary, John suggests, comes to the tomb alone. Remembering the other gospels, we are puzzled. Why does he not mention the other women? Why is this story so different from the one we find in Matthew, Mark, and Luke? What is this unfamiliar story about Peter and "the other disciple...whom Jesus loved"? The other evangelists tell us nothing of their visit. Rather than worrying about these differences, however, we should be asking *why* the fourth evangelist has chosen to tell these particular stories. When we ask that question, we notice immediately that all his resurrection stories highlight the reactions of particular disciples to the news of Jesus' resurrection: Mary Magdalene, the beloved disciple, Thomas, and (in the following chapter) Peter. All four stories concern what these characters see –and how they *interpret* what they see; how they at first misunderstand what has happened –and then believe. We are going to look at two of them.

The two stories are clearly linked together. Mary Magdalene is the first to come to the tomb, and she rushes off to tell two disciples what she has seen. We're told about how they run there to see what has happened for themselves, and then we return to the story of Mary. So we have a kind of "sandwich" –first Mary, then the two men, then Mary once again. This sandwich proves to be a double-decker one, however! For the story of the two disciples begins with one who is never named, then moves to Peter, and finally returns to "the other disciple." Is this interweaving accidental? Or has the evangelist told the story this way to draw our attention to something? Is he perhaps pointing us to the way in which these three disciples see things and interpret them?

Mary sees the empty tomb, but doesn't comprehend; the beloved disciple comes to the tomb, sees, but apparently doesn't comprehend; Peter enters the tomb; but he, too, fails to comprehend. Then a great change occurs. The beloved disciple enters the tomb, sees the grave clothes, and believes. Mary sees Jesus, and at first is uncomprehending; but when he speaks, she believes. Peter's turn comes later. Gradually, incomprehension gives way to understanding and to faith.

When Mary first comes to the tomb, she sees that the stone has been removed and that the body of Jesus is gone; but *"it was still dark,"* and so naturally she misinterprets what she sees. "Someone has removed Jesus' body," she tells the disciples, "and we don't know what they have done with him" (20:2b, paraphrase). But how else *could* she explain what she has seen? Dead bodies don't get up and walk! Mary's feet are planted firmly on the ground. The Jesus she knew and loved was flesh and blood, as she is; now he is dead. If his body is no longer in the tomb, it must be because someone has removed it. She doesn't yet realize that from now on Jesus is not going to be limited by his physical body.

Returning to the tomb, she sees two angels, but clearly doesn't comprehend why they are there. By now, day has dawned, but Mary is still in inner darkness. Then she sees Jesus himself! Once again she misinterprets what she sees—hardly surprising, since he is the last person she is expecting to see. What she had expected to see was his dead body laid out in the tomb. She is not prepared to see him walking upright in the garden. Naturally enough, she assumes him to be the gardener—possibly it is he who has moved Jesus' body? Only when Jesus addresses her by name does she recognize him.

"Rabbouni," she responds, "My Rabbi." In case we do not see the significance of her words, the evangelist explains that they mean "my Teacher." She still doesn't really understand. She knows only that Jesus has come back, the old Jesus, the Jesus she knew and loved. She supposes that in spite of everything that has happened, life will now go on just as before.

Her actions tell the same story. "Do not hold on to me" (20:17a), says Jesus, and clearly that is precisely what Mary is doing. But what else would we expect? She has come to the tomb and found it empty. Distraught with grief, she has rushed back to tell the disciples, returned to the tomb, and has searched for someone who can tell her where the body has gone. Now she is suddenly confronted by the living Jesus!

She is certainly not going to say, "How nice to see you—shall we take a turn round the garden?" She flings herself at Jesus, clings to him, rejoicing that the old Jesus has been restored to her—the one she knows as "Teacher." But this is her mistake.

"Do not hold on to me," says Jesus, "because I have not yet ascended to the Father." His words puzzle us; how, we wonder, could she hold on to him *after* he ascends? She will not be able to touch him then, because he will not be present in the flesh—but why should she not do so now? Then we realize that in ascending, he is leaving the world below for the world above. When she calls him "Rabbouni," Mary is clearly thinking in terms of her old relationship with the earthly Jesus. When she holds on to him, she is wanting to perpetuate that relationship. The time for that is past. A new era has begun. From now on, she must learn to "hold on" to him in a new, spiritual, way.

Jesus instructs Mary to take a message to the disciples. Even this is a surprise. We *expect* him to say, "Go and tell them that *I have been raised* from the dead." Instead, he says, "Go…and say to them, '*I am ascending* to my Father and your Father, to my God and your God'" (20:17b, emphasis added).

Jesus' words remind us that he is not from "below," but from "above," and that he is returning to God. He has not just been raised to life again. Not long before, Jesus had raised Lazarus—a great miracle indeed, but one day Lazarus would die again. His body of flesh was raised—but flesh is mortal and must die. Jesus has been raised to a new kind of life, to which there is no end—and he is returning to God.

The fourth evangelist never *describes* the ascension (any more that he *describes* the resurrection!), but clearly it is important to him. With Jesus' resurrection and ascension comes a new kind of relationship with God for ordinary men and women. From now on they will regard him, as Jesus does, as "Father." Of course, they will have a new relationship with Jesus himself. Mary obeys Jesus' instructions, rushes off to find the disciples, and declares—not "I have seen the teacher"—but "I have seen *the Lord*" (20:18). Astonishingly, it is *a woman* who is the first to see the risen Jesus, and the first to acknowledge him as "Lord." Clearly, things are very different in this new era!

Mary Magdalene has figured prominently in popular piety. She is commonly identified (though incorrectly, many scholars say) with the woman described as "a sinner" who appears elsewhere in the gospels, and who is never named. Nowadays, of course, as a result of Dan Brown's novel, everyone is familiar with later apocryphal stories and more recent imaginative embellishments. In fact, however, we know very little about Mary Magdalene! Apart from a comment by Luke, who tells us that Jesus had saved her from seven demons and that she was one of a number of women who supported Jesus financially, she appears only at the very end of the story, as a witness—in all four gospels—to Jesus' death and resurrection.

For John, she is not simply the first to see Jesus, but the witness to a profound truth about the significance of his resurrection. During his lifetime, men and women were able to see and touch Jesus, for he was the Word made flesh. With the resurrection, death has been defeated, and light has triumphed over darkness. With the coming ascension, a new relationship begins—one that is spiritual rather than physical. We remember Nicodemus, who came to Jesus by night. He, too, addressed Jesus as "Rabbi." He was told that he needed to be born "from above," which meant that he must be born of the Spirit rather than the flesh. The reason, the evangelist explains, is that Jesus, who descended from heaven, has ascended there again. Those who believe in him must comprehend "heavenly things." When Mary acknowledges Jesus to be not just her teacher but her Lord, she grasps the meaning of heavenly things and is born "from above."

The story of Mary Magdalene is wrapped around another story—that of two disciples who ran to the tomb when she brought news that it was empty. Peter is merely a foil to the central character, the so-called "beloved disciple." Once again, we have a disciple about whom we know almost nothing. This time we do not even know his name! Is he perhaps the author of this gospel—or at least, the source of much of the tradition it contains? A comment at the very end of the gospel (21.24) states that this is the case. Why are we told that Jesus loved him? Did he not love *all* his disciples? Why is he not named? Intentionally or not, leaving him nameless helps *us* to identify with him. We find that *we* are looking into an empty tomb—and being challenged to believe. We may not be able to see the risen Lord in the garden, and yet we know that he is alive.

For this disciple, the penny drops much faster than it does for Mary. What is it that leads him to make this extraordinary leap of faith? When he first came to the tomb, John tells us, the disciple looked in. In the gloom he could see the linen wrappings that had been wound round Jesus' body. Peter arrived, rushed in, and saw not only the linen clothes, but also the cloth that had been used for Jesus' head, lying separately. Then the other disciple went in, saw, and believed. *What* he saw was presumably what Peter saw: the head-covering laying apart, near the position it had been when the body had been buried. Once again, we're reminded of the story of Lazarus. When he came out of the tomb, his hands and feet were still bound with linen, his face wrapped in a cloth.

Jesus' resurrection is no simple restoration to life in this world. His body has been transformed. He ascends to the Father, leaves the mortal for the eternal. His spiritual body has no need of linen wrappings, so they are discarded. The disciple whom Jesus loved believes. He has not yet seen the risen Lord, but with the eyes of faith he has comprehended what those linen cloths signify. We, who cannot see the risen and ascended Lord with physical eyes, are invited to "see" the truth of what has happened, and to share the beloved disciple's faith.

6

Jesus' Voice in John

Thomas E. Boomershine

How did Jesus sound? What was the character and tone of his voice? High tenor or deep bass? Was there warmth and sympathy in his voice, or did he always speak in an authoritative and emotionally detached manner? What was his attitude toward his listeners: the disciples, the Pharisees, the crowds? Was he sympathetic or cynical, confrontational or engaging? Did he ever laugh or have a sense of humor, or was he always serious?

These questions about Jesus and his voice can also be asked about the performances of the stories and speeches of Jesus in the gospel tradition. Given that the stories of the gospels were normally told or read to groups and virtually never read in silence and rarely alone, how did the storytellers of the early Jesus community present his voice? Specifically, how did Jesus sound in the ancient performances of the gospel of John? That is, how was the voice of Jesus presented in the early recitals of John's gospel? Of course, we have no direct evidence for how Jesus' voice sounded, either his actual voice or the voice he was given by ancient storytellers. There were no tape or digital recorders 2,000 years ago, so we have no way of answering the question on the basis of actual sounds.

Yet we answer these questions every time we read the gospels aloud in worship. We perform the gospels every week in churches and classes around the world, and most of those gospel readings contain some words of Jesus. When we pronounce Jesus' words and perform the stories about Jesus, several things happen. We present Jesus' voice, its tone, volume, and attitude. This voice is a primary dimension of our presentation of Jesus as a person and of the dynamics of his relationships with the other people in the stories. That is, every time we perform the gospels, we make decisions about these questions, and our answers are experienced in our performance.

Furthermore, we have answered these questions with a high level of consistency in contemporary performances of the gospel of John. A very distinctive performance tradition seems to have developed for the presentation of Jesus' voice in the readings of John's gospel. Jesus' words in these speeches have generally been performed in solemn and serious tones. Jesus almost always has a deep voice in which he delivers a series of authoritative, theological pronouncements. The voice has a strong tone with considerable volume. The tone frequently drops at the end of the sentences creating a note of authority. It is an emotionally detached and highly objective voice. In fact, in much of the English-speaking world, the voice of Jesus might be compared to that of a British theologian or rector. The tone is often almost a monotone with little or no variation in pitch.

The tradition of Jesus' voice in the gospel of John is integrally related to the distinctive role of the gospel of John in the Christian tradition. Along with the letters of Paul, especially Romans, the gospel of John has been the major source of Christian theology. The major doctrines of the Church—the Nicene doctrine of the Trinity, the Chalcedonian doctrine of the unity of the human and divine in Jesus—have been based on the gospel of John. In part for this reason, the gospel has always been heard as addressed to Christian believers, and this remains the dominant conclusion of modern scholarship. Jesus is presented then as speaking theological truth to believers. Furthermore, with the exception of the reading of the Johannine passion narrative on Good Friday, John's gospel is usually performed as a series of short readings that precede homilies or sermons addressed to "the faithful."

This voice of the Johannine Jesus in the memories of our collective ears has one very substantial downside. When performed in this way, the character of Jesus frequently comes off as what can best be described in the vernacular as pompous and arrogant. I would suggest that you read the following passage aloud in the traditional voice:

> "No one can come to me unless drawn by the Father who sent me; and I will raise that person up on the last day. It is written in the prophets, 'And they shall all be taught by God." Everyone who has heard and learned from the Father comes to me. Not that anyone has seen the Father except the one who is from God; he has seen the Father." (Jn. 6:44–46)

The combination of the provocative content of these sayings and the authoritative, detached voice creates a highly alienating overall effect.

Furthermore, Jesus says a lot of very negative things about "the Jews," such as "You are from your father the devil, and you choose to do your father's desires" (Jn. 8:44). When performed as solemn pronouncements, these statements have been experienced as the announcement of theological truths.

When spoken and heard in this way, many of the sayings are experienced as profoundly anti-Jewish. This conclusion is also related to our picture of John's audience. The dominant conclusion in Johannine scholarship is that John's audience was a congregation of Christian believers. When read as addressed to Christians, the words of the gospel about Jews are heard as being about "them," the Jews, not about "us," Christians.

Ancient Recordings and the Original Voice of Jesus

The question is whether this voice is appropriate. Specifically, is this how Jesus' voice sounded in the original performances of John's gospel? At first blush, this question appears unanswerable. After all, we have no analog or digital sound recordings of Jesus' voice. But we do have *ancient* recordings of Jesus' voice. A foundational shift has taken place in recent research on the ancient world. It has now been established that ancient manuscripts were "published" by public performances and were written for those performances.[1]

When the evangelists wrote the gospels, they were making a recording of the sounds of the stories, with the assumption that every reader of their gospel would reproduce the sounds, usually having learned the words by heart. When they wrote, the evangelists were like composers writing a musical manuscript. They were not writing for readers as we now read: silently with a book in hand. They were composing sounds that would be reproduced by storytellers and readers, even if, like the Ethiopian eunuch, they were reading alone (Acts 8:28–30). The writers of the gospels were not composing texts that would be read in silence by individual readers. Relatively few people could read in antiquity. Current estimates are that not more than 10 percent in the Greco-Roman world of the first century could read.[2] Ancient writers wrote with the assumption that their writings would be published by public performances for audiences. In most instances, the texts were performed "by heart." Thus, the gospel of John, like virtually all of ancient literature, was written for performance. We can appropriately think of the text of John as an ancient recording of performances of John's story.

For twenty-first–century folk, it is important to distinguish our current concept of memorization from the ancient practice of learning "by heart." Dennis Dewey makes the distinction between "memorization" as head memory and "internalization" as heart memory.[3] Head memory is associated with rote memorization and the "mindless" recitation of words or repetition of notes. Heart memory is embodied memory that involves the whole of the body. It includes emotion as well as thought. Thus, Dewey notes that we have a selective memory of the injunctions following the Shema:

> Most pastors can remember the last four of the five "corollaries" to the Shema (Deuteronomy 6.4ff): catechize (teach these things to your children), theologize (talk about them continually), symbolize (wear them on your wrists and foreheads), publicize (inscribe them on your

doorposts and gates). But few can remember the important corollary that follows immediately upon the commandment to love God with heart, soul and strength: "Keep these words that I am commanding you today in your heart" (Deut. 6:6) (internalize).[4]

If we are going to imagine performances of John's story as the normative medium of experience of John in the ancient world, we need to imagine persons who were telling the story and presenting the speeches of Jesus "by heart."

Could someone have told John all at one time? Of course. Ancient storytelling performances were often long, four to six hours or more. Storytellers were the primary providers of an evening's entertainment. Performances of Homer's epic often went on all night. The performance of written narratives such as *The Iliad* and the gospels was a continuation of the traditions of ancient storytelling. Storytelling was the most widely practiced art in the ancient world. Stretching back into the millennia of preliterate human culture, storytelling was the foundation of tribal life.[5] Thus, the sources of the performance traditions of internalized *written* narratives were developments of the performance traditions of traditional *oral* narratives. Thus, it is highly likely that the gospel of John was learned "by heart" and told in a three-to-four-hour evening of storytelling. More than any of the other gospels, John's story was an interweaving of stories of events with a series of long speeches by Jesus. But how can we determine the character of Jesus' voice?

Storytelling and Audience Address

A constant feature of storytelling performance is the storyteller's address to the audience. The storyteller is always talking to the audience. Storytellers are, first of all, themselves. A storyteller addresses his or her audience as himself or herself. Think in detail about what is happening at the beginning of the recital of John's story: "In the beginning was the Word." Who am I in this moment of story introduction? I am Tom retelling the words of John by heart. And who are you? You are the audience, the object and receiver of this story. Storytelling is an extensive and dynamic interaction of a storyteller and an audience. The dynamics of that interaction profoundly shape the meaning of the story for the audience. One set of clues, therefore, to the character of Jesus' voice is to observe the dynamics of interaction between the storyteller and the audience.

In the gospel of John, the interaction of the storyteller with the audience is often as the character of Jesus. One of the stock-in-trade traditions of storytellers is the presentation of multiple characters. During the telling of the story, the storyteller presents various characters. In John's story, the storyteller presents Jesus, Nicodemus, the blind man, the Samaritan woman, etc. In presenting these characters, the storyteller gives each of them a distinctive presence with gestures, accents, tones, and ways of relating to other characters in the story. Thus, the blind man is different from the Pharisees and his parents in the story. An integral part of the fascination and joy of storytelling is this playful representation of the different characters of the story.

The storyteller, in a sense, becomes different characters and presents each character's gestures, facial expressions, attitudes, and voice. This presentation of various characters is a major factor of audience address. When various characters are interacting in the story, the audience is often addressed as one or more of those characters. Sometimes the storyteller may present the interactions of the different characters as addressed to an imaginary character on the imaginary stage of the story. Most of the time the words of the various characters are addressed directly to the audience.

This is a foundational difference between storytelling and drama. In a drama, the actors relate to each other on a stage. The members of the audience are spectators who watch the actors interacting with each other. In storytelling, the audience is frequently addressed as one of the characters in the story. Notice, for example, what happens in the story of Jesus and Nicodemus. The audience is addressed as Nicodemus, especially in the later parts of the story (3:10–21). In this speech I, as the storyteller, present Jesus and you, as the listeners, become Nicodemus who is addressed by Jesus. This dynamic of changes in the characters of the storyteller and the audience happens throughout the gospel. Just as the storyteller imaginatively becomes the various characters, so also the members of the audience are invited to become the characters who are addressed. Furthermore, just as the storyteller frequently changes character, so also the audience frequently changes its imaginary identity. Thus, right after the storyteller's speech as Jesus to the audience as Nicodemus, the storyteller presents John the Baptist, and the audience is addressed as John's disciples (3:26–36).

This storytelling dynamic is especially present in long speeches. The storyteller presents one of the characters in the story giving a speech to some person or group. The storyteller's audience is addressed as that character or group. Long speeches make it possible for the audience to live into the character who is being addressed, in part because the speech goes on for a long time. Just as the storytelling fiction leads to an experience of the storyteller as the character who is speaking, so also the members of the audience have an extended period of time in which to experience themselves as the character being addressed in the speech.

An important dimension of audience identification is that we, as part of an audience, can identify with an audience that is different than our actual identity. It is possible, for example, for a white person to experience a story told to a black audience as an integral part of that community. This can include giving verbal responses, laughter, and standing up. This is equally possible for a black person in a white audience. This dynamic happens in the screening of films every day. One of the unique dynamics of watching "foreign" films is that the films were created for audiences that are significantly different from the audience to whom the film is marketed and screened. People from all over the world watch films that were produced for American audiences. I have experienced this dynamic watching French, Indian, and German films—including Nazi films produced for German audiences in the Nazi era. I have experienced these dynamics as a member of an audience in synagogues, Russian and Greek Orthodox churches, and Roman Catholic communities. I may not be Jewish, Orthodox, or Roman Catholic, but I can participate in worship services as if Jewish, Orthodox, and Roman Catholic. This is also true of audiences in another period of history. As a twenty-first–century, highly literate, white male Christian, I can still identify with the audiences of ancient Israelite stories, to a certain degree, and vicariously experience some dimensions of the experience of ancient tribal audiences listening to stories told by ancient Israelite storytellers.

Thus, listening to storytelling, both ancient and contemporary, is an opportunity for vicarious participation in a community of which I am not actually a member. However, as a member of that audience, one is quite aware of the fact that this is an imaginative experience. At the same time, there is reality to this participation and identity. While there is a clear realization that the story assumes experiences and knowledge that one does not fully share, one can experience and vicariously identify with feelings, experiences, and attitudes of that community's particular experience. There can be a feeling of oneness and identification that is transformative. You can learn a lot about another community by listening to that community's stories.

Audience Address in the Gospel of John

Let us then identify the interactions of the Johannine storyteller and his audience. Among the four gospels, John is distinctive in its manner of audience address. One of those distinctive features of John's gospel is a lot of long speeches by Jesus, more than in any other gospel. For example, Mark has two long speeches, while Matthew and Luke both have five. John contains eight long speeches and several shorter speeches by Jesus. These comprise nearly half of the gospel.

Furthermore, Jesus' speeches in John are addressed to the audience as a much wider range of characters than in any of the other gospels. Just for comparison, Matthew has five long speeches all addressed to the audience as the crowds and/or the disciples. Jesus' five major speeches in Luke are similar in their audience address. Yet in John the speeches are addressed to a wide range of different characters: Nicodemus, various groups of Jews, the Pharisees, and the disciples. Thus, the storyteller's imaginative interactions with the audience in John are more complex than in any of the synoptics.

Another distinctive feature of Jesus' speeches in John is that several of the stories—Nicodemus, the feeding of the 5,000, the trip to Jerusalem for the Feast of Tabernacles, the healing of the man born blind, and the triumphal entry—function as introductions to long speeches to the audience as characters in the preceding story. In these speeches, the story moves imperceptibly from a third person description of an event to a first person address by Jesus to the audience. An example is the story of Nicodemus. (3:1–21) The storyteller tells the story of Nicodemus coming to Jesus at night and reports their conversation. After several exchanges, Jesus is talking to Nicodemus in the first person: "Truly I say to you, we speak of what we know and we bear witness to what we have seen; but you do not receive our testimony. If I have spoken to you about earthly things and you do not believe, how will you believe if I speak to you about heavenly things?" (3:11–12).[6]

But in the next sentences, Nicodemus fades into the background, and Jesus is talking in the third person: "And just as Moses lifted up the serpent in the world, so also must the Son of Man be lifted up, so that everyone who believes in him may have eternal life.... For God so loved the world that he gave his only Son..." (3:14–16a).[7]

In the telling of the story, the storyteller as Jesus is now talking directly to the audience as if the audience were Nicodemus.[8] The audience has imaginatively become Nicodemus, and Jesus' speech is addressed to each member of the audience as a "seeker" Pharisee.

The most distinctive feature of John's gospel is the clearly marked structure of the addresses to the audience. In chapters 1–4, the audience is addressed as various groups of first-century Judaism: the Pharisees (1:26–27), the Jews in the temple at Passover (2:16–19), Nicodemus/the Pharisees (3:1–21), the followers of John the Baptist (3:27–30), and the Samaritans (4:21–24).

After the story of the healing of the lame man at the pool of Bethzatha (5:1–15), John makes a sudden and radical change in the identity of the audience that Jesus addresses. Jesus' speech to the audience as the Jews that follows this healing story is by far the longest speech to this point in the story. It is introduced by this narrative comment: "For this reason the Jews were seeking all the more to kill him, because he was not only breaking the sabbath, but was also calling God his own Father, thereby making himself equal to God" (5:18).

Throughout the next seven chapters of the story following this radical and sudden shift (Jn. 5–12), the audience is addressed as various groups of Jews who are both drawn to Jesus and repelled by him. Jesus' dialogue partners in this long section of the story are torn between believing in Jesus and not believing in him. There is constant change in the specific identity of the character(s) to whom Jesus is speaking in these stories: for example, as Jews who want to kill him (ch. 5), then as the crowd and the disciples (ch. 6), then as Jews who believe in him (ch. 8), then as Pharisees and as Jews who took up stones to stone him (ch. 10), then as Andrew and Philip (ch. 12), and frequently throughout this section as simply Jews. In this section of the gospel (chs. 5–12) the audience is addressed as Jews who are constantly changing in their attitude and response to Jesus—from total alienation, to belief, and everything in between.

Finally, another sudden change in the identity of the audience appears with the story of Jesus' last supper. The climax of the speeches of Jesus to the audience is Jesus' long talk with the disciples after washing the disciples' feet (chs. 13–17). In this long speech, the audience is addressed as Jesus' disciples.

Thus, the structure of audience address in the gospel as a whole is clearly marked and moves from Jesus addressing various groups of Jews (chs. 1–4) to Jesus addressing Jews who believe and don't believe in him (chs. 5–12) to Jesus addressing his disciples (chs. 13–17). The audience is thereby invited to move in its relationship with Jesus from being Jews, to Jews who are violently torn between belief and unbelief, to disciples who are in a highly intimate relationship of mutuality and love with Jesus.

The most striking dimension of the audience address is that, with the exception of the Samaritans, all of these characters are identified as Jews. The only characters who are not *explicitly* named as Jews are "the crowd" and "the disciples." But "the crowd" is clearly identified as Jews who were fed (6:24, 41) or were in Jerusalem (7:11, 35). "The disciples" are likewise identified as Jews (1:47). That is, no non-Jews are directly addressed in the interactions of the storyteller and the audience. The audience is never addressed as a character other than various groups of Jews. Throughout the story, the storyteller as Jesus addresses the audience as Jews. The structure of Jesus' speeches moves from speeches to various groups of Jews who are interested in him, to Jews who are conflicted about believing in him or being hostile toward him, to his long talk with the audience as his Jewish disciples. To participate fully in the hearing of the story, the audience of the gospel, regardless of their actual ethnic or religious identity, must imaginatively become Jews. Furthermore, throughout the first half of the gospel, the audience is explicitly addressed as Jews who are torn between believing and not believing in Jesus.

The Historical Audience of John

This fact raises the further question of the relationship between the audience as addressed in the story and the actual historical audiences of the gospel. The cultural horizon of the gospel is congruent with the cultural horizon of diaspora Judaism in the Hellenistic cities of the Greco-Roman world. This was the same cultural world in which Paul carried out his missionary work and that is reflected in his letters. However, in contrast to the letters of Paul, the audience of the gospel of John reflects no explicit inclusion of Gentiles. The probability is, therefore, that the actual historical audiences of the gospel of John correspond to the audiences addressed in the gospel itself: Jews, Pharisees, the followers of John the Baptist, perhaps Samaritans, and Jews who believed in Jesus. However, the gospel does not exclude Gentiles from its audience. It only requires that they become Jews in their imaginative participation in the story. That is also true for later participants in John's audience. To participate appropriately in the interactions of the Johannine storyteller and the character of Jesus with the audience, later Christian audiences must become Jews in their identity as listeners.

Thus, the structure of audience address in the gospel of John does not support the conclusion that the gospel is addressed to Christian believers, Jewish or Gentile. All of the storyteller's speeches addressed to the audience prior to the Last Supper (Jn. 1–12) do not presume belief. The prologue talks explicitly about those who have believed in his name (1:12) but addresses this to the audience without presuming that they share that belief. The structure of audience address in its movement from Jews (chs. 1–4) to Jews who are conflicted about believing in Jesus (chs. 5–12) to Jews who are disciples (chs. 13–17) is the clearest internal sign of the purpose of the Johannine storyteller.

The gospel is structured to invite the audience as Jews to move from being interested in Jesus, to considering the issues involved in believing in Jesus as Messiah, to full identification as disciples. This does not exclude believers. They can live through this process of coming to belief in Jesus many times. But the story is structured for nonbelievers and does not exclude them by presuming belief at any point (with the possible exception of chapter 21). The character of audience address, therefore, indicates that the gospel was conceived as an evangelistic story directed to Jews who did not believe that Jesus was the Messiah. The purpose of the story is stated explicitly to each member of the audience at the end of Jesus' appearance to Thomas: "These are written so that you may come to believe that Jesus is the Messiah, the Son of God, and that through believing you may have life in his name" (20:31).

The Original Voice of Jesus

What then can we learn from this about the tone of Jesus' voice in the first-century performances of John's gospel? The actual character of audience address in the gospel of John makes it highly improbable that the voice of Jesus in the original recitals of his words in John's gospel was the impassive, deep, and authoritarian voice of the performance tradition. This traditional tone only makes sense if the audience was predominantly Christian believers who are non-Jewish. Whatever the historical identity of the audiences of the gospel of John may have been in its early performances, a storyteller told the story from memory, either with or without a manuscript, to audiences who were addressed as Jews. The patterns of audience address in the gospel are clearly designed to engage the audience in an encounter with Jesus as a highly sympathetic character who invites them to believe in him as the Messiah and to identify themselves as his disciples. He is trying to win them and to invite them into a deeply personal relationship. He is not giving them a long series of pronouncements.

The tone of Jesus' voice throughout the recitals of the gospel of John was, then, most likely sympathetic and emotionally warm. But perhaps most importantly, it was the honest voice of a friend.[9] Jesus' voice probably modulated over a wide range of volume, from soft to loud. A strong and confident voice, yes, but a voice that invited the listeners to reflect on their responses to his words and to him. The tone is inviting, explorative, and probing. It is even possible that some of these statements are said with a smile and even laughter. The tone of these speeches is the tone of a rabbi who is inviting the listeners to think. It is a tone associated in contemporary experience with Yiddish. The character of Jesus has credibility because the storyteller is presenting a story about the most engaging martyr in the history of Israel. But the tone of Jesus' speeches in early performances must have been radically different from the way in which we have come to consider the speeches to have been traditionally performed.

In fact, a sympathetic, honest, and engaging voice of Jesus is the only way in which the gospel can be told as a whole and hold the attention of an audience. If Jesus' words are presented in the way in which the gospel is now usually performed, Jesus becomes a very alienating character. He is a kind of pompous figure, constantly making arrogant statements. It is impossible to maintain the attention and good will of an audience if Jesus' statements are performed in this manner. This effect may be somewhat more pronounced in the modern world, but the same dynamic was operative in the ancient world. Even when enacted in a more sympathetic manner, Jesus' statements are often extremely provocative. They are only credible when they are presented in a self-confident but humble manner. Furthermore, the authoritative, theological Jesus is also boring. Without human warmth and engagement in his manner, the character of Jesus in John becomes untenable as a character who can sustain this "one man show."

Thus, the conclusion that flows from the analysis of audience address in John is that the speeches of Jesus throughout the gospel were performed in a warmly engaging tone addressed to the audience as various groups of Jews. His tone throughout the story is loving, peaceful, and deeply centered. It remains strong, confident, and self-assured, yet humble and inviting. This is most pronounced in the long speech to his disciples, but it is true throughout the gospel. Jesus' words are often provocative and shocking. As a character Jesus is aggressive and persistent, constantly appealing for the audience to listen to him, to receive his words, and to believe in him. In response to ongoing rejection and plots to kill him, Jesus is persistent in his determination to engage in dialogue with the audience as various Jews and to invite them into a deeper relationship with him and with God. Jesus' words do not have their origin in a spirit of hostility or judgment. In fact, he explicitly says this at several points in the gospel, most notably in the: last speech of Jesus that is addressed directly to the audience:

> Whoever believes in me believes not in me but in him who sent me. And whoever sees me sees him who sent me. I have come as light into the world, so that everyone who believes in me should not remain in the darkness. I do not judge anyone who hears my words and does not keep them, for I came not to judge the world, but to save the world. (12:44–47)

Jesus is presented as a person who knows that people are seeking to kill him. The listeners to John's gospel sixty or so years after Jesus' death know that those people finally succeeded. But Jesus never responds with hostility or violence to these attacks.

Furthermore, the gospel invites anyone who wants to enter into the story to identify themselves with the audience of Jews to whom the story is addressed. This is stated explicitly in the prologue: "He came to what was his own, and his own people did not accept him. But to all who received him, who believed in his name, he gave power to become children of God" (1:11–12). However, it is striking that no Gentiles are in the horizon of the gospel. The audience is never addressed as Gentiles. In the story, when some Greeks ask Andrew and Philip to see Jesus, his response is, "The hour has come…," and, the Bible does not report any meeting with them. The only significant Gentiles in the entire story are Pilate, who condemns Jesus to death, and the Roman soldiers, who execute him. Furthermore, the audience is never addressed as Christians. The audience is addressed as disciples in the most intimate speech of the entire gospel tradition, the Last Supper speech in chapters 13–17. But the disciples are addressed as Jews who believe in him.

Therefore, all those who identified themselves as non-Jews, both then and now, are required by the character of John's story to imagine themselves as Jews for the appropriate telling and hearing of this story. That may be difficult. There may be dimensions of the storyteller's story of which the listener may be unaware as a result of not being Jewish. But just as all ethnic stories require sympathetic listening and identification with the story's audience, the gospel of John implicitly invites all of its listeners to become Jewish as listeners to this story.

The Gospel of John Then and Now

Thus, an analysis of audience address in the gospel reveals the basic character of the gospel of John. The gospel of John is addressed to Jews throughout the gospel. The storyteller/author presents himself as a Jew who believes that Jesus is the Messiah.

This also clarifies the basic problem in the interpretation of the gospel of John now. The gospel is almost exclusively read by and for Christians who do not think of themselves as Jews. Most Christians hear the words in the gospel about "the Jews" as being about "them" rather than "us." Our task as performers of the gospel is to enable our audiences to identify with the original audience and to hear Jesus' words to the Jews as addressed to them. That means presenting Jesus' words in a manner that is thoroughly Jewish, and, therefore, engaging, provocative, warm but probing, confident yet humble. It is the voice of a discerning and true friend.

The challenge for those who would tell the gospel of John, therefore, is to find a tone for the character of Jesus that will make him credible and appealing. Part of the challenge is that the liturgical theological voice is so dominant that we virtually cannot hear Jesus' voice in any other tone. Therefore, I would invite each of you to perform Jesus' words in a way that is warm, nonauthoritarian, strong, friendly, and inviting.

Finally, some brief observations about performing and preaching the gospel of John. The readings/tellings need to be contextualized for Christian audiences who identify themselves as "not Jews." This is a complex and difficult issue. If our congregations have spiritually identified with the traditions of Israel, they can think of themselves as Jews and hear this gospel as addressed to them as Jews who believe that Jesus is the Messiah. It is, therefore, important that we tell the stories of the Hebrew Scriptures and encourage our congregations to become fully a part of the spiritual heritage of Israel.

I would also highly recommend that any texts of John to be recited in worship be embodied and told rather than read from a text. In this way, the address to the audience is made more explicit. But, most important, telling Jesus' actions and words makes Jesus more human, more accessible, more Jewish, and more attractive. Performing the gospel as a story told "by heart" counteracts the inevitable tendency of readings to become emotionally distant, and that is particularly dangerous with the gospel of John. The sermon is also a time when the connections to the traditions of the Old Testament and to John's setting in the 90s after the Jewish war can be made more explicit.

Finally, this traditional style of presenting Jesus' voice works against the greatest strength of John's story, namely, the building of intimacy between the audience and Jesus. The authoritative voice makes Jesus into a distant and intimidating person. The great value of John is that Jesus is presented as a more accessible and intimate person than in the other gospels. In John's gospel, Jesus becomes a true friend. You can get closer to Jesus in John than anywhere else in the gospels.

Perhaps paradoxically, he is also more human, even while making a series of statements about himself and his relationship with God that are unprecedented for any figure in human history. The dynamic structure of John's gospel creates an experience for the listeners of growing steadily closer to Jesus. In part, this is because there is so much conflict with him. Because of Jesus' spirit, this is an experience of growing intimacy. It is also an experience of growing closer to God. That intimacy with God is directly connected to intimacy with Jesus. As a listener, you have the potential of growing in love with Jesus, with God, and with others. As Jesus says, "Abide in my love," and, "Love one another." In the experience of the gospel, Jesus' voice is the connection with that experience of being loved by Jesus and by God, even when you are so angry at him that you want to kill him. Therefore, I would invite you to learn and tell the gospel of John to others "by heart" and to listen for Jesus' voice.

SERMON _____

No Dead End in Christ
John 10:11–18

PAUL SCOTT WILSON

Compositional Comments

Thomas Boomershine maintains that we often perform Jesus' voice as deep, impassive, authoritarian, and monotonous. Jesus comes across as pompous. However, when we understand that Jesus' audience in John are Jews, and his intention is to invite them into relationship with him, our performance of his voice changes. The performance changes not just in reading the story but in preaching it as well. The contemporary audience is invited to identify with John's audience as it moves in its relationship with Jesus from curious Jews (chs. 1–4), to Jews who are divided between belief and unbelief (chs. 5–12), to disciples who are in a highly intimate relationship with Jesus (chs. 13–17).

As Paul Wilson preaches from this particular part of John's story, the Jewish audience is strongly divided over Jesus (10:19). Jesus offers them an invitation: *Come to me all you who are filled with anxiety, loss, guilt; all you who have reached a dead end in your life, and I will give you rest.*

In this part of the story, Jesus as shepherd issues the invitation. The audience are the sheep. The sheep know the voice of their shepherd (10:5, 16). What kind of voice would the sheep recognize as their shepherd's voice? What kind of voice would the preacher perform as this text is proclaimed? The sheep would know Jesus' voice as compassionate, strong, and caring. Wilson's sermon performs this voice. Most importantly, Wilson performs the voice of Jesus, to use Boomershine's language, as "the honest voice of a friend."

Sermon

I am so pleased to be sharing in this worship service marking the forty-fifth anniversary of this congregation. One aspect of this marvelous building is that if one looks up at the cross at the front, on the other side of the wall, exactly, is the statue outdoors of the Good Shepherd, Jesus Christ, holding a shepherd's crook in his hands. Several small details are telling; for example, each wrist has a nail hole. In other words, the Good Shepherd is not only the historical Jesus, but the resurrected Christ. The sculpture stands on a small platform that juts out from the wall, like an inverted pyramid. Since early times, the church has been imaged as a boat. If one stands outside the church looking at that statue, as I did this morning, one can imagine that that inverted pyramid is in fact the prow of a ship and that Jesus is standing at the prow. It is a beautiful symbol of this church in our troubled times. Jesus is still at the prow, leading us onward as the Good Shepherd he is. We have no need to fear when Christ is at the prow; there is no dead end in Christ.

Here in North America, Christianity is declining. Many people brought up in the church are not attending, and many immigrants are not from Christian backgrounds. Since the church has so much to offer this hurting world, why do not more people attend, apart from the fact that today they are on holiday? At our church we have some folks who attend regularly whom we still do not know, and that is because "regular" for them is every Christmas or Easter. I always feel saddened that something keeps them away.

I'd like to think that the service last year was so meaningful that it kept them spiritually inspired all year long, that when they are brushing their teeth at night they are still humming the anthem the choir sang twelve months before. I would like to think that the sermon was so deep and memorable, they have put its words to memory and are still savoring its meats. I would also like to think that they have enough meaning in their lives that, when they wake up in the middle of the night and contemplate their lives they are not anxious, that they have found deep contentment, that amidst the busyness of life they have time to think about what really matters.

I suspect, however, that they are like the rest of us. They have periods of doubt, anxiety, real need for community, and God. In fact, there is only one helpful guideline for being in church: you have run out of fuel or experienced some dead end in life. At minimum, all one needs is a longing for meaning, a broken dream, some sense of loss, guilt, loneliness, or addiction. If that is your situation, if you have known disappointment or need, if you still carry it with you, if you know life occasionally to be like a dead end, you are where you need to be. In Christ there is no dead end. Whatever reason you may think you have for being here today, the real one is that your Shepherd called you here to fill you with what you need.

Our text is about a lot of people who have reached dead ends in life. Jesus says we are all sheep and have all chosen a shepherd. He says he is the good shepherd, the one who is willing to die for his sheep so that they may live. The way Jesus sees it, everyone has selected a shepherd, and a lot of folks have chosen another shepherd, a shepherd of death. These false shepherds are hired hands, folks who do not own the sheep, who only pretend to be shepherds, who trick the sheep into thinking they are safe.

Nearly everything about them seems to indicate that they are legitimate. They call the sheep to follow. They lead them to green pastures. They lead them by streams and offer them drink. They pretend to restore the soul. In the evening they take the sheep into the sheepfolds, stone-walled enclosures, and allow them a place to sleep. In this they are doing the duty of a shepherd. Here is the problem: when the wolf comes, the bad shepherds are out of there. They hightail it. They are gone with the wind, footloose and fancy free, looking out only for themselves. Jesus says that many folks choose the bad shepherd.

Choosing the bad shepherd is the same thing as choosing an agent of death to be your shepherd.

Some folks may say of themselves, "I don't believe in anything," but everyone believes in something. Some folks believe in savings, some in having a good time, some in possessions. If you aren't going with the good shepherd, you may be going with the bad. Sometimes it is hard for us to know. Some people choose death and race to it with cocaine or heroine. Some take a shortcut to death by bearing anger, withholding forgiveness, nursing grudges. Some try to avoid death by exercising at the gym; but one way or the other, the wolf approaches us all. No matter what sheepfold you are in, the wolf is always out there, ready to strike. The question is, whom do you trust, the good shepherd or the bad?

Whenever we sin, we choose death. If by some strange reason, you choose death, there is bad news for you. Whatever sheepfold you are in, Jesus comes and stands in the gate. If you want to reach the wolf out there, you have to get past Jesus. He is the Good Shepherd. If you are intent on finding death, you have to choose some other route than Jesus. You cannot get to death through Jesus. He offers life and only life. He says, "If you are looking for death, you've come to the wrong shepherd. I am the Good Shepherd, trust me." That's what he said to Mary at Easter by the empty tomb, "If you are looking for death, you've come to the wrong place." It is what he said to the disciples gathered in a locked room, "If you are honoring death, you won't find it here." It is what he said to Thomas, "If you are guessing death, guess again." It is what he said to Paul on the road to Damascus, "If you are choosing death, you are blind." It is what he said to Mother Teresa, and Martin Luther King Jr., and Jean Vanier, and you and me, "If you want death, you've come to the wrong place. I am the Good Shepherd. I am the Shepherd God ordained for you. I am at watch in the night. I am attentive at noon. I am your way, your path."

Sometimes I like to take a familiar psalm and change the words so that it is no longer the psalmist saying them but Jesus Christ speaking them directly to us. It might be rewarding for you to go out and study that statue of the Good Shepherd and revise the words of Psalm 23 such that you hear the Good Shepherd saying them to you:

> I am your shepherd, you shall not want.
>   I make you to lie down in green pastures,
> I lead you beside still waters,
>   I restore your soul.
> I lead you in paths of righteousness
>   for my name's sake.
> Yea though you walk through the valley of the shadow of death,
> you will fear no evil: for I am with you;
>   my rod and my staff, they comfort you.

I prepare a table before you
in the presence of your enemies: I anoint your head with oil;
    your cup runs over.
Surely goodness and mercy shall follow you
    all the days of your life;
and you will dwell in the house of the LORD
    forever. (NKJV)

When Jesus stands in your way, the road to death is blocked. A key problem with summer is the road crews. You want to go somewhere, and you have to detour. That is how it is when you meet Jesus. He is so concerned for his sheep that he went to the cross and died. He took our death on himself. He died our death for us, and he rose again, that in faith we might receive his eternal protection. He wears a sign: "Road to Death Closed." Oh, alternate routes lead over the walls of the sheep pen left and right, but Jesus stands in the middle of the gate between you and death. If you insist on death, you have to avoid Jesus because if you go his way, you will only find eternity.

A lot of people are hell-bent on finding death. A woman with a broken heart sees Jesus and detours left. She does not want to risk being hurt in love again. Jesus says to her, "Believe in me, and I will never let you go." A teen snorting coke sees Jesus and detours right, afraid to face the day without drugs. Jesus says, "Believe in me, and I will be your strength." "Believe in me," Jesus says to everyone. "I love you, no matter what you have done. I will make you part of my community." It is surprising how much energy some people put into saying no to Jesus, instead of saying, "The Lord is my Shepherd, I shall not want."

I heard of a woman in her thirties. She met a young girl aged eleven in foster care. She got along so well with her she decided to see if she could adopt her. She knew it would be hard for the girl to find adoptive parents, and this woman felt led by her faith to share what she had. Her whole family has rejoiced in welcoming this new member to the family. The new granddaughter took her new grandmother upstairs to see her room. Passing her mother's room, she observed that it was not as tidy as it might be. Her own room was meticulously clean, all the teddy bears neatly arranged, the books on the desk piled neatly. We may not all be able to show our faith in such life-changing ways as adopting a child, but we can all show the love of Christ to whomever we meet in the week.

Our Good Shepherd leads us to new life. An amazing thing about Christ is that all of the detour roads to death eventually lead back to him. If you are afraid to come to Jesus, Jesus will come to you. If you have been trying to bypass the Good Shepherd, why not instead say, "my Lord." He died for you. He rose for you. Through the Holy Spirit he sends good things every day to you. In Jesus there is no "dead end." In Christ there is *no* end. In Christ there is only new beginning, new dawn, and new you, a new tomorrow. With him at the prow of this ship, the church, we have nothing to fear about tomorrow.

"I am the good shepherd. The good shepherd lays down his life for the sheep. The hired hand, who is not the shepherd and does not own the sheep, sees the wolf coming and leaves the sheep and runs away—and the wolf snatches them and scatters them. The hired hand runs away because a hired hand does not care for the sheep. I am the good shepherd. I know my own and my own know me, just as the Father knows me and I know the Father. And I lay down my life for the sheep. I have other sheep that do not belong to this fold. I must bring them also, and they will listen to my voice. So there will be one flock, one shepherd. For this reason the Father loves me, because I lay down my life in order to take it up again. No one takes it from me, but I lay it down of my own accord. I have power to lay it down, and I have power to take it up again. I have received this command from my Father. (Jn. 10:11–18)

Notes

Chapter 1: The Materiality of John's Symbolic World

[1]Ernst Käsemann, *The Testament of Jesus* (Philadelphia: Fortress Press, 1968). The quoted phrases are found on p. 26 and p. 9.

[2]Rudolf Bultmann, *The Gospel of John* (Philadelphia: Westminster Press, 1971).

[3]This is the hermeneutical approach that George Lindbeck calls "intratextual theology" in his *The Nature of Doctrine: Religion and Theology in a Postliberal Age* (Philadelphia: Westminster Press, 1984), 112–38.

[4]See Thomas Olbricht essay here.

[5]On John as a "two-level drama," see especially the classic work of J. Louis Martyn, *History and Theology in the Fourth Gospel*, 3d. ed. (Louisville: Westminster John Knox Press, 2003).

[6]Archibald MacLeish, "Ars Poetica," in *The Collected Poems of Archibald MacLeish* (Boston: Houghton Mifflin, 1962), 50–51.

[7]John Ciardi, *How Does a Poem Mean?* (Boston: Houghton Mifflin, 1959), 910.

[8]Laurence Perrine, *Sound and Sense: An Introduction to Poetry*, 2d. ed. (New York: Harcourt, Brace & World, 1963), 124.

[9]This paragraph reiterates observations I made in Richard B. Hays, *The Moral Vision of the New Testament: Community, Cross, New Creation* (San Francisco: HarperSanFrancisco, 1996), 156.

[10]T.S. Eliot, "The Dry Salvages," in *The Complete Poems and Plays* (New York: Harcourt, Brace & World, 1962), 133.

[11]The verbal link is even closer to Psalm 78:24, a retelling of the same story.

[12]This sermon, "Standing by the Fire," was originally preached at First Presbyterian Church, Nashville, Tennessee, April 22, 2007.

Sermon: Standing by the Fire

[1]Rowan Williams, *Resurrection: Interpreting the Easter Gospel* (Harrisburg, Pa.: Morehouse, 1994), 34.

[2]From "Ah, Holy Jesus," words by Johann Heerman, 1630, translated by Robert S. Bridges, 1899.

[3]*The News and Observer*, Raleigh, N.C., April 13, 2007, available online at http://www.newsobserver.com/1185/story/563705.html.

[4]T.S. Eliot, "Little Gidding," in *The Complete Poems and Plays* (New York: Harcourt, Brace & World, 1962), 142. For the connection of these lines to John 21, I am indebted to Williams, *Resurrection*, 32.

Sermon: God in the Flesh

[1]Frederick Buechner, "The Good Book as a Good Book" in *The Clown in the Belfry: Writings on Faith and Fiction* (San Francisco: HarperSanFrancisco, 1992), 44.

[2]Robin Scroggs, *Christology in Paul and John*, Proclamation Commentaries (Philadelphia: Fortress Press, 1988), 63–77, especially p. 65.

[3] Jon L. Berquist, *Incarnation*, Understanding Biblical Themes (St. Louis: Chalice Press, 1999), 83.

[4]William C. Placher, *Jesus the Savior: The Meaning of Jesus Christ for Christian Faith* (Louisville: Westminster John Knox Press, 2001).

[5]Ibid., 16.

Chapter 2: Friendship as the Theological Center of the Gospel of John

[1]See three recent book-length studies of friendship and John: E. Puthenkandathil, *Philos: A Designation for the Jesus-Disciple Relationship. An Exegetico-Theological Investigation of*

the Term in the Fourth Gospel (Frankfurt: Peter Lang, 1993); J.M. Ford, *Redeemer–Friend and Mother: Salvation in Antiquity and in the Gospel of John* (Minneapolis: Fortress Press, 1997); Sharon Ringe, *Wisdom's Friends: Community and Christology in the Fourth Gospel* (Louisville: Westminster John Knox Press, 1999).

[2]Words written by Joseph M. Scriven in 1855.

[3]See, for example, S. McFague, *Metaphorical Theology: Models of God in Religious Language* (Philadelphia: Fortress Press, 1982); E. Johnson, *She Who Is: The Mystery of God in Feminist Theological Discourse* (New York: Crossroad, 1994); C.M. LaCugna, *God for Us: The Trinity and Christian Life* (San Francisco: HarperSanFrancisco, 1991); E. Moltmann-Wendel, *Rediscovering Friendship,* trans. J. Bowden (London: SCM, 2000).

[4]See, for example, the two collections of essays edited by J.T. Fitzgerald, *Greco-Roman Perspectives on Friendship,* SBLRBS 34 (Atlanta: Scholars Press, 1997); and *Friendship, Flattery, and Frankness of Speech,* NovTSup 82 (Leiden, The Netherlands: Brill, 1996).

[5]Of the three recent books on friendship and John cited in n. 1 above, two, those by Ford and Ringe, are attentive to the first-century social and rhetorical context.

[6]F.M. Schroeder, "Friendship in Aristotle and Some Peripatetic Philosophers," in *Greco-Roman Perspectives on Friendship,* 36.

[7]David Konstan, "Problems in the History of Christian Friendship," *Journal of Early Christian Studies* 4 (1996) 90. See, for example, M. Nussbaum, *The Fragility of Goodness: Luck and Ethics in Greek Tragedy and Philosophy* (Cambridge: Cambridge University Press, 1986); Schroeder, "Friendship in Aristotle"; L.S. Pangle, *Aristotle and the Philosophy of Friendship* (Cambridge: Cambridge University Press, 2003). Athens was a small slice of the ancient world, even the Greek world, and the other city-states did not share the Athenians' enthusiasm for democracy. Sparta, for example, was more of a military state, and led a confederacy called the Peloponnesian League in defeating Athens in the Peloponnesian War (431–404 B.C.E.).

[8]Aristotle, *Ethica Nicomachea.* 9.8.9 [translation, LCL].

[9]Plato, *Symposium* 179B, also 208D. See also Aristotle, *Ethica Nicomachea* 9.8.9; Lucian, *Toxaris* 36; Epictetus, *Dissertationes* 2.7.3; Seneca, *Epistulae morales* 9.10. In the New Testament, see Romans 5:6–8.

[10]See the collection of essays, edited by J. T. Fitzgerald, *Friendship, Flattery, and Frankness of Speech.*

[11]Plutarch, *How to Tell a Flatterer from a Friend* [Translation, LCL], 51.

[12]David Konstan, "Friendship, Frankness and Flattery," in *Friendship, Flattery, and Frankness of Speech,* 8–12. See, for example, Plutarch, *How to Tell a Flatterer from a Friend* (*Quomodo adulator ab amico internoscatur*); Cicero, *On Friendship* (*Laelius; de amicitia*).

[13]Plutarch, *How to Tell a Flatterer from a Friend,* 61.

[14]A fuller discussion of the social context of friendship in John can be found in Gail R. O'Day, "Jesus as Friend in the Gospel of John," *Interpretation* 58 (2004): 144–57. Much of the discussion that follows in this essay was originally explored in that essay.

[15]For example, R. Brown, *The Gospel According to John XIII–XXI,* AB 29A (Garden City, N.Y.: Doubleday, 1970), 664.

[16]Both Ringe, *Wisdom's Friends,* and Ford, *Redeemer–Friend and Mother,* discuss the first motif and its relationship to the love commandment (13:33–35 and 15:12), but neither of them even allude to the motif of boldness. An essay by William Klassen ("PARRESIA in the Johannine Corpus," in *Friendship, Flattery, and Frankness of Speech,* 227–54) studies *parrēsia* but does not link it with friendship. Rudolf Schnackenburg, *The Gospel According to St. John,* 3 vols., trans. Kevin Smyth (New York: Crossroad, 1982) 3.111, alludes to the connection between *parrēsia* and friendship in John 15 but does not develop the connection.

[17]For an excellent discussion of "noble death" and its connections to John, see J. Neyrey, "The 'Noble Shepherd' in John 10: Cultural and Rhetorical Background," *JBL* 120 (2001): 267–91. Oddly, though, Neyrey never explicitly links the noble death motif with the motif of friendship, even though both John and Greco-Roman philosophers do.

[18]Lucian, *Toxaris,* 36.

[19]See Gail R. O'Day, "The Gospel of John: Introduction, Commentary, and Reflections," in vol. 9 of *The New Interpreter's Bible,* ed. Leander E. Keck (Nashville: Abingdon Press, 1995), 727–28.

[20]Neyrey, "Noble Shepherd," 291.

[21]See O'Day, "John," , 713–15. The real contribution of Ford (see note 1) is her attempt to reclaim friendship as a soteriological category for John. Her effort is not completely successful, however, because she tends to treat friend and mother as if they share the same set of conventions, and so both terms lose their distinctiveness.

[22]For a discussion of this aspect of John, see R.A. Culpepper, *Anatomy of the Fourth Gospel: A Study in Literary Design* (Philadelphia: Fortress Press, 1983); Gail R. O'Day, *Revelation in Fourth Gospel: Narrative Mode and Theological Claim* (Philadelphia: Fortress Press, 1986).

[23]Interestingly, Schnackenburg, who noted the connection between *parresia* and friendship in connection with 15:15, makes no connection between "speaking openly" and friendship here (*St. John*, 161–66).

[24]Schnackenburg, *St. John*, 110. Ambrose, in *De officiis ministrorum* 3.22.135, sees in John 15:15 one of the core practices of Christian friendship: "Let us reveal our bosom to [a friend], and let him reveal his to us. *Therefore*, he said, *I have called you friends, because all that I have heard from my Father, I have made known to you.* Therefore a friend hides nothing, if he is true: he pours forth his mind, just as the Lord Jesus poured forth the mysteries of his Father," (Ambrose, *De officiis, Edited with an Introduction, Translation, and Commentary*, Ivor J. Davidson, Oxford, OUP, 2001). See Konstan, "Problems in the History of Christian Friendship," *Journal of Early Christian Studies* 4 (1996) 106–10.

Sermon: Blessed If You Do Them

[1]"*Jesu, Jesu*," Tom Colvin, hymn text, *The United Methodist Hymnal* (Nashville: United Methodist Publishing House, 1989), no. 432.

[2]Wes Howard-Brook, *Becoming Children of God: John's Gospel and Radical Discipleship* (Maryknoll, N.Y.: Orbis Books, 1994), 297.

Sermon: Once I Was Blind, But Now...?

[1]Dallas Willard, *The Spirit of the Disciplines–Reissue: Understanding How God Changes Lives* (New York: HarperCollins, 1991), 259.

[2]Lynna Williams, "Personal Testimony," in *Texas Bound* (Dallas: SMU Press, 1994).

[3]"Love Lifted Me," words by James T. Rowe, 1912.

[4]Author is paraphrasing the quotes of story in John 9 about Jesus' healing a blind man.

[5]Dialogue taken from the transcript of the trial as found in Daniel Berrigan, *The Trial of the Catonsville Nine* (Boston: Beacon Press, 1970).

[6]Thomas Merton, *A Thomas Merton Reader,* ed. Thomas P. McDonnell (New York: Doubleday/Image, 1974), 18.

Chapter 3: The Paraclete as Friend

[1]See Rudolf Schnackenburg, *The Gospel According to St. John*, 3 vols., trans. Kevin Smyth (New York: Crossroad, 1982), 3.110.

[2]See, for example, Gail R. O'Day, "The Gospel of John: Introduction, Commentary, and Reflections," in vol. 9 of *The New Interpreter's Bible,* ed. Leander E. Keck (Nashville: Abingdon Press, 1995), 738.

[3]Plutarch, *How to Tell a Flatterer from a Friend* [Translation, LCL], 61.

[4]The Greek verb *elench* is difficult to translate. The English translation that best conveys the sense of the Greek is "expose," which communicates both "bring to the light" and "hold accountable." See Edwin C. Hoskyns, *The Fourth Gospel*, ed. F.N. Davey (London: Faber and Faber, 1947), 484.

[5]See C.H. Dodd, *The Interpretation of the Fourth Gospel* (Cambridge: Cambridge University Press, 1953), 414.

[6]Rudolf Bultmann, *The Gospel of John* (Philadelphia: Westminster Press, 1971), 573.

Sermon: Moving beyond Normal Belief

[1]See Raymond E. Brown, *The Gospel According to John,* Anchor Bible (Garden City: Doubleday, 1966), I.425–26. More emphatic is Gail O'Day in "The Gospel of John:

Introduction, Commentary, and Reflections," in vol. 9 of *The New Interpreter's Bible,* ed. Leander E. Keck (Nashville: Abingdon Press, 1995), 690.

[2]O'Day, "The Gospel of John," 694.

Sermon: A Call to Courage

[1]Gail R. O'Day, "The Gospel of John: Introduction, Commentary, and Reflections," in vol. 9 of *The New Interpreter's Bible,* ed. Leander E. Keck (Nashville: Abingdon Press, 1995), 784.

[2]Gail R. O'Day, "Jesus as Friend: Courage for the Present," Sermon Seminar, Rochester College, May 21, 2007.

Chapter 4: The Word as Sign

[1]I have published two books on the Johannine writings: Thomas H. Olbricht, *Lifted Up: John 18–21: Crucifixion, Resurrection and Community in John* (Webb City, Mo.: Covenant Press, 2005), and *Life Together: The Heart of Love and Fellowship in 1 John* (Webb City, Mo.: Covenant Press, 2006).

[2]Rudolf Bultmann set forth the most discussed claim, that the gospel contains more than one source and shows signs of redaction: Rudolf Bultmann, *The Gospel of John: A Commentary,* trans. G. R. Beasley-Murray (Oxford: Blackwell, 1971). Robert Fortna offered some of the most important modifications of Bultmann's views: Robert Fortna, *The Gospel of Signs: A Reconstruction of the Narrative Source Underlying the Fourth Gospel* (Cambridge: Cambridge University Press, 1970).

[3]Robert Kysar, *Voyages with John: Charting the Fourth Gospel* (Waco: Baylor University Press, 2005), 244.

[4]Rudolf Bultmann, *Theology of the New Testament,* trans. Kendrick Grobel (New York: Charles Scribner's Sons, 1955), 2:60–61.

[5]Ibid., 2:71.

[6]I have worked out this point in some detail in Thomas H. Olbricht, "The Theology of the Signs in the Gospel of John," in *Johannine Studies in Honor of Frank Pack,* ed. James E. Priest (Malibu, Calif.: Pepperdine University Press, 1989).

[7]Raymond E. Brown, *The Gospel According to John, I–XII,* Anchor Bible (Garden City: Doubleday, 1966), 528.

[8]Ibid., 527.

[9]Rudolf Schnackenburg, *The Gospel According to St. John,* trans. Kevin Smyth (New York: Crossroad, 1982), I:349. Note pp. 357–59 in which Schnackenburg is bothered by these "signs" occurring before the second sign in Cana (4:54). Schnackenburg, however, does not perceive that the two signs in Cana are in some manner special and by no means proposes to offer a definite catalog of signs in which the words of Jesus are as much signs as the actions that follow.

[10]Gail R. O'Day, "The Gospel of John: Introduction, Commentary, and Reflections," in vol. 9 of *The New Interpreter's Bible,* ed. Leander E. Keck (Nashville: Abingdon Press, 1995), 532. I commend this exemplary commentary to all who proclaim the Word.

[11]George R. Beasley-Murray, *John,* 2d ed. (Nashville: Thomas Nelson, 1999), 386.

[12]See Hays' essay here. Hays builds on this observation by linking the Spirit to preachers who live in John's symbolic world and "say new things to our time."

[13]Bultmann, *The Gospel of John,* 609. This point continues on 610.

[14]Beasley-Murray, *John,* 254–57.

[15]O'Day, "The Gospel of John," 610.

[16]From "I Love to Tell the Story," words by Katherine Hankey, 1868.

[17]My early thinking about the stages in how the signs lead to faith in John was stimulated by Robert Kysar in his book *John: The Maverick Gospel* (Atlanta: John Knox Press, 1976), in his chapter, "Seeing Is Believing–Johannine Concepts of Faith," 65–83.

Sermon: Nathanael, a Disciple by Water and the Word

[1]From "The Church's One Foundation," words by Samuel J. Stone, 1866.

[2]From "Will You Not Tell It Today," composed by Jessie Brown Pounds and James H. Fillmore.

Sermon: He Always Had Some Mighty Fine Wine

[1]This is an estimate. According to the text, the actual amount would have been more than 120 and less than 180 gallons.

[2]John 6:1–13.

[3]John 4:10; 7:38.

[4]John 15:5.

[5]John 3:25.

[6]John 3:26; 4:1–2.

[7]John 1:12–13, NIV.

[8]John 2:5.

[9]John 1:1.

[10]John 5:39–40, NIV.

[11]From a letter Steve Orduño sent me following the Pepperdine Lectures.

Sermon: Signs and Wonders and Faith

[1]Scripture quotes in sermon are author's paraphrases.

[2]Gail R. O'Day, "The Gospel of John," in vol. 9 of *The New Interpreter's Bible*, ed. Leader Keck (Nashville: Abingdon Press, 1995), 576.

[3]Gary Burge, *John: The NIV Application Commentary* (Grand Rapids: Zondervan, 2000), 166–67.

[4]Robert Kysar, *John: The Maverick Gospel* (Atlanta: John Knox Press, 1976), 70.

[5]A statement made by Fred Craddock in a sermon on cassette tape, "Sermons Preached at the Alter," sermon 2 on Romans chapter 1, JBC Cassette Service, nd.

Chapter 5: Believing Is Seeing

[1]Author's translation. Except where otherwise noted, all scriptural quotations come from the *New Revised Standard Version*.

[2]Author's translation.

[3]Jouette M. Bassler, "Mixed Signals: Nicodemus in the Fourth Gospel," *Journal of Biblical Literature* 108 (1989): 643–46.

[4]Author's translation.

[5]Author's translation.

[6]R. Alan Culpepper, "The Theology of the Gospel of John," *Review and Expositor* 85 (1988): 419–20.

[7]Author's translation.

[8]James M. Howard, "The Significance of Minor Characters in the Gospel of John," *Bibliotheca Sacra* 163 (2006): 76.

[9]Etienne Trocmé, "Light and Darkness in the Fourth Gospel," *Didaskalia* 6 (1995). 6.

[10]Author's translation. The Greek in this verse is particularly emphatic.

[11]R. Alan Culpepper, "The Johannine *Hypodeigma*: A Reading of John 13," *Semeia* 53 (1991): 141–42.

[12]The earliest Greek manuscripts have no punctuation in them, and the grammar of verse 31 can be read either as a statement or a question. Given that Jesus follows it with a reference to them all abandoning him, it makes the most sense to read it as a question.

[13]Craig R. Koester, "The Passion and Resurrection According to John," *Word & World* 11 (1991): 91.

[14]Gail O'Day and Susan E. Hylen, *John* (Louisville: Westminster John Knox Press, 2006), 196.

Sermon: I've Always Liked Nicodemus

[1]Jouette M. Bassler, "Mixed Signals: Nicodemus in the Fourth Gospel," *Journal of Biblical Literature* 108 (1989): 643–46. I must identify here the import of a community of resources when preparing a sermon. In an e-mail exchange just prior to the sermon's composition, Alyce McKenzie recommended her colleague's (Bassler's) work. This encouragement, coupled with Stevenson's reference, sent me to the copy of *JBL* in which the article appears.

²Joshua Fleer, "The Johannine Concept of Belief," unpublished manuscript, Pepperdine University, 2002.

³Author's paraphrase.

⁴Author's paraphrase.

⁵Author's paraphrase.

⁶Author's paraphrase.

Sermon: Do You Want the Living Water?

¹Gail O'Day, *The Word Disclosed: John's Story and Narrative Preaching* (St. Louis: CBP Press, 1987), 13–15.

²Ibid., 13.

³Ibid.

⁴Ibid., 29.

Sermon: Do You Want to Be Made Well?

¹Author's paraphrase.

²Words by John Newton, 1779.

Chapter 6: Jesus' Voice in John

¹Whitney Shiner, *Proclaiming the Gospel* (Harrisburg: Trinity Press, 2003); Paul Achtemeier, "*Omne Verbum Sonat:* The New Testament and the Oral Environment of Late Western Antiquity," *Journal of Biblical Literature* 109 (1990): 3–27.

²While some instances of private, even silent reading, have been identified, these are relatively minor exceptions to the general pattern. See Paul Saenger, "Silent Reading: Its Impact on Late Medieval Script and Society," *Viator* 13 (1982): 367–414.

³Dennis Dewey, "Great in the Empire of Heaven," in *Preaching the Sermon on the Mount: The World It Imagines,* ed. David Fleer and Dave Bland (St. Louis: Chalice Press, 2007), 69–74.

⁴Ibid., 71.

⁵The handing down of sacred stories was the most central cultural and religious practice of ancient tribes. The stories were passed down from generation to generation by learning them "by heart" and repeatedly telling the stories to children (Deut. 6:4–7).

⁶Author's translation.

⁷Author's translation.

⁸The punctuation of different translations reflects different decisions about the narrative character of this speech. In the RSV, NIV, and NAB there are no quotation marks enclosing John 3:16–21, thereby indicating the editors' conclusion that this was not part of the speech of Jesus but is a comment by the narrator. The TEV and *The Complete Gospels* end the quotation marks and begin the narrative comment at 3:13. The NRSV (also NEB, CEV, JB) has the more accurate punctuation of quotation marks around the entire speech (Jn. 3:10–21), thereby indicating that all of these words were part of Jesus' speech.

⁹Gail O'Day's description of the tradition of friendship in the ancient world and of the characterization of Jesus as a true friend is completely congruent with the dynamics of audience address in the gospel. The tone of Jesus' words in the gospel, including those addressed to those who are seeking to kill him, is the tone of a friend who steadily tells them the truth. See her two essays earlier in this volume.